Fiscal Policy, Decentralization and Economic Growth in India

# Fiscal Policy, Decentralization and Economic Growth in India

**Pradeep S. Chauhan**
Fellow, South Asian Study Centre,
St. Antony's College,
University of Oxford, UK.

New Century Publications
New Delhi, India

NEW CENTURY PUBLICATIONS
4800/24, Bharat Ram Road,
Ansari Road, Daryaganj,
New Delhi – 110 002 (India)

Tel.: 011-2324 7798, 4358 7398, 6539 6605
Fax: 011-4101 7798
E-mail: indiatax@vsnl.com • info@newcenturypublications.com
www.newcenturypublications.com

*Editorial office:*
LG–7, Aakarshan Bhawan,
4754-57/23, Ansari Road, Daryaganj,
New Delhi – 110 002

Tel.: 011-4356 0919



First Published: **July 2010**

ISBN: **978-81-7708-231-9**

Published by New Century Publications and printed at Salasar Imaging Systems, New Delhi.

Designs: Patch Creative Unit, New Delhi.

PRINTED IN INDIA

# Contents


About the Book x
Author's Profile xi
Preface xii-xv

**1. Fiscal Policy: Theoretical Framework** 1-9
1.1 Introduction
1.2 Keynes on Fiscal Policy in General Theory
1.3 Post-Keynesian Views

**2. Fiscal Policy and Economic Growth** 10-36
2.1 Introduction
2.2 Allocative Efficiency and Growth
  2.2.1 Tax Policy
2.3 Public Expenditure Policy
2.4 Budget Policy
2.5 Stability and Growth
  2.5.1 Tax and Expenditure Policies
2.6 Income Distribution and Growth
2.7 Concluding Remarks

**3. Indian Fiscal System** 37-58
3.1 A Brief Prelude
3.2 Fiscal Consolidation
3.3 Fiscal Sector Development at the Central Level
  3.3.1 Taxation Developments
  3.3.2 Disinvestment, Privatization and Restructuring of Public Sector
  3.3.3 Borrowings by Government
  3.3.4 Expenditure Reforms Commission
3.4 Fiscal Sector Development at the Level of States
  3.4.1 RBI Initiatives on State Finances
3.5 Trends in Fiscal Imbalances
  3.5.1 Global Financial Crisis and Set Back to

Fiscal Consolidation
3.6 Robust Economic Growth and Buoyant Tax Revenue
3.6.1 Indirect Taxes
3.6.2 Tax Expenditures
3.7 Expenditure Trends
3.7.1 Interest Payments
3.8 Subsidies
3.9 Government Debt
3.10 Eleventh Plan on Government Finances

**4. Fiscal Reforms in India** 59-79
4.1 Fiscal Responsibility and Management Act
4.1.1 FRBM Act and Transparency of Budgetary Policy
4.1.2 Implementation of FRBM by States
4.1.3 FRBM Act and Check on Public Debt
4.2 Tax Structure Reforms at the Central Level
4.2.1 Introduction of CENVAT
4.2.2 Exemptions Causing Distortions
4.2.3 Tariff Reductions
4.2.4 Proposed National Goods and Services Tax (GST)
4.3 Modernisation of Public Pension System
4.4 Introduction of VAT at the Level of States
4.5 Effectiveness and Transparency of Subsidies
4.6 Summing Up

**5. Fundamentals of Fiscal Decentralization** 80-126
5.1 Introduction
5.2 Historical Basis of Fiscal Centralization
5.3 Emerging Fiscal Decentralization Trends
5.4 Conventional Fiscal Decentralization Theory
5.4.1 Primary Responsibility of Stabilization
5.4.2 Redistributive Function
5.4.3 Allocation Function

5.5 Relevance for Developing Countries
5.6 Decentralization and Economic Development
5.7 Macroeconomic Effects of Decentralization
5.8 Growth-retarding Effects of Fiscal Decentralization
5.9 Fiscal Decentralization and Distribution
5.10 Fiscal Decentralization and Revenue Generation
5.11 Fiscal Decentralization and Accountability of Local Participation
5.12 Elements of a Good Fiscal Decentralization Programme
5.12.1 Adequate Enabling Environment
5.12.2 Assignment of Appropriate Functions to Local Governments
5.12.3 Assignment of Appropriate Revenues to Local Governments
5.12.4 Appropriate Inter-governmental Transfer System
5.12.5 Adequate Local Access to Investment Capital

**6. Fiscal Decentralization and Economic Growth** 127-150
6.1 Introduction
6.2 Decentralized Government Expenditure and Growth
6.3 Estimation of Relationship between Decentralization and Growth
6.4 Direct and Indirect Linkages between Decentralization and Growth
6.5 Linkage between Efficiency and Measured Growth
6.6 Sub-national Governments, Competition and Development
6.7 Corruption and Fiscal Decentralization
6.8 Summing Up

**7. Fiscal Decentralization in India** 151-175
7.1 The Indian Polity
7.2 Distribution of Powers between the Centre and the States
7.3 Centrally Biased Constitution
7.4 Extent of Fiscal Devolution to State Governments
7.5 Mechanism of Transfer of Resources from the Centre to the States
7.6 Controlling Debt of States by Central Government
7.7 Significant Role Played by Postal Savings System
7.8 Constitutional and Legal Framework for Local Bodies
7.9 Local Bodies Remain Underdeveloped
7.10 Assessment of Effectiveness of Local Bodies
7.11 Summing Up

**8. Progress, Prospects and Challenges of Indian Economy** 176-224
8.1 India's Development Experience: Pre-reforms Period
8.2 Economic Policies in the 1980s
8.3 Initiation of Economic Reforms in Early 1990s
8.4 Fiscal Consolidation in the Indian Economy
8.5 Response of the Economy to Reforms
8.6 Gains in Labour Productivity: Main Driver of Growth
8.7 Total Factor Productivity Growth and GDP
8.8 Sterling Performance of Services and the IT Sector
8.9 Special Economic Zones (SEZs)
8.10 Faster Growth in Relatively Developed States
8.11 Prospects and Challenges
8.12 Need for Further Deregulation

8.13 Employment Aspect of Accelerated Growth
8.14 Need for Enhanced Efficiency of the Financial System
8.15 Reorientation of Public Expenditure
8.16 Modernization of Tax Structure
8.17 Centre-State Financial Relations
8.18 High Demand for Infrastructure Services
8.19 Urban Renewal and Development
8.20 Summing Up

**Appendix** 225-244
Fiscal Policy Strategy Statement, as Part of the Budget Papers, Presented to Parliament by Shri Pranab Mukherjee, Minister of Finance, on February 26, 2010

**Bibliography** 245-272

**Index** 273-280

# About the Book

When the Indian economy faced an unprecedented macroeconomic crisis in 1991, fiscal consolidation constituted a major objective of the policy response. For this purpose, it became necessary to (a) enhance tax and non-tax revenue, (b) curtail current expenditure growth, (c) restructure public sector undertakings (d) improve fiscal-monetary co-ordination and (e) deregulate financial system. The need for improvements in budgetary practices led to the enactment of the Fiscal Responsibility and Budget Management (FRBM) Act, 2003 which ushered the Indian economy in an era of fiscal consolidation based on fiscal policy rules.

The passage of the Constitution (Seventy-third Amendment) Act, 1992 marked a watershed in the history of modern India. With this amendment, a uniform structure of *panchayats* emerged throughout the country. Similarly, the passage of the Constitution (Seventy-fourth Amendment) Act, 1992 was a landmark in the history of municipal administration in India. Resultantly, *panchayats* and municipalities are now constitutional bodies forming third tier to the federal polity of India. This decentralisation initiative poses challenges and offers opportunities.

To counter the negative fallout of the global meltdown on the economy, Indian Government took prompt action by providing substantial fiscal stimulus.

This book provides an account of fiscal developments in India during the post-liberalisation period, with particular emphasis on decentralization initiatives. It also examines prospects and challenges facing the Indian economy. An appendix included in the book contains Fiscal Policy Strategy Statement presented to Parliament by Shri Pranab Mukherjee, Minister of Finance, on February 26, 2010.

# Author's Profile

Dr. Pradeep S. Chauhan, a noted economist, is based at South Asian Study Centre, St. Antony's College, University of Oxford, UK as a Fellow. He is M.Phil. (Gold Medallist) and Doctorate in Economics. He has taught in many world-known universities and institutions in his 17 years of academic career. His scholarship ranges over the fields of international economics, economics of climate change and economic theory. His illustrious academic career includes a prestigious French Government Fellowship for which he pursued his research and teaching at Paris School of Economics, Paris. He was awarded Agatha Harrison Memorial Fellowship to pursue his research at the University of Oxford, UK.

Dr. Chauhan has published many books and completed a number of research projects. He is member of many national and international academic bodies including Kastler Foundation, France, International Forum of Young Scientists, Hungary and Indian Economic Association. He has presented papers at many national and international conferences and seminars.

# Preface

Fiscal policy is an important instrument of the general economic policy of a government. It is concerned with the use of a government's taxation and expenditure powers to influence economic activities in an economy at the aggregate level. It also deals with financial relations between different tiers of government in a federal polity. Through the medium of budget, it determines government expenditure, borrowing requirements and issue of new currency. It also determines private spending through taxation measures.

**Fiscal Policy Reforms**

It may be recalled that the external payments crisis of 1991, which led to the initiation of economic reforms in India, was the result of deteriorating fiscal situation during the latter half of 1980s. This period was marked by high and persistent fiscal deficits, accompanied by large revenue deficits. This had led to a significant enlargement of Government borrowings from financial intermediaries and increased financing of Government deficit through automatic monetisation which aggravated price rise.

When the Indian economy faced an unprecedented macroeconomic crisis in 1991, fiscal consolidation constituted a major objective of the policy response. This consolidation was to be achieved through reduction in the size of budget deficit and public debt in relation to GDP. For this purpose, it became necessary to (a) enhance tax and non-tax revenue, (b) curtail current expenditure growth, (c) restructure public sector undertaking, including disinvestment, (d) improve fiscal-monetary co-ordination, and (e) deregulate financial system.

Apart from these reforms aimed at fiscal consolidation, a number of institutional measures were also taken during the 1990s. Public sector restructuring and disinvestments were undertaken with a view to increase the efficiency of the public sector undertakings and also to provide additional resources to the Government.

The need for improvements in budgetary practices led to the enactment of the Fiscal Responsibility and Budget Management (FRBM) Act, 2003 which ushered the Indian economy in an era of fiscal consolidation based on fiscal policy rules.

The financing of fiscal deficit is another area, which underwent significant changes in the post-reform period. With the discontinuation of *ad hoc* 91-day Treasury Bills in April 1997, automatic monetisation of deficits was eliminated. Greater reliance on borrowing at market-related interest rates has led to a substantial lowering of statutory pre-emption of institutional resources for the Government. This has also facilitated development of the market for Government securities which has witnessed remarkable changes in the last few years.

**Decentralisation Initiative, 1992**

The passage of the Constitution (Seventy-third Amendment) Act, 1992 marked a watershed in the history of modern India. With this amendment, a uniform structure of *panchayats* emerged throughout the country.

Article 243G read with Eleventh Schedule of the Constitution explicitly requires the States to devolve powers and authority on *panchayats* which may be necessary to enable them to function as institutions of self-government.

Similarly, the passage of the Constitution (Seventy-fourth Amendment) Act, 1992 was a landmark in the history of municipal administration in India. Article 243W read with Twelfth Schedule of the Constitution provides the illustrative list for the devolution of functions to the municipalities. Many States have amended their municipal laws to ensure conformity with the new constitutional provisions.

In short, *panchayats* and municipalities are now constitutional bodies forming third tier to the federal polity of

India. India's decentralisation initiative in the form of Seventy-third and Seventy-fourth Amendments poses challenges and offers opportunities.

## Global Financial Crisis and Fiscal Policy

The current global financial situation continues to be uncertain and unsettled. What started off as a sub-prime crisis in the US housing mortgage sector has turned successively into a global banking crisis, global financial crisis and now a global economic crisis (recession).

To counter the negative fallout of the global slowdown on the economy, Indian Government took prompt action by providing substantial fiscal stimulus. The Central Government invoked the emergency provisions of the FRBM Act to seek relaxation from the fiscal targets and launched two fiscal stimulus packages in December 2008 and January 2009. These fiscal stimulus packages, together amounting to about 3 percent of GDP, included additional public spending, government guaranteed funds for infrastructure spending, cuts in indirect taxes, expanded guarantee cover for credit to micro and small enterprises, and additional support to exporters. These stimulus packages came on top of an already announced expanded safety-net for rural poor, a farm loan waiver package and salary increases for government staff, all of which should stimulate demand.

## Prospects and Challenges

Recent developments in the World economy have brought forward several new realities that pose severe challenges to macro-economic management, in particular to monetary and regulatory policies globally. Concerns relating to the US slowdown and its intensity have mounted in view of the potential spill over on to the global economy. Threats to the global economy are emanating from advanced economies in sharp contrast to earlier crises which stemmed from the emerging world.

Similarly, there are indications that protectionist tendencies have increased around the world in anticipation of the growing possibilities of slower growth in advanced economies.

India, with its strong internal drivers for growth, may escape the worst consequences of the global financial crisis. Indian banks have very limited exposure to the US mortgage market, directly or through derivatives, and to the failed and stressed financial institutions.

In spite of the severity and multiplicity of the adverse shocks, India's financial markets have shown admirable resilience. This is in large part because India's banking system remains sound, healthy, well capitalized and prudently regulated. India's comfortable foreign exchange reserves position provides confidence to overseas investors.

Since a large majority of Indians do not participate in equity and asset markets, the negative impact of the wealth loss effect that is plaguing the advanced economies should be quite muted. Consequently, consumption demand should hold up well. The farm loan waiver package implemented by the Government should further insulate the agriculture sector from the crisis.

Over the years, India has built an extensive network of social safety-net programmes, including the flagship rural employment guarantee programme. These uniquely Indian versions of automatic stabilizers should protect the poor from the extreme impact of the global crisis.

*April 2010* **Pradeep S. Chauhan**
U.K.

# 1

# Fiscal Policy: Theoretical Framework

## 1.1 Introduction

The term fiscal comes from the Latin word *fiscalis* which in turn comes from *fiscus*, i.e. a basket used for collecting money. In Italian, *il fisco* refers to the agency that collects taxes. Thus, fiscal policy means policy related to taxes. The same is the case in Spanish, French, and Portuguese. In English, the expression fiscal policy was apparently first used by Edwin R.A. Seligman, a prominent professor of public finance at Columbia University in the early part of the 20th Century. He used the expression to criticize Adolf Wagner, a German economist, who suggested that governments should engage in some redistribution of income through their budgetary activities. This seems to be the genesis of the *redistribution branch* of the trilogy made popular by Richard Musgrave (1959). The Keynesian revolution changed the meaning of fiscal policy, moving it away from the tax or revenue side of the budget to include both revenue and spending. For the Keynesians, fiscal policy refers to the manipulation of taxes and public spending to influence aggregate demand. Thus, we had the genesis of the *stabilization branch* in Musgrave's trilogy.

The theory of fiscal policy owes much to North European economists such as Jan Tinbergen, Bent Hansen, Leif Johansen, and others who developed it five decades ago. In spirit, if not in geography, Richard Musgrave could be placed among this group. There were also obviously, contributors from North America such as Alvin Hansen, Lawrence Klein, Abba Lerner, Robert Solow, Paul Samuelson, and others, but, in their writing, they focused mostly on the stabilization role of fiscal policy. The Keynesian stabilization policy is only a part, though an important part, of the modern theory of fiscal policy. In the conception of this theory, especially well developed in Musgrave's (1959) and in Johansen's (1965) treatises, the goals of fiscal policy extend beyond stabilization, because fiscal tools can be used also for redistributing income and for reallocating resources.

The impact of fiscal policy on economic growth has long been a focus of interest and discussion in macroeconomic analyses. The effects of fiscal policy and fiscal deficit on aggregate demand — on absorption with the consequent impact on domestic inflation; on the level and composition of economic activity and growth; and on the external balance, have been at the core of the study and research. Studies have been made of fiscal policy's role in promoting growth and in sustaining the development process by improving the quantity and quality of investments and savings.

"Perhaps the most fundamental achievement of the Keynesian revolution was the reorientation of the way economics viewed the influence of government activity on the private economy. Before Keynes, it was a commonplace that government spending and taxation were powerless to affect the aggregate levels of spending and employment in the economy — they could only redirect resources from the private to the public sector." (Blinder, Solow, 2005). "With a classical supply curve, every dollar increase in real government spending is offset by a dollar reduction in private spending, hence, the crowding out is complete" (Dornbusch, Fischer, Startz, 1998). Do these statements hold in real life? Generally, Keynesian approach is considered to be valid in the short run where prices are given and output and employment depend on the demand. The supporters of that school believe that lower taxes and bigger government consumption have a positive impact on the economy.

On the contrary, the favourites of classical school say that it cannot be sustainable in the long run where prices adjust and where output and employment are at their potential levels.

These approaches are tested in this chapter to see if and how fiscal policy decisions affect economy, especially the Gross Domestic Product (GDP) growth. Keynesian analysis is based on theoretical analyses, which later on provides for understanding of empirical analysis of long-run classical effects. The theoretical part relies on national accounts, which is a simple way to show that GDP components (consumption, investment and net export) can be further divided into sub-components whereas most of these sub-components are fiscal policy indicators—different government sector revenue and expenditure categories. It is equally important to note that these fiscal indicators are interrelated with each other (for example, budget deficit is the gap between total revenue and total expenditure) and that they have a direct impact on other macroeconomic indicators (like private consumption, current account balance, GDP etc).

In the long run, there are so many additional factors (human capital quality, price level, initial economic stance, technological development etc.) that influence economic growth. This is due to the fact that not only the relationships of the same time period matter here, but rather the consequences of the events of one period on the events of the following period are also important. The longer the period, the more complicated it becomes to analyse the relationship between the events of the current period and the ones of the preceding and the following periods. No theoretical model can perfectly explain why things are as they are. Therefore, empirical approach is used to find out fiscal policy effects on economic growth in the long run.

Altogether, the key is hidden in understanding that if one is analyzing the effect of any fiscal policy decision on economic growth, one should take into account all possible simultaneous changes in other fiscal and macroeconomic indicators. For example, the effect of budget balance on growth is not necessarily the same at all levels of revenue and expenditure. Or, the effects of government total expenditure depends on whether there is an increase in government wage costs, social benefits, government investments or any other expenditure category. The opposite is also valid in this case. If one is interested in understanding the impact of private consumption on growth, it is absolutely necessary to find out whether changes in consumption are due to changes in taxes, social benefits, private saving or other component.

## 1.2 Keynes on Fiscal Policy in General Theory

In popular textbook presentations, Keynesianism is represented by deficit spending. Keynes himself defended public works and deficit spending since the late 1920s, and particularly during the long debates of the Macmillan Committee (Clarke, 1988). [1] In particular, he did not believe that such spending would crowd out private spending as argued by Treasury officials. Public spending did not use, in Keynes' view, a given pool of savings—which would reduce the loanable funds to private agents—but, on the contrary, by increasing the level of activity, which led to higher aggregate savings. [2]

However, Keynes emphasized the importance of balanced budgets in the long term (Carvalho, 1992; Brown-Collier and Collier, 1995). Keynes was keenly aware of the limitations of fiscal policy in times of recession. He noted that time lags would make fiscal policy a second best solution for a recession (1980b, p. 22 and 1973, p. 49). More importantly, Keynes noted that budget deficits have a cyclical component and that deficits were just a symptom of insufficient spending and investment above all. In other words, in a recession, tax revenues decrease and spending programs (e.g. unemployment insurance) increase, implying higher government expenditures, thereby resulting in deficit. Deficits are an effect of a recession and do not represent a reliable solution. If deficits were the result of a recession, the best way to avoid them was to stabilize the cycle by stabilizing investment and the best instrument at hand was public investments.

In the General Theory itself, Keynes (1936, p. 378) argues, in one of his most controversial propositions, for "a somewhat comprehensive socialization of investment." Keynes (1936, p. 378) also warned that the socialization of investment did not preclude "all manner of compromises and devices by which public authority [would] cooperate with private initiative." Socialization of investment was not devised as "a terrific encroachment on individualism, [but], on the contrary...as the only practicable means of avoiding the destruction of existing economic forms [that is, capitalism] in their entirety and as a condition of successful functioning of individual initiative," (Keynes, 1936, p. 380).

Consistent with his emphasis on counter cyclical public investment, Keynes argued for a separation of the current or ordinary budget and the capital budget.

The first was related to the government consumption and should be balanced on an average or even in surplus to finance the capital. The latter was related to public investment and should be used for counter cyclical purposes. The main difference between the two types of expenditure is that whereas consumption implies immediate fruition, capital expenditures provide a real return over time.

Further, by creating a favourable expectational environment for private investment, capital expenditures would help stabilize the level of output. In that respect, tax policies and public works which involved deficit budgeting should be relegated to secondary plane and capital budgeting should be the central instrument of fiscal policy.

It is clear that as much as deficit budgeting, capital budgeting may also lead to the accumulation of public debt. Keynes (1980b, p. 366) notes, however, that government debt is of no concern provided it does not get "out of proportion to the growth of the national income." His ideas on debt sustainability are in line with the notion of functional finance as developed by Lerner (1943), and with the debt sustainability theorems developed in line with Domar (1944).

However, Keynes' never became a Lernerian, in the sense of being in favour of deficit spending as a solution for unemployment. [3] Hence, Keynes favoured public investment to be financed by public borrowings and taxes should be budgeted with a view of making debt servicing payments over the life of the investment projects. However, it would be incorrect to presume that Keynes views on fiscal policy stop at this stage. [4] The euthanasia of the rentier was an integral part of the analytical framework of the General Theory. The euthanasia of the rentier would imply low rates of interest, which not only would provide a better environment for private investments and full employment, but also it would make debt servicing and, hence, public investment, economical.

Keynes (1936, p. 335) noted that "in a society where there is no question of direct investment under the aegis of public authority, the economic objects, with which it is reasonable for the government to be preoccupied, are the domestic interest rates and the balance of foreign trade." That is why to guarantee the euthanasia of the rentier, Keynes pointed out that the central bank should be able to set the rate of interest independently from any international pressure.

Keynes especially insisted upon the idea that movements of capital could not be left unrestricted. During the long preparatory works and the negotiations for the Bretton Woods conference, Keynes argued "we cannot hope to control rates of interest at home if movements of capital money out of the country are unrestricted" (1980a, p. 276). If, however, the government permits capital funds to freely move across national boundaries, then according to him (1936, p. 336) "the authorities had no direct control over the domestic rate of interest or the other inducements to home investment." Hence, capital controls are the necessary complement to Keynes' fiscal policy proposals for current and capital budgeting and the socialization of investment. [5]

## 1.3 Post-Keynesian Views

Developing from Keynes' General Theory and Bretton

Woods' writings, post-Keynesian analysis (e.g. Davidson, 2003) [6] demonstrates what most orthodox economists mean by a policy of fiscal discipline that it will not produce a fully employed economic system. This point is corroborated here, since primary surpluses cum high interest rates—the former imposed by the IMF and the latter resulting from an open and deregulated capital account—will continue to constrain the ability of the government to pursue counter cyclical fiscal policies.

Post-Keynesians have long emphasized the need for greater regulation of global capital markets, and some propose new international institutions such as a World Financial Authority (Eatwell and Taylor), an International Monetary Clearing Union (Davidson) or a publicly controlled international transaction system (D'Arista). [7] A more comprehensive reform of the international financial system, along Keynes' proposals at Bretton Woods, as advocated by post-Keynesians, however, is necessary not just to stabilize financial markets but also to reduce balance of payments crisis. A more closed capital account would allow lower rates of interest, lower debt servicing spending, and more space for public investment. International financial reforms are a necessary complement for sound fiscal policy in the periphery.

Keynesian short-run principles do not generally seem to hold and in the long run, expansionary fiscal policies are not beneficial for the economy generally. For a government, it is essential to recognize that changes in different revenue and expenditure categories may have the same impact on budget balance and on total government revenues and expenditure, but they have different effects on economic growth. By extending the fiscal policy analysis to the sphere of economic growth, we may take an essential step towards attaining greater realism and relevance for fiscal policy — for conclusions derived from static analysis may no longer be applicable when we permit dynamic considerations.

Regrettably, however, it must be conceded that the theory

of fiscal policy within a dynamic setting is still very much in its infancy. Whilst much has been done, it can be concluded with the observations made by Peacock and Shaw (1976), that most of the policy discussion has been concerned with specific proposals designed to influence actual short-term growth rates, whereas the greater part of growth theorizing has been concerned not with actual growth rates but rather with the required rates needed to fulfil certain long-term conditions. It can hardly be considered surprising if the economic policy maker should feel somewhat remote from the concerns with golden age solution.

**Notes**

1. Pérez Caldentey (2003) suggests that Keynes' recanted from his early support of public works, and used the framework developed in the General Theory, which put emphasis on stabilizing investment, as the main tool of counter cyclical fiscal policy. The argument is further developed below.
2. In fact, as Keynes (1936, p. 64) notes "savings is a mere residual [and] the decisions to consume and the decisions to invest between them determine incomes."
3. For a discussion of functional finance see Forstater (1999). For a discussion of Keynes' views on Lerner's functional finance see Colander (1984). Colander (1984, p. 1574) suggests that the main reason for Keynes' objections towards functional finance were related to the political implications of such policies. However, the distinction between ordinary and capital budgets hints that sustainability implications of consumption versus investment spending might have had a role too.
4. Note that Brown-Collier and Collier's (1995) well written and otherwise detailed analysis of Keynes' fiscal policies views omits discussion of interest rates and the euthanasia of the rentier.
5. It is important to mention that during the Bretton Woods capital controls were widespread, but Keynesian policies regarding current and capital budgeting were not. On the second point see Brown-Collier and Collier (1995).
6. Williamson (2003) has recanted some of his original views, but not the main thrust of his initial proposal.

7. For the Argentinean fiscal efforts see Damill et alli (2003), and for the Brazilian fiscal experience see Câmara and Vernengo (2002). In both cases the idea that fiscal crisis were behind the balance of payments problems is refuted.

# 2

# Fiscal Policy and Economic Growth

## 2.1 Introduction

Fiscal policy has occupied centre stage in recent policy deliberations in many developed, developing, and transition economies alike, as concerns with fiscal dimensions, such as high unemployment, inadequate national savings, excessive budget deficits and public debt burdens, and looming crises in the financing of pension and health care systems, have intensified. Timely policy responses to these concerns have taken on a sense of urgency. Under these circumstances, issues relating to the appropriate scope, nature, and conduct of fiscal policy, in the context of both mitigating macroeconomic instability in the short run and fostering growth in the long run, have naturally come to the fore in policy debates.

The division of fiscal policymaking into three hypothetical but interdependent branches and allocation, distribution, and stabilization — first formalized by Musgrave (1959) almost 60 years ago, remains to this day, a useful conceptual framework with which to discuss, analyze and evaluate alternative fiscal policy measures, even though the world today is much more complex than the one that existed at the time when Musgrave wrote on the subject. Musgrave's framework has endured largely because it helps organize one's thoughts, in an elegant way, on the fundamental issues of interest to policymakers — efficiency in resource utilization, equity in income distribution, and cyclical fluctuations.

This chapter considers the positive and normative aspects of the impact on growth of different instruments of fiscal policy. These instruments fall broadly under the three conventional classifications of taxation, public expenditure, and aggregate budgetary balance. Each is analyzed from the perspective of Musgrave's three economic branches. While a multiplicity of factors, some of which are of a non-economic nature, could plausibly affect the performance of an economy from period to period, a country's growth over a reasonably long period of time is ultimately determined by three factors. (1) the state of technical know-how in that country, meaning, the efficiency with which any existing stock of resources is utilized (which would depend, *inter alia*, on cultural, institutional, political, as well as economic, parameters); (2) the accumulation over time of productive resources (which would include, *inter alia*, human and other forms of intangible capital); and (3) technological progress (which for most countries would depend, *inter alia*, on their ability to absorb new technology from abroad). [1]

While for ease of exposition, the growth effects of different fiscal policy instruments are discussed separately below, it does not imply that they are independent of each other. The impact on growth of taxes would depend, for example, in addition to their level and structure, on how the tax revenue is spent (the composition of public expenditure), as well as on how they affect the overall budgetary balance (for any given total level of public expenditure). This interdependence underscores the danger in policy deliberations of focusing too narrowly on the value of one variable (e.g. the budgetary balance) to the neglect of its underlying components — a conceptual equivalent to not properly controlling the relevant variables in empirical estimation. In general, the empirical growth literature has shown that estimation results could be materially affected by the presence or absence of controlled variables.

The relevance of considering the growth effects of fiscal policy must be predicated, of course, on the basic proposition that policy matters for the long-run growth. Although this may seem intuitively obvious, it is in fact a relatively new idea; it became established in mainstream economic thinking only with the recent advent of the endogenous growth literature. [2]

As an alternative paradigm to the neoclassical growth theory of Solow (1956) and Swan (1956) [3] in which long-run growth is completely determined by factors exogenous to the theory itself (and, therefore, is invariant to policy), the endogenous growth literature has been largely motivated as an attempt to overcome the former's failure in reconciling theory with some of Kaldor's (1961) six celebrated stylized facts of growth, most notably the seeming absence in the data of any discernible sign of growth convergence along income levels across countries—-a fundamental implication of the neoclassical paradigm. [4] While this chapter is not a survey per se of the variety of models, results and policy implications of the voluminous endogenous growth literature, it takes as given the basic premise of this literature, that a country's growth performance in the long run is endogenously determined by a set of variables which are responsive to (and affected by) policy, and in this particular case, the fiscal policy.

A legitimate question that could be raised is the appropriateness of adopting national output, rather than welfare, as the yardstick for evaluating policy, since it is presumably the latter which is the ultimate concern of policymakers. The problem of the gap and in more extreme circumstances, that of changes in opposite directions, between output and welfare, is well known. It follows from the fact that national income accounts omit imputed values for household production, leisure, and environmental externalities, among others. [5] Hence, it is theoretically possible for some policy measures to stimulate output and yet reduce welfare (e.g. excessive tax incentives provided to certain industries without properly taking into account the possible pollution costs associated with their activities). While this problem is conceptually important (and hence worth noting explicitly), its resolution in practice would present formidable measurement problem, because the more encompassing welfare effects of policy are not directly and objectively observable. Moreover, in discussing issues of long-run growth, the bias in evaluating policy on the basis of output effects is somewhat lessened, as any persistent difference between changes in output and those in welfare is unlikely to be sustainable in the long run. Accordingly, this chapter will adopt the conventional approach in assuming that output growth is positively correlated with the welfare improvement.

In what follows, the impact of fiscal policy on growth will be taken up first from the point of view of allocative efficiency and then from that of stability. The relatively new literature on the growth effects of fiscal policy from an income distribution perspective will be considered last.

## 2.2 Allocative Efficiency and Growth

**2.2.1 Tax Policy:** Some of the clearest and most direct conceptual links between fiscal policy and growth have traditionally been associated with tax policy. This reflects, of course, the tact that the allocative impacts of taxation (e.g., on labour-leisure choice, on consumption-saving behaviour, and on the relative profit abilities of different industries, among others) are easily appreciated by theorists and policymakers alike, and, consequently, have long been one of the best researched areas in economics. The various links between taxation and growth have, however, different conceptual underpinnings, so it will be useful to consider them separately.

One link is built on the idea that all taxes are non neutral, with the singular exception of lump sum levies (which are largely irrelevant as a practical instrument, and may even be non neutral in an inter-temporal context if planning horizons are finite or in open economies). With non neutral taxes, private economic agents' allocative decisions will be different from those that would be made in the absence of such taxes. This tax-induced distortion in economic behaviour results in a net efficiency loss to the whole economy, commonly referred to as the excess burden of taxation, even if the government engages in exactly the same activities and with the same degree of efficiency as the private sector with the tax revenue so raised. [6] "It then follows that higher the level of taxation, the larger would be the efficiency loss. Moreover, the loss typically grows disproportionately with increase in the tax level when there are other existing tax distortions in the economy. This result would go through even if the taxes are optimally structured, in the sense that the excess burden of each tax is equalized (proportionally) across all taxes." It must be pointed out that while it is straightforward to conceptualize a negative relationship between the level of taxation and the level of output, it is not clear why the former would adversely affect the long-run growth of output. To obtain a growth effect, the appropriate variable to consider should instead be the rate of change in the level of taxation.

The above link between taxation and growth is established on the basis of the former's excess burden in a static context. A second and more conspicuous link has to do with the impact of taxation on factor accumulation, particularly capital — it relates, therefore, to the excess burden of taxation in a dynamic sense. Because in the neoclassical growth paradigm, long-run growth is invariant to policy, as noted earlier, the focus of the traditional analysis of capital income taxation employing such a paradigm is on the long-run tax impact on the level rather than on the growth of output. [7]

Policy implications are entirely different, only when growth is responsive to policy, as in the case of the endogenous growth theory. Here, all other things equal, a tax on income from (physical) capital would lower the after-tax return to savings, and is, therefore, a disincentive to accumulate (physical) capital. However, the ultimate impact of this on growth turns out to be a priori ambiguous; it is dependent on how the other factor, such as human capital, which cooperates with physical capital in the production process, is affected by the tax (assuming the other factors are not taxed). A comparison between two simple cases, both with human capital as the only other factor of production, will illustrate the difference in outcome in a particularly transparent manner.

In one case, we can assume that the production of human capital requires only human capital (Lucas, 1988). Then the growth-depressing effect of the tax on physical capital will be entirely offset by an increase in human capital accumulation. Hence, the net impact on growth is zero. Alternatively, suppose the production of human capital requires both human and physical capital. In this case, the offset will only be partial, and the net impact on growth is negative (Rebelo, 1991). This simple comparison underscores the important point that the growth effects of (physical) capital income taxation are sensitive to the specification of production technology. In general, however, it can be reasoned that the lighter the tax burden on the production of human capital relative to that on other sectors that are human capital intensive, the smaller will be the adverse impact on growth of taxing physical capital.

The above discussion suggests that the structure of taxation could have important implications for growth. This consideration actually is not limited to simply the area of capital income taxation or even to income taxation in general. It embodies in fact, broad significance for the overall design of the structure of the entire tax system. For a given total tax level, a relative shift from income to consumption taxation would, for example, reduce the disincentive to save, and consequently, provide a boost to capital accumulation. [8] While a tax on consumption distorts labour-leisure choice, it is neutral with respect to the relative price between consumption today and tomorrow, and thus, can only produce a level (rather than growth) effect. In addition to its impact on resource accumulation, the structure of a tax system may have other growth consequences also. A heavy reliance on trade taxes could, for example, impede an economy's capacity to absorb or develop new technologies, thereby harming its growth prospects, by reducing the exposure of domestic industries to international markets and competition. [9]

Another channel through which tax policy could have a significant impact on both resource accumulation and technological progress is the provision of tax incentives (also known otherwise as a form of tax expenditure) which in one form or another exists in almost all (developing and developed) countries, for promoting investment and research and development (R&D) type activities. While there is broad consensus among economists that general, i.e. non-targeted incentives are of questionable value — relative to other factors such as stability, simplicity and neutrality of a tax system with internationally comparable tax rates, in achieving their stated objectives, there is much less agreement on targeted incentives. By their very nature, all tax incentives create distortions. However, if targeted incentives are designed to mitigate certain market failures, then the distortions they cause may well be outweighed by the benefits that can be reaped from their use. For example, the social benefits from enhanced growth produced by many investments and R&D type activities could exceed their private returns. Without corrective public measures, such activities would be below their optimal levels. Such arguments usually neglect, however, political-economy costs of providing tax incentives, as they tend to encourage rent-seeking behaviour, corruption, and the development of special interest groups. While these costs are not easy to measure, their adverse impact on growth may be significant.

The empirical evidence of the impact of various aspects of tax policy on growth has so far been mixed. While there is some general indication that the relationship between either the total or income tax level and growth is negative, this relationship is not robust and is sensitive, showing that inter-sectoral spill over effects of industrialization would call for the implementation of investment promotion policies in a coordinated manner to model specification, particularly with respect to the list of non-tax variables that are controlled. Easterly and Rebelo (1993) experimented with 13 different tax measures and found only one, a marginal income tax rate computed by a time series regression of income tax revenue on GDP, to be statistically significant in explaining the growth variations among the sample countries. By including the initial real GNP per capita as a variable in the regressions, the authors found the strikingly negative correlation between the ratio of income tax revenue to GDP and growth shown in Plosser (1992) and subsequently much cited by others to be statistically insignificant. As noted earlier, Engen and Skinner (1992) found statistically significant relationships between growth and the rate of change in tax levels.

The most severe difficulty in isolating the impact of taxation on growth clearly lies in the fact that key non-tax fiscal variables, webbed as public expenditure and budget policies and which are often not independent of tax policy, can also affect the growth levels, let alone the complex interactions among the fiscal and other macroeconomic variables? For example, there is also some evidence suggesting that the growth effects of fiscal policy variables are dependent on income levels, and the negative relationship between tax levels and growth rates is the strongest among the least developed countries. Overall, the general conclusion that can be drawn is, that the empirical evidence on the relationship between taxation and growth is much weaker than what the theory would have led one to expect.

## 2.3 Public Expenditure Policy

The financing of any level of public expenditure whether through taxation or borrowing, involves the absorption of real resources by the public sector that otherwise would be available to the private sector. From a purely static allocative point of view, this absorption would improve overall efficiency if the social return (benefit) from public expenditure exceeds its private opportunity cost. While public expenditure may displace private sector output (the crowding-out effect), it may also improve private sector productivity (the externality or public good effect). Its total social return must, therefore be interpreted as the sum of both of these effects. [10] The net impact on aggregate output of the crowding-out effect of public expenditure is clearly dependent on the relative marginal productivities between the public and private sectors. There is a widespread belief that in view of absence of externalities, public production tends to be less efficient than private production. Hence, on account of this effect alone, the higher the level of public expenditure, the greater the inefficiency and the lower the level of output. To relate public expenditure to long-run output growth, however, it should be the rate of change in the level of public expenditure that matters — a point that is analogous to the case noted earlier involving the level of taxation.

The externality effect of public expenditure, in contrast, enhances the growth by raising private sector productivity. Here a high growth rate could be achieved by a higher level of such expenditure. In the recent endogenous growth literature, the focus has been on the stock of public infrastructure (or the level of services that flows from it) as a productive input, although conceptually there is no reason why this effect should be limited to infrastructure spending only; there is a range of public expenditures such as those on elementary education and vocational training that enhance human capital (a key variable in endogenous growth) which potentially could have a similar impact.

The opposing nature of the crowding out and externality effects implies that the structure of public expenditure, rather than merely its level would be of considerable importance. In analyzing the composition of public expenditure, the traditional approach has been to divide it broadly into the categories of public consumption and public investment, with the idea that the former tends to retard, and the latter to promote growth. While intuitively appealing, this classification can quickly become problematic. Many public investment projects could be wasteful, for example, in the sense that their marginal net present values could be negative for the society as a whole. At the same time, many public consumption expenditures, such as certain kinds of educational training, operations and maintenance spending on existing infrastructure and even targeted funding for R&D type activities, could be enormously beneficial for long-run growth. Hence, a more useful classification - one that is gaining popularity recently- would divide public expenditure into productive (i.e. growth-inducing) and unproductive (i.e. growth-retarding) categories, taking into consideration the levels and mixes of both the resources absorbed and outputs produced, by different expenditure programs. [11]

The usefulness of the productive-unproductive classification for growth analyses is particularly apparent in a dynamic context, because it focuses one's attention on the impact of public expenditure on private savings and investment and hence capital accumulation. There are three dimensions to this impact. *First,* public expenditure needs to be financed and this reduces resources for private savings. *Second*, to the extent that it improves private productivity, it stimulates private savings. *Finally,* the degree of complementarity substitutability between it and the private expenditure is important. The lower (higher) the complementarity (substitutability), the smaller the impact on private savings. The combined impact of these effects on private savings would suggest that the relationship between the level of public expenditure and growth is typically not monotonic. For a given degree of complementarity/ substitutability, growth may first, be enhanced by public expenditure up to a point, after which the relationship between the two turns negative. This has provided a basis for determining the growth-maximizing level of public expenditure, as well as for government intervention in a decentralized economy.

As with the case of taxation, the empirical evidence of the growth effects of public expenditure (as a share of GDP) is inconclusive. Based on cross-country regressions, Ram (1986) found that growth in general is positively correlated with the rate of change in total public expenditure but is negatively correlated with the level of such expenditure. This latter result was also obtained by Levine and Renelt (1992). When public expenditure is broadly disaggregated, there is a stronger indication that growth is negatively correlated with public consumption, net of defence and education spending (Barro and Sala-i-Martin, 1995), Easterly and Rebelo (1993), and to a certain extent Levine and Renelt (1992). One possible explanation for this negative relationship is that, in the aggregate, such public consumption is viewed by economic agents as a less-than-perfect substitute (or possibly even a complement) for private consumption, whereby private savings decline as a result. Karras (1994) also found evidence of complementarity between public and private consumption.

As regards more specific categories of public consumption, Knight et al. (1996) found a significant adverse impact of military spending on growth. While and Chauer (1989) found that the impact of such spending on private sector productivity in the United States, though negative, is insignificant. [12] A significantly positive impact on growth of public spending on education was found by Barro and Sala-i-Martin (1995), who interpreted the results to represent the growth effect of improved quality in human capital, although it is also consistent with the Tanzi (1995) argument that such spending increases a country's ability to absorb technology from abroad and invent new technologies. Levine and Renelt (1992) found neither military nor public education expenditures as having a robust correlation with the growth.

The finding by Aschauer (1989) of strong and positive correlation between non-military public capital stock and private sector productivity in the Unites States has been widely cited as evidence of the importance of public investment in promoting growth. Of particular interest here is the identification of a subset of core infrastructure (utilities and transportation facilities) as having the greatest impact. In a cross-country setting, Easterly and Rebelo (1993) also obtained strong support for a positive correlation between growth and public investment especially that in transportation and communication. However, Levine and Renelt (1992) found that the growth effects of public investment are not robust. Those researchers who have used functional categories of public expenditure in their growth regressions have also found mixed results.

For example, Devarajan *et al.* (1993) found government expenditure on health and transport and communications to be growth promoting but found no positive impact of education and military spending. Albala and Mamatzakis (2001), using time series data covering 1960-1995 to estimate a Cob-Douglas production function that includes public infrastructure for Chile, found a positive and significant correlation between public infrastructure and economic growth. These results reinforce the argument that empirical outcomes are likely to differ from country to country and time to time even when same estimation techniques are employed. We therefore, believe the solution to the fiscal policy-growth conundrum rests in specific country studies.

The difficulties noted earlier in properly estimating the growth effects of taxation clearly apply to public expenditure as well. Even if the correlation between growth and public expenditure (or a subset thereof) is found to be robust (in the sense that other relevant variables have been adequately controlled), it would still be unclear as to the direction of causation underlying the correlation. Higher income growth may well generate higher demands for some or all types of public expenditure, which in turn may necessitate higher levels of taxation.

A further problem that has not been addressed in this literature is that the relationship between growth and fiscal variables may not be monotonic, either over the levels of the fiscal variables themselves or over income levels, or both. As noted earlier, it is analytically plausible to argue that increasing levels of public expenditure would first raise and then reduce growth. If countries pursue approximately growth-maximizing public expenditure policies, then one would expect little correlation between growth and the level of public expenditure in a cross country regression. Similarly, a case could be made that the growth effects of fiscal variables, if any, may well change direction as income rises. [13] These and other problems suggest that there is much scope for further empirical research in disentangling the complex interactions among different fiscal variables.

## 2.4 Budget Policy

Another broad fiscal variable that could have implications for growth is the budget policy, in the sense that the level of public revenue relative to that of public expenditure, i.e., the budget balance, may have growth effects that are separate from those related to the absolute level of either taxation or public expenditure discussed earlier. One type of effect stems from the stability implications of budget imbalances. Another type is related to a possible behavioural response from the private sector triggered by such imbalances. If the private sector regards budget deficits (even if financed by debt) simply as taxes delayed, then it may choose to increase its own savings to neutralize the public dissavings, thus leading to an unchanged level of national savings. Alternatively, budget deficits might not induce a response in private sector savings, in which case, national savings would be reduced and growth hampered.

The question of whether there is neutrality between debt and tax financing has been the focus of much recent research. A crucial condition for the neutrality to hold is that, when the planning horizons of economic agents are finite (as would be the case under the intuitively appealing notion of life-cycle savings), there are operative private transfers (gifts and bequests) between generations, so that the implied tax burden of public dissavings on future generations is not ignored by the current generation. It is now widely recognized that strict neutrality would also depend on the absence of a host of other factors, such as tax distortions, income uncertainties and imperfect credit markets.

While conceptually intriguing, the importance of the above neutrality result clearly lies in the empirical evidence. Unfortunately, similar to the case of the growth effects of taxation and public expenditure, the empirical support for debt neutrality is mixed. On the whole, the evidence, particularly from cross-country data seems to suggest that the response from private sector savings to public sector dissavings does not completely neutralize the latter. Direct tests of the impact of budget deficits on growth based on cross-country data have also been recently performed by a number of studies. Easterly and Rebelo (1993) found the correlation between the two significant and negative; Martin and Fardmanesh (1990) found the correlation significant and negative only for middle-income countries; and Levine and Renelt (1992) found the correlation fragile.

## 2.5 Stability and Growth

**2.5.1 Tax and Expenditure Policies:** From the point of view of stability, the most direct link between tax policy and growth has to do with the fact that, when the tax regime is uncertain, it injects volatility to the returns to an investment project. In the recent literature investment under uncertainty, it has been established that, since most projects are to some extent irreversible, increased uncertainty to their returns would generally lead to a reduction (postponement) in investment. [14] Hence, uncertainty about the tax regime, which in turn leads to uncertain after-tax returns, is likely to discourage investment and hamper growth.

Tax regime uncertainty could be attributable to a number of factors. The difficulty in forecasting the direction of prospective tax reforms under political debate is one obvious example. Another example would be the possible changes to the tax regime necessitated by unexpected shocks to income and/or interest rates, 'or by unforeseen public expenditure needs. A tax system that is not indexed and/or has significant collection lags would also give rise to uncertain real effective tax rates in an unstable inflationary environment. Hence, there is, however, one type of uncertainty that is unrelated to such unanticipated factors, but that nevertheless could arise even in a framework of an optimizing government whose objective coincides with that of the representative economic agent — if the optimal tax regime changes from one period to the next, there would be uncertainty as to weather the government would maintain the same regime over time.

The above problem which is generally known as the time-inconsistency of optimal policy, can best be understood intuitively by considering a simple two-period model with endogenous savings and labour supply. The government in period 1 optimizes and determines the optimal tax rates on labour and capital for period 2. When period 2 comes around, savings undertaken in period 1 have become fixed capital (sunk cost) and, if taxed, would not give rise to any excess burden. Hence, it would be optimal for the government in period 2 to tax only capital, which is a policy that, in general, will not be the same as the optimal policy set by the government in period 1. [15] While it is tempting to interpret the foregoing result as simply another consequence of investment being irreversible, the time-inconsistency problem is in fact fairly general and can occur even in models without capital. [16]

The likely adverse impact on growth of tax regime uncertainty, irrespective of its origin, raises quite naturally questions about the possible ways by which the uncertainty (or at least some types of such uncertainty) could be alleviated. For the time-inconsistency problem, various potential mechanisms have been advanced to pre-commit the government in a given period to maintain an optimal policy over time. If the uncertainty stems instead from unexpected shocks to income and/or interest rates, or from unforeseen public expenditure needs, then an appropriate debt management policy could obviate the need for altering the tax regime as a response to such occurrences. Finally, if inflation is the source of uncertainty about the real tax burden, the first-best solution is clearly to implement appropriate policies to reduce macroeconomic instabilities. Indexing the tax system and adopting administrative measures to reduce tax collection lags are possible second-best solutions.

Based on cross-country regressions of a large sample of developing countries, Aizenman and Marion (1993) presented empirical evidence which suggests that, to varying degrees, there is a significant and negative correlation between growth and uncertainty in a number of fiscal variables, such as levels of revenue, public expenditure, and budget deficits. Easterly and Rebelo (1993) also found that the standard deviation in the ratio of domestic tax revenue to consumption and investment had a significant and negative impact on growth.

Assume for the moment that monetary financing of budget imbalances is not available. Under such circumstances, the evolution of the stock of real public debt is entirely governed by the path of cumulative real budget imbalances over time. If the economy is dynamically efficient (i.e. its long-run real interest rate exceeds its long-run growth rate) and the government is to be solvent, then any indebtedness of the government would have to be eliminated eventually through appropriate budget policy that would bring the present value of the stock of public debt at some future date (which could be infinity) to zero. An important implication of this solvency requirement for the conduct of budget policy is that the government would be obligated to accumulate a sufficient level of net primary budget surpluses (in present value terms) over time to pay off its initial debt. [17] This implication, in turn, provides a natural basis for evaluating whether current budget policy, if maintained, is sustainable (Wilcox, 1989), and, if not, to what extent tax rates must be raised (for a given path of public expenditure) to ensure government solvency (Blanchard et al.,1990).

The relevance of policy sustainability for growth is two-fold. If current policy is deemed to be unsustainable, then either a regime change in tax (and/or expenditure) policy would be expected to occur, or monetary financing would be resorted to. The former would increase policy uncertainty, whose impact on growth has already been discussed earlier. The latter would lead to inflation, which raises the important issue of possible growth effects of inflation.

There are a number of conceptual links between inflation and growth. One of the oldest is built on the idea that inflation can be viewed as a distortive tax on real money balances and therefore has efficiency consequences in much of the same way as other more traditional distortive taxes. As pointed out earlier, from a purely allocative perspective, any adverse growth impact from distortive taxes would have to stem from increase in the level of taxation which would result in acceleration of the inflation. From a stability perspective, however, arguments have been advanced that higher inflation rates would lead to greater uncertainty about future inflation (Olron, 1971; and Friedman, 1977). Thus, larger efficiency losses would result simply from higher levels of inflation.

The impact of inflation on growth has also been examined directly in growth models. In the earlier growth literature, the focus was on the issue of the super neutrality of money. i.e. whether inflation could affect the steady-state capital-labour ratio, rather than on the growth effects of inflation per se (as the long-run growth in these models is exogenous). With endogenous growth models, however, a number of direct channels through which inflation could affect growth, open up, such as the potential impacts of inflation on both physical and human capital accumulation, as well as the interaction between inflation and a tax system that is based on nominal rather than real magnitudes. On the whole, however, the theoretical results in both the old and new growth models seem to be too dependent on model specifications to render them useful as yet for policy purposes.

While further theoretical explorations of the growth effects of inflation are certainly called for, there is increasing empirical evidence which suggests that there exists a significant and negative correlation between high inflation and growth. Based on panel data, the inflation threshold above which growth effects become significant, ranges from 8 percent to 40 percent. Furthermore, Judson and Orphanides (1996) found that inflation volatility is robustly and negatively correlated with growth at all levels of inflation. Hence, there seems to be a compelling case for believing that an expansionary budget policy that results in high rates of inflation would most likely exact a growth penalty.

## 2.6 Income Distribution and Growth

While economists may disagree on the relative importance of the allocative and distributional objectives of fiscal policy, most will accept the proposition that some trade-off is involved in pursuing the two policy objectives. The trade-off stems, of course, from the disincentive effects of distortive taxes that are required to finance direct or indirect transfer payments from the rich to the poor. Indeed, in a static framework, it is easy to demonstrate that, under fairly general assumptions about (heterogeneous) individual preferences regarding income and work effort, the efficiency cost of pursuing an egalitarian policy could be prohibitively high. Hence, in the traditional view, policies effecting a redistribution of income toward equality would exact a price of (aggregate) output loss that is likely to rise disproportionately to the reduction in income inequality achieved by such policies. When extended to a dynamic context, such a view leads quite naturally to the conclusion that there is increasing marginal cost, in terms of growth forgone, of income redistribution, on account of the saving depressing effects of taxation.

The validity of this traditional view has however been challenged recently by several strands of research. One strand argues that redistributive taxation and the expenditure it finances are a form of social insurance against certain types of risk over an economic agent's lifetime for which private insurance may not be available. Consequently, it could stimulate productive risk.

The threshold is found to be 8 percent in Sarel (1996), 10 percent in Judson and Orphanides (1996), 15 percent in Barro (1995a), and 40 percent in Bruno and Easterly (1995).

Inflationary effects of an expansionary budget policy are countered by a restrictive monetary policy, in which case the growth penalty would be exacted through high interest rates. Moreover, even though the statistical relationship between growth and low inflation is weak, Feldstein (1996) showed that the interaction between an existing distortive tax system and inflation would result in substantial welfare losses even at low inflation rates.

Taking an output growth, it is argued that such behaviour does not necessarily result in greater equality in the post tax distribution of income. [18]

A second strand emphasizes the importance of various aspects of financial market imperfections for growth. A central idea here is that the potential productivity of the poor cannot be fully realized unless they are given the opportunity to do so. If financial markets were perfect, the poor would be able to borrow against their future earnings to acquire, for example, basic needs (nutrition, health care, education, etc.) and human capital. In the absence of such markets, however, redistributive policies are needed to raise the standard of living of the poor at least beyond some threshold for them to become productive members of society and, consequently, contribute to output growth. Once gainfully employed, the poor could then begin to acquire assets, accumulate human capital, and gain access into financial markets to further raise their earnings potential. The financial markets, in turn, by benefiting from the increased participation in the intermediation process by economic agents, would become more developed and the growth prospects for the whole economy would be enhanced as a result. An implication for fiscal policy from this strand of literature is clearly that redistributive policies that result in less income inequality could well promote growth.

Yet another strand of research focuses on the impact of various political-economy factors on growth. While model structures differ across different studies, at the core of this literature is the idea that income distribution affects political outcomes, which, in turn, affect the kind of policies that are actually implemented through the voting process. By invoking the standard median-voter theorem, this literature is able to demonstrate that the greater the inequality of income, the higher will be the voted level of taxation, either for the provision of public goods (Alesina and Rodrik, 1994) or for purely redistributive transfers (Persson and Tabellini, 1994), as a poorer median voter faces a lower tax price of public expenditure than a richer one. Since higher taxes in turn lower growth by depressing either physical or human capital accumulation, or both, a direct causal effect of income distribution on growth is thus established.

The above political-economy approach takes into account the initial distribution of income (or wealth). Consequently, it cannot be used to explain how such a distribution is arrived at in the first place. A potential solution to this limitation could be found in an older but voluminous literature, associated with the seminal work of Kumets (1966) that focused on just the reverse causation, i.e. the impact of growth on income distribution. Kuznets (1966) argued that growth would first increase income inequality, and then would reduce it after some level of income is reached. This relationship can often be derived from a two-sector economy setting comprising, say, a high growth urban sector and a low growth rural sector. As labour migrates from the rural to the urban sector with economic development, various conventional measures of inequality would first rise and then fall. By combining these two bodies of literature, and perhaps in conjunction with elements of the financial market imperfections literature noted above, it is possible to derive a two-way causal relationship between income distribution and growth. Hence, the trade-off between the allocative and distributional objectives of fiscal policy is not absolute - growth with redistribution is possible.

Most of the above cited studies employing the political-economy approach present cross-country empirical evidence, based on various samples of developed and developing countries, that supports to varying degrees a negative correlation between income inequality (measured in some base year close to the beginning of the sample period over which growth rates are computed) and growth. Clarke (1995) has recently confirmed that this negative correlation is robust across a broad sample of countries and with alternative measures of inequality.

While the evidence on the adverse impact of initial income inequality on growth seems compelling, what remains unclear is the precise channels through which this impact operates.

In the models constructed by Alesina and Rodrik (1994) and Persson and Tabeini (1994), a high degree of income inequality generates an outcome of heavy taxation for high public investment expenditure or large public transfers, but Perotti (1993a) has found rather weak support in the data for these chains of events. Recently, Alesina and Perotti (1996) have identified an alternative transmission mechanism — income equality creates social unrest and political instability, which in turn depress investment and growth. Their empirical analysis, which involves the construction of an index of social-political instability (SPI), found cross-country evidence for negative correlations both between income equality and SPI and between SPI and investment. The latter finding is consistent with other empirical studies that found a negative correlation between political instability and growth, e.g. Barro

(1991) and Mauro (1995).

## 2.7 Concluding Remarks

Economists working in public finance have always believed that fiscal policy, interpreted as the manipulation of fiscal instruments to achieve specific objectives, can affect economic growth. This belief is reflected in the title of many books and articles which refer to the assumed connection between fiscal policy and economic growth. This connection has been thought to originate from various channels such as the negative effect of distortive taxes, the negative effect of progressive taxes on the propensity to save, the scope for mobilizing resources through higher taxation and of using the additional resources to increase the level of public investment, and so on.

While public finance economists seemed to have no doubt that they could influence growth through the policy changes they recommend, the prevailing neoclassical growth theory did not leave much role to policy, except for relatively short-run effects on growth. This dichotomy resulted in part from various assumptions implicit in the theory and in part from the different time horizons contemplated by the public finance economists and the growth theorists. For example, while the neoclassical growth theory gives no role to policy for long-run growth, its definition of the long run could be long enough to leave ample scope for the effects of policy over the time horizon, which would be of interest to most governments and individuals.

This chapter has attempted to consider in a systematic and comprehensive way the relationship between various public finance instruments and the growth of countries' economies. It has surveyed a large body of literature, both theoretical and empirical, in an attempt to arrive at the conclusion as to the way in which taxes, public spending, and budgetary policy can influence growth by affecting the allocation of resources, the stability of the economy and the distribution of income. The existing literature is very extensive and very rich and at times, it is hard to interpret. Yet it is much less definitive on some of these issues than one would have thought. Especially, the empirical literature is somewhat disappointing in its support of theoretically reached conclusions.

In spite of the lack of robust results in the empirical literature, the conclusion of this chapter been that, when interpreted from the perspective of the new endogenous growth theory, fiscal policy could play a fundamental role in affecting the long-run growth performance of countries. Thus, economists should not hesitate to recommend changes in the instruments of public finance in the direction in which theory has deemed it important for enhancing growth, such as policies to improve the neutrality of taxation, promote human capital accumulation and lessen income inequality.

## Notes

1. While the second factor-resource accumulation-has traditionally been the focal point of growth economics, Schumpeter (1934) made the case for the first and third factors, which together imply productivity improvement, as the main ingredients for growth. Tanzi (1995) expanded on the Schumpeterian theme and emphasized the importance of a country's social absorptive capacity (with respect to technology) in determining its development. The resource-accumulation versus productivity-improvement debate has raged in recent years as researchers have tried to understand the factors which have contributed to the impressive growth of a small number of East Asian economies. For an argument supporting the resource accumulation thesis in this context, see Young (1995).
2. While the early roots of this literature go some ways back to Arrow (1962) and Uzawa (1965), its present analytics owe much to Romer (1986) and Lucas (1988).
3. The inter-temporal utility maximization-based neoclassical growth models that have become familiar today are actually due to Cus (1965) and Koopmans (1965).
4. For an illuminating discussion, see Romer (1989). There is, however, no consensus among researchers on the question of convergence. Studies by Baumol (1986). Barro and Sala-i-

Martin (1995), Mankiw et at. (1992), and Sala-i-Martin (1996a, 1996b) tended to confirm the existence of convergence, provided that variables other than income (such as human capital) are properly controlled. For a dissenting view, see Quah (19968, 1996b).

5. An early influential investigation into this problem was provided by Nordhaus and Tobin (1973). A different aspect of the problem commonly found in most centrally planned economies is that of the suboptimal mix of outputs-often heavily biased toward the production of capital goods.
6. The concept and measurement of excess burden has a long and controversial history in economics dating in its modern formulation at least as far back as the work of Dupuit more than a century ago. For a recent comprehensive survey of this literature, see Auerbach (1985).
7. The voluminous literature on this subject is succinctly surveyed in Sandmo (1985). Two well-known results from this literature are worth noting. Atkinson and Sandmo (1980) showed that, in a two-period, life cycle, overlapping-generations model, the optimal capital income tax rate in the long run is not necessarily zero, but instead would generally depend on the relative tax elasticities of labour supply and savings, as well as on their cross elasticities. The nature of this outcome is characteristic of the optimal taxation literature. In contrast, Charnley (1986), using an infinite-horizon model, demonstrated that the long-run optimal capital income tax rate is in fact zero. The two results differ because the intergenerational inefficiency resulting from taxing capital income is not fully capturable in a life cycle framework.
8. It is common to note that, in the absence of a labour-leisure choice, the inter temporal budget constraint of an economic agent implies that taxing wage income (and inherited wealth) only (leaving interest income untaxed) is equivalent to taxing consumption (and bequests), with national savings unaffected by the choice between these two taxes (unless there are other distortions). Tanzi and Zee (1993) showed, however, that if consumption requires time, a wage tax would discourage savings in a manner similar to that of a tax on interest income.
9. Trade taxes are frequently the most administratively reliable tax handles, and consequently heavily relied upon to produce

revenue in many developing countries. On an average, trade taxes (especially import duties) amount to about a quarter of total tax revenue in a broad group of non-OECD countries, compared to about 2 percent in OECD countries. See Zee (1996a).

10. For a clear separation of these two effects, see Ram (1986).
11. For a recent development of this argument, see Devarajan et aI. (1996). for a discussion of the various aspects of the productive-unproductive classification of public expenditure. One type of unproductive public expenditure that has received much attention recently is military spending. See, for example, Knight et al. (1996). It should, however, be noted that not all public expenditure programs are designed to promote growth. Hence, some public expenditures could be unproductive in the growth sense, and yet simultaneously effective in the sense of achieving their objectives.
12. In the United States, military spending has often produced technologies potentially beneficial to the whole economy. This is less likely to happen in other, and particularly in developing, countries.
13. In an investigation of Wagner's law, Tanzi and Zee (1995) found the correlation between the levels of public wage expenditure and income to be positive for middle-low income countries and negative for high income countries.
14. This result comes about because it may pay to wait for a favourable state of nature to occur. Depending on the nature of the uncertainty, however, uncertain returns could, under some circumstances, stimulate investment. One reason is that the act of investing itself sometimes provides additional information that could act to reduce the uncertainty; another reason is that a mean-preserving spread of variance (i.e., an increase in variance with the same mean) with respect to returns would increase the expected value of a project, if the valuation function displays diminishing marginal value of returns. For a recent comprehensive treatment of this literature, see Dixit and Pindyck (1994); for an illustration that the impact of uncertainty on investment is dependent on the way tax regime uncertainty is modelled, see Hassett and Metcalf (1994).
15. See Fischer (1980) for a particularly illuminating discussion of this example. Kydland and Prescott (1980) examined essentially

the same example in greater generalities. The same demonstration can be made with respect to human capital investment, where a government could find it optimal to tax such investment lightly in the early periods of an individual's life, but to tax the returns from human capital heavily once the capital has been formed.

16. See, for example, the well-known demonstration by Lucas and Stokey (1983). As it turns out, in a typical inter temporal model with endogenous labour supply but with no capital, whether an optimal tax regime is time-inconsistent or not depends critically on the tax instruments at the disposal of the government. If only an income tax (either on wages or on interest income, or both) is available, the outcome is time inconsistent (Turnovsky and Brock, 1980; and Lucas and Stokey, 1983). Rogers (1987) found that a consumption tax is time consistent under a Cobb-Douglas utility function. When the utility function has a general specification., however, Zee (1994) showed that an optimal tax regime would be time consistent only if both the income and consumption taxes are available. Moreover, Zee (1994) also showed that an optimal time-consistent tax structure could be distortive.
17. Whether an economy is dynamically efficient or not is an empirical question; theory cannot rule out the possibility that its long-run growth rate could exceed the long-run real interest rate (see Diamond. 1965). In the latter case, the solvency requirement is no longer meaningful, as the government could sustain some positive stock of public debt forever simply through additional borrowing without having to run budget surpluses (this phenomenon has sometimes been referred to as a Ponzi finance scheme), because by assumption the debt service cost is lower than income growth. The determination of a sustainable positive stock of public debt was examined by Zee (1988). Recently, however, Abel et al. (1989) found that most capitalistic economies are dynamically efficient.
18. For this argument, see Sinn (1995, 1996). The link between redistributive taxation and social insurance was explored earlier in Eaton and Rosen (1980) and Varian (1980). While the connection between taxation and risk taking is not new, the existing literature on it by and large focuses on the impact of taxation on portfolio investment decisions (see Atkinson and

Stiglitz (1980) for a review) rather than on issues of income redistribution.

# 3

# Indian Fiscal System

Fiscal system refers to the mechanism through which financial resources for the government and its agencies are procured, channelled or raised, and the scale and pattern of allocation of such resources is determined. In the Indian fiscal system, the budgetary resources and expenditures are determined through the annual budget of the Central Government and the State Governments. The five yearly as well as annual resources and expenditure for development plans of the public sector as a whole are determined by the Planning Commission.

## 3.1 A Brief Prelude

Even before Independence, there was a broad consensus, across the political spectrum, that once Independence was achieved, Indian economic development should be planned, with the state playing a dominant role in the economy and achieving self-sufficiency across the board as a major objective (Srinivasan 1996). Within three years of independence, a National Planning Commission was established in 1950, charged with the task of drawing up national development plans. Broadly, during the first 30 years of Independence, between 1950 and 1980, the fiscal deficits of both the central and the state governments were not excessive. This was a period of revenue surplus in general. However, automatic monetization of government deficit by the RBI, which started as an exception during the mid 1950s, became a regular practice thereafter. Simultaneously, there was also a distinct shift in the management of the financial sector with the nationalization of major commercial banks in 1969 and 1980.

These two developments had a significant bearing on the

relationship between the monetary authority (RBI) and the fiscal authority (Government). There was a significant deterioration in the fiscal situation in the 1980s, accompanied by large and automatic monetization of government deficits. The process involved issue of ad-hoc Treasury bills at rates initially on par with 91-day Treasury Bills. Since July 1974, the ad-hoc Treasury bills were offered at off-market discount rate of 4.6 percent which was less than half of the prevailing market rates. There were two immediate consequences.

Firstly, when large government deficits were monetized, there was excess liquidity in the system, which prompted the monetary authorities to increase the cash reserve ratio (CRR) for banks at regular intervals with a view to mop up the excess liquidity.

Secondly, to facilitate the central government to borrow comfortably, the monetary authority, which is also the debt manager for the government, periodically increased the statutory liquidity ratio (SLR) to be maintained by banks. This process went on to an extent that CRR and SLR, together, pre-empted more than 50 percent of banking sector liabilities, for a period. In other words, more than 50 percent of the resources of the banking sector were pre-empted to primarily finance the budget deficits of the governments.

Further, the deposit and lending rates of banks were, for most part, administered. This situation impacted the health of the banking system and the consequential adjustments during the banking sector reform process were, naturally, somewhat complex. The large fiscal deficit and its monetization had some spill-over effect on the external sector, which reflected in the widening current account deficit in the late 1980s and early 1990s. Triggered by the balance of payments crisis in the early 1990s, when India's foreign currency assets depleted rapidly to the extent that it could barely finance just two weeks of imports, it had started the reform process in 1991-92. A credible macroeconomic structural and stabilization programme encompassing trade, industry, foreign investment, exchange rate, public finance and financial sector was put in place, which created an environment that was conducive for the expansion of trade and investment. Simultaneously, several reform measures towards the mercerization of government borrowings were initiated.

The First Supplemental Agreement between the RBI and the Government of India was signed in 1994 setting out a system of limits for creation of ad hoc treasury bills during the three-year period ending 1996-97. Then in 1997, soon the second agreement with the government was signed, in pursuance of this Second Supplemental Agreement between the RBI and the Government of India on March 6, 1997, the ad hoc Treasury Bills were completely phased out from April 1997, replaced by a scheme of Ways and Means Advances, subject to limits. In order to smoothen the transition, the Government of India was allowed to incur also an overdraft, but at an interest rate higher than the rate applicable for Ways and Means Advances (WMA). With effect from April 1, 1999 these overdrafts were allowed only for a maximum of ten working days.

These features placed the Central Government on par with the State governments which were brought under an "Overdraft Regulation Scheme" since 1985. Furthermore, it was agreed that the RBI would trigger fresh floatation of Government securities whenever 75 percent of the WMA limit was reached. It was also agreed that the government's surplus cash balances with the RBI, beyond an agreed level, would be invested by it in government securities. While the transition to a full-fledged WMA and overdraft mechanism was gradual, non-disruptive and consensual, the successful implementation of this mechanism made it possible to incorporate some of these practices into a law—the Fiscal Responsibility and Budget Management Act (FRBM Act). It is noteworthy that this law also practically prohibited RBI from participating in primary issues of all government securities.

As a result of the concerted efforts to restore fiscal balance through tax reforms, expenditure management, institutional reforms and financial sector reforms in the first half of the 1990s, there was significant reduction in the magnitude of fiscal deficit and the proportion of debt relative to GDP during the period 1991 to 1997. However, during the period 1997 to 2003, there was a reversal in the trend of fiscal consolidation, and the cumulative impact of industrial slowdown, fifth pay commission award, and a lower than expected revenue buoyancy culminated in fiscal deterioration. This deterioration in the Indian fiscal position happened at an inopportune time when there was fiscal improvement the world over and India was trying to globalize. It is important to remember that India's fiscal situation has been significantly divergent from the global fiscal situation and continues to be so even now. This is the background one should keep in view whenever discussing the pace and the content of economic reforms in India. The coming into force of the FRBM Act, 2003 on July 5, 2004, which established a framework for a rule based fiscal consolidation, should be viewed in this background (Y.V. Reddy, 2008).

In the period subsequent to 2003, the central government's fiscal position has been improving, though there are several underlying fiscal pressures that are not entirely evident in the numbers, as will be explained later. The states' fiscal positions have also improved significantly during this period and their revenue deficits are close to being virtually eliminated. However, as in the case of the Centre, there are some underlying pressures that are not reflected in the fiscal numbers of the States.

Despite considerable improvement in the fiscal scenario, both at the centre and in the states, India's combined fiscal deficit (centre and state), as a percentage of GDP, still continues to be one of the highest in the world. In this context, the UK-based weekly the Economist (dated November 17, 2007, pages 75-77) ranked India, along with Turkey and Hungary, as the riskiest economies among select leading emerging market economies. The Economist based its conclusion on standard parameters such as current account balance, budget balance, inflation and growth in bank lending, for assessing the degree of risk. One cannot disagree with the relevance of these parameters in assessing risks. Yet it is noteworthy that most of these risky elements were present in the Indian economy for several years, almost all through the reform period, and yet the economy exhibited macro-stability and impressive growth even while withstanding some significant domestic and global shocks. In view of this evidence, India needs to explore the reasons for such risks not de-stabilising our economy so far and the measures that are needed, in future, for insulating the economy from such de-stabilising effects, to the extent feasible.

### 3.2 Fiscal Consolidation

Fiscal policy is the building block for an enabling macro-environment, which not only provides stability and predictability to the policy regime, but through its tax transfer mechanism, also ensures that national resources are allocated in terms of its defined priorities. Unproductive expenditure, tax distortions and high deficits are considered to have constrained the economy from realising its full growth potential. The medium-term fiscal policy stance of Government, therefore, has been to reduce deficits, prioritise expenditure and ensure that this results in intended outcome and augment resources by widening the tax base and improving the compliance while maintaining moderate rates. At the beginning of the fiscal reforms in 1991, the fiscal imbalance was identified as the root cause of the twin problems of inflation and the difficult balance of payments position.

The fiscal consolidation, which followed in response, in the absence of a defined mandate, however, failed to sustain itself. For medium-term management of the fiscal deficit, and to provide the support of a strong institutional mechanism, the Fiscal Reforms and Budget Management Act (FRBMA) was enacted on August 26, 2003 and the Act and the rules were notified to come into effect from July 5, 2004. FRBMA is an important institutional expression to ensure fiscal prudence and support for macroeconomic balance. With the enactment of the FRBMA, the traditional annual budgeting moved to a more meaningful medium-term fiscal planning framework. According to the Rules, revenue deficit is to be reduced by an amount equivalent to half percent or more of the estimated GDP at the end of each financial year and eliminated by March 31, 2009. Fiscal deficit is to be reduced by an amount equivalent to 0.3 percent or more of the estimated GDP at the end of each financial year and reduced to no more than three percent of the estimated GDP by the financial year ending on March 31, 2009. The process of fiscal consolidation under FRBMA has been continuous and essentially an incremental one. Some of the important fiscal measures that are being implemented include: reducing the peak rates of customs duties; rectifying anomalies like inverted duty structure; rationalising excise duties with a movement towards a median CENVAT rate; revisiting the tax exemptions; relying on voluntary tax compliance through taxpayer facilitation; introduction of State-level VAT for achieving a non-cascading, self enforcing, and harmonized commodity tax.

### 3.3 Fiscal Sector Development at the Central Level

Fiscal sector reforms were perhaps the most critical part of the macroeconomic stabilization and reforms initiatives taken by the government after the 1991 economic crisis. Notwithstanding the initial fiscal adjustment measures for correcting the fiscal imbalances immediately after the crisis and the subsequent fiscal reforms, a high level of deficits in the government budgets particularly during the second half of 1990s, continue to constrain growth impulses for the economy. The level of fiscal deficit combined both for the Central government and State governments is more or less at the same level at the end of 1990's as it was at the beginning.

Government debt is approaching a critical mark beyond which it could be labelled as unsustainable.

**3.3.1 Taxation Developments:** Tax reforms during 1990s have been mainly guided by the report of the Chelliah Committee on Tax Reforms (1993). The main objectives have been simplification of the tax system, rationalization of tax rates, fairness in tax system, improvement in tax administration and above all providing a growth promoting tax structure. The wide range of reform measures taken during the last decade include in the case of direct taxes: moderation of tax rates, widening of tax base, incentives for development of infrastructure and housing and strengthening of enforcement, and in the case of indirect taxes: reduction in multiplicity of rates, rationalization of the rate structure, drastic reduction in the scope for discretionary changes and uniform floor rates for sales tax by the States. Further, rationalization and improvements in tax administration, of course, is a continuing process.

**3.3.2 Disinvestment, Privatization and Restructuring of Public Sector:** The strategy towards public sector enterprises reform encompasses a judicious mix of strengthening strategic units, privatizing non strategic ones through gradual disinvestment or strategic sale and devising viable rehabilitation strategies for weak units. The latest policy announced by the Finance Minister has the following as main elements:

1. Restructure and revive potentially viable PSUs.
2. Close down PSUs which cannot be revived.
3. Bring down Government equity in all non-strategic PSUs to 26 percent or lower, if necessary.
4. Fully protect the interests of workers.

During the last two years, financial restructuring of 20 PSUs has been approved by the Government. As a result, many PSUs have been able to restructure their operations, improve productivity and achieve a turnaround in performance. Even so, a large number of procedural as well as policy issues continue to constrain the progress on disinvestment process.

Various fiscal reform measures relating to Central Public Enterprises (CPEs) undertaken by the Central Government have shown some noticeable improvements in the finances of these enterprises during the decade of 1990s. In particular, it needs to be noted that the budgetary support (Plan + Non-Plan) to CPEs as a percent of GDP came down to only 0.5 percent in 1998-99 from 1.5 percent in 1990-91 and CPEs deficit GDP ratio came down to 1.3 percent in 1998-99 from 3.0 percent in 1990-91. Moreover, profitability trends also depicted a distinct improvement. The profit after tax, as percent of net worth, for CPEs, had increased to 10.4 percent in 1997-98 from 3.9 percent in 1990-91.

**3.3.3 Borrowings by Government:** Though largely treading on financial sector reforms, the significant changes in the process of central government borrowings to meet the budgetary deficits and temporary mismatches have been part of the fiscal sector reforms as well.

Switchover to borrowings by government at market related interest rates, abolition of the system of automatic monetization of the budget deficit, implementing a new system of ways and means advances, and developing as well as deepening government securities market have changed the whole system of financing the budgetary deficit and its relation with monetary policy stance The new system of ways and means advances (WMA), implies vacation of advances made by the RBI to the government with limits fixed for a given time period (Ten days). This system has provided scope for a judicious credit creation, possibilities for monetary targeting, a closer monetary and fiscal policy interactions, and mechanisms for open market operations to take care of surges in inflows of foreign capital (Reddy, 2000b).

Notwithstanding the fact that greater reliance on market borrowings and bond finance (BF) and that too at market related rates rather than less borrowing along with monetization route, has led to an excessive debt burden for the government, empirical testing in a recent research study (Moorthy et.al. 2000 June) has shown that move to market borrowings has been beneficial as (a) there is no evidence of a systematic shift to an unstable debt regime during the 1990s, (b) reduction in monetization has helped curb the fiscal deficit by inducing a fall in primary expenditures larger than the rise in interest payments, (c) the decline in private sector interest rates due to the move to market borrowing indicates that overall costs of private borrowings are likely to have declined, and (d) there has been a surge in private investment relative to public investment.

Nevertheless, the study points out that Central and State government finances are in precarious condition due to large non-market debt, unfounded liabilities and contingent liabilities.

**3.3.4 Expenditure Reforms Commission:** To carry the process of reducing the growth in non-developmental expenditure, the government has set up (in February, 2000) an Expenditure Reforms Commission. The main terms of reference for the Commission were as follows:

1. To suggest a road map for reducing the functions, activities and administrative structure of the Central Government.
2. To review the framework of all subsidies, both explicit and implicit for maximizing their impact on the target population and minimize cost.
3. To review the framework for determination of user charges of Departmental and Commercial activities: suggest an effective strategy for cost recovery.
4. To review the adequacy of staffing under Central government Ministries, attached offices etc.
5. To review the procedure for setting up of government funded autonomous institutions.
6. To consider any other relevant issue concerning expenditure management in government and make suitable

recommendation.

The Commission has already submitted to the government a few interim Reports.

## 3.4 Fiscal Sector Development at the Level of States

Of late, several State governments have been facing acute financial problems due to various structural rigidities as well as ad hoc compulsions including steep pay hikes to their employees. Specific time bound fiscal reform programs have, therefore, been discussed in the National Development Council (represented by the Chief Ministers of States) and with the Finance Minister. It was felt that joint effort on the part of the Centre as well as Sates is required to devise a medium term strategy for fiscal reform programs in the States. This strategy has taken the form of a package of advance financial assistance to be provided by the Centre to the States for an appropriate time bound reform program by signing a Memorandum of Understanding (MOU).

The main objective of the program is to wipe out the revenue deficit in the State budget in the medium term. The programme components are:

1. Reduction in Non Plan Revenue Expenditure, through appropriate taxation and expenditure measures and down-sizing of Government, where possible;
2. Pricing/subsidy reforms, to reduce fiscal burden of the State and improve allocative efficiency;
3. Institutional reforms, to improve regulation and efficiency in delivery of public services and;
4. Reduction in the role of Government in nonessential areas, through decentralization disinvestment and privatization;

**3.4.1 RBI Initiatives on State Finances:** In response to the emerging new balances, it has been recognized that finances at the provincial level are critical to the realignment of the role of the state in the economy. Contextually, the Reserve Bank started a close and more intensive interaction with State Governments on a regular basis, and on a wide range of relevant issues. Accordingly, several significant initiatives have been taken during the recent years, which include the following:

1. Reserve Bank in its role as adviser to the States, had examined the implications of contingent liabilities/guarantees granted by the States to facilitate economic activities. A Committee of State Finance Secretaries has, with the active involvement of Reserve Bank, recommended limits on Government guarantees.
2. With the support from Reserve Bank, a Committee of Finance Secretaries of State Governments is presently working on the issue of transparency and voluntary disclosure norms for State Budgets.
3. Recently, the States have also been encouraged to access the market for a part of their market borrowings. Within the approved borrowing program, the State Governments are provided with the option of raising resources in a flexible manner in terms of method, timing and maturates. The State Governments can borrow from the market between 5 percent to 35 percent of the approved borrowing limit under the new scheme. The State of Punjab, Andhra Pradesh, Tamil Nadu and Karnataka have raised funds directly from the market. The gains from the auction mechanism were seen from the fact that the auction based yield were below the pre announced rates.
4. A Committee of the State Finance Secretaries is currently acting in an advisory capacity to oversee the indicators of financial parameters by the Reserve Bank.
5. The Reserve Bank has been advising the State Governments in areas such as cash management, funds management and reforms in budgetary practices. Cash management techniques relate to updating of accounts, data analysis, technology improvements, updating of financial accounting and other codes and prompt analysis of monthly data. Modernization of budgetary procedures and financial practices and development of forecasting

models or expert systems are some of the issues being examined as a part of reforms in budgetary practices.

6. Mounting debt of the State Governments is increasing the burden on future generations. To achieve some inter-generational equity, Reserve Bank has, in consultation with State Finance Secretaries, developed a scheme for Consolidated Sinking Fund which is optional for State Governments.

## 3.5 Trends in Fiscal Imbalances

Revenue deficit is the difference between revenue expenditure and revenue receipts. Broadly, the revenue deficit indicates the excess of current expenditures over revenues, or dis-savings by the Government. The fiscal deficit captures the excess of overall expenditure over revenue comprising current receipts and non debt capital receipts. Revenue deficit implies an increase in the liabilities of the Central Government without a corresponding increase in its assets. The existence of revenue deficit indicates that a part of the borrowings by the Government is not being used for financing public investment. When the focus is only on reducing the fiscal deficit, the brunt of fiscal correction is often borne by compression in capital expenditure. The change in revenue deficit on the path of fiscal adjustment indicates the quality of fiscal correction, which is as important as the level of fiscal correction itself. FRBMA highlights the significance of keeping the revenue expenditure under control and envisages elimination of the revenue deficit by the end of 2008-09.

At the beginning of reforms in 1991, the fiscal imbalances were identified as the root cause of the balance of payments crisis and domestic inflation. The fiscal consolidation, which followed in response, however, failed to sustain itself as it lacked a statutory mandate and the required institutional support. The enactment of the Fiscal Responsibility and Budget Management Act (FRBMA), 2003 provided the required mandate and lent credibility to the fiscal reforms process. States have also joined the process of fiscal consolidation in line with the Twelfth Finance Commission's (TFC) recommendations and are complementing the efforts of the Central Government.

As recommended by TFC and following the example of the Central Government, States have already enacted fiscal responsibility legislations. The fiscal situation of the States has shown considerable improvement, which in fact is even better relative to the performance of the Central Government, post-FRBMA. As a proportion of GDP, the fiscal deficit of the States declined from 4.4 percent in 2003-04 to 2.3 percent in 2007-08.

**3.5.1 Global Financial Crisis and Setback to Fiscal Consolidation:** The fiscal stimulus packages to arrest slowdown in the domestic economy have involved additional expenditures and tax cuts, putting stress on government finances.

Government finances, which had exhibited a noteworthy correction starting 2002-03, came under renewed pressure in 2008-09 on account of higher expenditure outgoes due to following factors: (a) higher international crude oil prices (up to September 2008) and the incomplete pass-through to domestic prices, (b) Sixth Central Pay Commission award and (c) debt waiver scheme.

Reflecting these and other factors, the Central Government's fiscal deficit more than doubled from 2.7 percent of GDP in 2007-08 to 7 percent in 2009-10 (revised estimates), and is slated to be 5.8 percent during 2010-11. Similarly, revenue deficit which stood at 1.1 percent of GDP in 2007-08 increased to 5.3 percent in 2009-10 and is estimated at 4.0 percent in the 2010-11 as mentioned in the 2010-11 Union Budget presented to Parliament on February 26, 2010 (Table 3.1). The previous low touched by revenue deficit was 4.4 percent of GDP during 2001-02 and 2002-03.

Various segments of the domestic financial market have been developed over a period of time to facilitate efficient channelling of resources form savers to investors and enable the continuation of domestic growth momentum. Investment has been predominantly financed domestically in India. The Government's fiscal deficit has been high by international standards but is also largely internally financed through a vibrant and well-developed government securities market, and thus, despite large fiscal deficits, macroeconomic and financial stability has been maintained.

**Table 3.1: Fiscal and Revenue Deficits of Central Government Budgets**

(as percent of GDP)

| | 2008-09 Accounts | 2009-10 R.E. | 2010-11 B.E. |
|---|---|---|---|
| Fiscal deficit | 6.0 | 6.7 | 5.8 |
| Revenue deficit | 4.5 | 5.3 | 4.0 |

B.E. = Budget estimates and R.E. = Revised estimates

Source: Government of India, Ministry of Finance, Budget Papers, 2010-11, *Budget at a Glance.*

## 3.6 Robust Economic Growth and Buoyant Tax Revenue

Robust economic growth and improved performance of the manufacturing and services sectors helped to keep tax revenues buoyant during the last five years.

The year 2007-08 was also the first year of the Eleventh Five Year Plan with the declared objective of "Faster and more inclusive growth". With growth accelerating from 5.5 percent per annum during the Ninth Five Year Plan to 7.8 percent per annum during the Tenth Five Year Plan, the Eleventh Five Year Plan has targeted an average growth of 9 percent. Consequently, gross budgetary support (GBS) for the annual plan 2007-08 was increased by 20.7 percent.

Bharat Nirman, a time-bound plan for rural infrastructure by the Government of India in partnership with State Governments and Panchayati Raj Institutions, remained the cornerstone of the Government's policy. The allocation for Bharat Nirman (including NER component) was increased by

31.6 percent in the 2007-08 Budget. The eight flagship programmes of the Government continued to receive high priority and significant increase in allocations were made in Sarva Shiksha Abhiyan, Mid-day Meal Scheme, Rajiv Gandhi Drinking Water Mission, Total Sanitation Campaign, National Rural Health Mission, Integrated Child Development Programme, National Rural Employment Guarantee Scheme and Jawaharlal Nehru National Urban Renewal Mission.

During the Tenth Five Year Plan, the buoyancy of tax revenue, with an average annual growth of 21.4 percent coincided with an acceleration in the growth of GDP. Considering such a performance, 2007-08 (BE) projected an increase of 23.4 percent in tax revenues over 2006-07. The shift in the structure of taxes from relatively regressive indirect taxes to direct taxes continued in 2007-08. The direct tax to GDP ratio has seen an uptrend because of the reforms in income and corporate taxes that simplified the tax system, reduced exemptions and tax rates, thus providing an incentive for better compliance. At the same time indirect tax GDP ratio has fallen because of reduction in custom duties and increasing exemptions in excise taxes.

The procedural reforms in direct taxes remained focused on expanding the tax base, improving tax compliance and making the tax administration more efficient. At the same time certain new initiatives and exemptions were provided to promote physical infrastructure, research and development in industry, development of the North-Eastern Region, and agriculture. To enable urban local bodies to raise funds for capital investment in urban infrastructure, exemption was provided on interest on notified bonds issued by a notified State Pooled Finance Entity on behalf of the urban local bodies.

To provide adequate stock of hotel rooms for the Commonwealth Games to be hosted in Delhi in 2010 and also to boost the number of convention centres, deduction was allowed in respect of profits and gains derived from the business of hotels and convention centres in the National Capital Territory of Delhi and districts of Faridabad, Gautam Budh Nagar, Ghaziabad and Gurgaon. Weighted deduction for expenditure on scientific research on approved in-house R&D facility in the case of a company engaged in the business of biotechnology or in the business of manufacture or production of any drugs, pharmaceuticals, electronic equipment, computers, telecommunication equipment, chemicals or any other article or thing notified by the Board was allowed for a further period of 5 years from March31, 2007 to March 31, 2012. A package of fiscal incentives and other concessions for the North-East Region, namely, the North-East Industrial and Investment Promotion Policy (NEIIPP) 2007 were provided. Bonds issued by NABARD and notified by the Central Government were included in Section 80C as an additional investment avenue for investors seeking tax benefit.

**3.6.1 Indirect Taxes:** As part of a continuous process of bringing about a moderate, rational and simplified tax structure and to reduce rates to ASEAN levels as per announced commitments, the peak rate of customs duty on non-agricultural products was reduced from 12.5 percent in 2006-07 to 10 per cent in 2007-08, with a few exceptions.

Service tax—a promising source of revenue Service tax was introduced in 1994-95 to redress the asymmetric and distortionary treatment of goods and services in the tax framework and to widen the tax net. It has been a buoyant source of revenue in recent years. The number of services liable for taxation was raised from 3 in 1994-95 to 75 in 2004-05 and then gradually to 114 in 2009-10. In 2010-11 Budget, certain more services have been included and process of refund of accumulated credit to exporters of services, especially in the area of Information Technology and Business Process Outsourcing has been made easy.

The peak rate of basic customs duty was brought down progressively from 150 percent in 1991-92 to 10 percent on non-agricultural products in the Budget for 2007-08 with a few exceptions. Owing to the calibrated reduction in custom duty, though resulting in a deceleration in the growth of revenue from it, there was an improvement in competitiveness of domestic industries and acceleration in the growth of manufacturing. Revenue from custom duty, in addition to the basic customs duty, also includes additional duty, which is the counterpart of the excise duty on domestically produced items, and special additional duty, a very partial counterpart of State taxes on domestic goods.

While the basic duty is the base level of protection to domestic industry, additional and special duties are in the nature of providing a level playing field to domestic industry. Since there were numerous rates and exemptions, the closest approximation to the average effective rates for import duty (Basic+AD+SAD) for different sectors is given by the relevant collection rates. The collection rate for all commodity groups fell from 15 percent in 2002-03 to 10 percent in 2005-06 and has remained at that level in 2006-07. Collection rate declined sharply for POL products, from 30 percent in 1995-96 to 5 percent in 2006-07. Decline was also sharp for non-POL products. Food products, paper and newsprint and natural fibres, however, did not experience a decline. In case of paper and newsprint and natural fibres the collection rate has remained low. Collection rate for chemicals, metals and capital goods also witnessed a decline. Lower rates for these products significantly contributed to acceleration in growth of these sectors and in improving overall competitiveness of domestic industry.

**3.6.2 Tax Expenditures:** The exemptions and incentives in the tax laws, which result in what are called tax expenditures, distort resource allocation by impinging upon the efficiency of the market. Further, they complicate the tax laws, increase litigation and raise the compliance cost for the taxpayers and the tax administration. Tax incentives and exemptions are being continuously reviewed so as to eliminate or provide a sunset clause to those that have outlived their rationale. A tax expenditure statement enables a more informed public debate on the efficacy of exemptions and discourages entrenched groups from demanding incentives in perpetuity.

Minimum Alternate Tax (MAT) base was widened to include the profits of STPI units and export-oriented units, which enjoy a tax holiday. Similarly, some incentives to the housing sector and to scientific research and development were allowed to sunset. Simultaneously, in the realm of indirect taxes, 7 exemptions in customs duties and 7 exemptions in Central excise duties were withdrawn.

### 3.7 Expenditure Trends

FRBMA stipulates that public expenditure must be reoriented for the creation of productive assets. Given the existing classification of expenditure, plan expenditure and capital expenditure are the closest approximation to such expenditure.

**3.7.1 Interest Payments:** Persistent and high deficits seriously impair the counter cyclical ability of fiscal policy, lead to unsustainable debt build up and adversely affect the composition of expenditure through larger interest outgo. As a proportion of GDP, interest payments after remaining at a high level of 4.8 per cent in 2002-03, started declining to reach 3.6 percent in 2006-07. It is budgeted to decline further to 3.4 percent of GDP in 2007-08. These declining trends, as proportion of both GDP and revenue receipts, were partly on account of the softening of interest rates which resulted in progressive reduction in the average cost of borrowing and slower growth of debt. The average cost of internal borrowing, including those under Market Stabilisation Scheme (MSS), is budgeted at 7.9 percent in 2007-08.

### 3.8 Subsidies

The impact of subsidies on specific goods and services is the opposite of that of excise and service taxes. By reducing relative prices, subsidies can increase the use of products like food, fertilizer and petroleum products. Market solutions often result in under consumption of various goods and services by vulnerable sections, either because of higher prices or because of competing claims on their income of other goods. By reducing the prices, across the board or for the specified groups, subsidies increase affordability, improve access, and correct under consumption of these goods with positive externalities. With direct provision by the Centre, major subsidies, mainly on food, fertilizer and petroleum, grew from Rs. 40,716 crore in 2002-03 to Rs. 52,935 crore in 2006-07, and were budgeted at Rs. 51,247 crore in 2007-08.

Though, as a proportion to GDP, major subsidies have declined in the last five years, as a percentage of total expenditure, these are still at a significantly high level of about 8 percent. These budgetary subsidies, however, do not include compensation provided through the issue of special securities to oil marketing companies, Food Corporation of India and fertilizer units. However, besides the issues relating to fiscal cost of subsidies and their distortionary impact on price mechanism, there are important governance issues of leakages, inefficient delivery mechanism and inclusion/ exclusion error associated with subsidies. The NCMP, therefore, mandates the Government to target all subsidies sharply at the poor and needy.

### 3.9 Government Debt

The RBI as the Government's debt manager fixes biannual indicative issuance calendar for the Government borrowings, in consultation with the Ministry of Finance.

Borrowings should generally be resorted to only for the purpose of asset creation. However, with the existence of a revenue deficit all through these years, a significant proportion of liabilities were contracted to meet the current expenditure commitments. Government accounting systems does not provide a comprehensive accounting of its assets, particularly land, building, etc., owned by it. But Government accounts do capture the assets created in the form of capital expenditure and outstanding loans receivable by the Central Government. These two together form the assets of Government created out of its annual fiscal operations.

Though the assets, for example, machinery and buildings, are of different vintages, their sum total nonetheless provides an assessment of Government's assets. Magnitude and trends in the outstanding liabilities of the Central Government (including external debt at historical exchange rate) are shown in Table 3.2.

**Table 3.2: Recent Trends in Outstanding Liabilities of the Central Government**

(end-March) (Rs. crore)

| | 2005-06 | 2006-07 | 2007-08 | 2008-09 | 2009-10 |
|---|---|---|---|---|---|
| 1. Internal liabilities | 21,65,902 | 24,35,880 | 27,25,394 | 30,14,441 | 33,57,772 |
| (a) Internal debt | 13,89,758 | 15,44,975 | 18,08,309 | 20,14,451 | 23,56,940 |
| (b) Other internal liabilities | 7,76,144 | 8,90,905 | 9,17,035 | 9,99,990 | 10,00,832 |
| 2. External debt (outstanding)$ | 94,243 | 1,02,716 | 1,12,031 | 1,21,634 | 1,37,680 |
| Total outstanding liabilities (1+2) | 22,60,145 | 25,38,596 | 28,37,425 | 31,36,075 | 34,95,452 |
| As percent of GDP | | | | | |
| 1. Internal liabilities | 58.4 | 56.9 | 55.1 | 54.1 | 54.5 |
| (a) Internal debt | 37.5 | 36.1 | 36.5 | 36.1 | 38.2 |
| (b) Other internal liabilities | 20.9 | 20.8 | 18.5 | 17.9 | 16.2 |
| 2. External debt (outstanding)$ | 2.5 | 2.4 | 2.3 | 2.2 | 2.2 |
| Total outstanding liabilities (1+2) | 61.0 | 59.3 | 57.3 | 56.3 | 56.7 |

2008-09 = Revised estimates; 2009-10 = Budget estimates.

$ External debt figures represent borrowings by the Central Government from external sources and are based on historical rates of exchange.

Source: Government of India, *Economic Survey*, 2009-10.

### 3.10 Eleventh Plan on Government Finances

The Eleventh Five Year Plan (2007-12) document points out the following major challenges in financing the plan.

1. The total resources for the Central and State Plans taken together have to increase from an average of 9.46 percent of GDP in the Tenth Five Year Plan to an average of 13.54 percent of GDP in the Eleventh Five Year Plan. It may be noted that while the total size of the Plan is projected at 13.54 percent of GDP, the total public investment in the economy is projected to be lower at 8.0 percent. This difference reflects the fact that a great deal of Plan expenditure finances current expenditure on various items of public service delivery which are not counted as investment.
2. The increase of 4.08 percent of GDP in total resources for the Plan has to be achieved while keeping borrowing within the FRBM requirement of reducing the fiscal deficit of the Centre and the States to 3 percent of GDP on each account.
3. The combined BCR of the Centre and the States has to increase by more than the projected increase in Plan resources. As against the Centre's BCR of an average of (-) 0.84 percent of GDP, realized in the Tenth Five Year Plan, it is projected to average 2.31 percent of GDP over the Eleventh Five Year Plan, i.e. an improvement of 3.15 percentage points of GDP.

Similarly, the BCR of States is also expected to improve substantially from (-) 0.18 percent of GDP as realized in the Tenth Five Year Plan to 1.41 percent of GDP in the Eleventh Five Year plan. The projected improvement required in the combined BCR of the Centre and the States taken together is therefore 4.74 percentage points of GDP. The achievement of these BCR targets is a key element in the financing of the Plan.

The Eleventh Five Year Plan also proposes to address many outstanding issues that have emerged up over the years with the changing structure of Centre-State financial relations such as increasing role of Centrally Sponsored schemes, financial discipline following the adoption of Twelfth Finance Commission Report and the distinction between Plan and non-Plan expenditure and revenue and capital expenditure. The traditional distinction along the above lines has created situations such as poor provision for maintenance expenditure, illogicality of treating certain expenditure for similar objectives as Plan and certain others as non-Plan. There are also issues relating to resource transfer to agencies of Government not getting captured in the accounting system and thus nullifying the larger objective of transparency in public finance. Furthermore, the issue of non-comparability of the size of the State Plans across different States, arising out of different practices being followed among States, has to be dealt with. Some States cover public sector entities (except Financial Intermediaries) within the scope of the State as an economic entity.

# 4

# Fiscal Reforms in India

India's economic development has brought tremendous success for the country with a better global image. Eight percent growth rate of India's national income for consecutive three years is a true indication of its growth story. India's fiscal system has been reformed significantly since the early 1990s, in particular in the area of taxation. This has, together with other fundamental economic reforms, contributed to a remarkable transformation of the Indian economy leading to significantly higher economic growth and for the first time since Independence, a decline in the absolute number of people living below the poverty line (OECD, 2007). This chapter describes fiscal reforms over the past two decades and examines a number of fiscal policy issues, such as the development of deficits and debt levels, government spending, taxation and fiscal relations between the different levels of government. It identifies areas where additional reforms could help to further reduce economic distortions and improve the provision of public services. It first looks at fiscal consolidation which has been addressed with some delay but has made progress more recently. It then analyses government spending and spending areas where reform has progressed. as in the pension system, or where additional controls are needed, as with subsidies and public-sector wages. This is followed by a description of the main elements of the tax system, which has been significantly improved during the past and suggestions for further reforms.

## 4.1 Fiscal Responsibility and Budget Management Act

In India, government saving (net of depreciation) has been persistently negative since the early 1980s implying a significant use of private savings to finance current government spending. In the second half of the 1980s, when the government had pursued expansionary fiscal policies to support growth from the demand side, the central and state governments ran large deficits averaging together 8 percent of GDP. These deficits contributed to the foreign exchange crisis in 1991 which then prompted the far-reaching economic reforms. The combined deficit then declined until 1996-97, but increased again in the following years. Net dis-savings of general government peaked in FY 2001. The government was then absorbing almost half of the nation's saving in order to finance its own consumption outlays. In addition, the government was borrowing to finance its investment, capital transfers and loans to state-owned enterprises. As a result, the borrowing requirement (fiscal deficit) of state and local governments had reached nearly 10 percent of GDP by 2001 and public debt was rising significantly.

In order to end this unsustainable situation, the central government enacted legislation to improve fiscal discipline. After close to three years discussion, the Fiscal Responsibility and Budget Management Act (FRBM) was adopted in August 2003. This Act sets a medium-term target of achieving a balance between current revenue and current spending (*i.e.* a zero-revenue deficit) by 2008 and limits the overall fiscal deficit for the central government to 3 percent of GDP.

**4.1.1 FRBM Act and Transparency of Budgetary Policy:** The FRBM Act also improved the transparency of budgetary policy. The Act provides that the government has to lay three documents before Parliament every year: one with an assessment of economic prospects, another with its strategy with regard to taxation and expenditure, and the final one giving a three-year rolling target for the revenue balance and the overall fiscal balance. Quarterly progress reviews have to be placed before Parliament. The second quarter review is the most important because a statement of the remedial steps that will be taken to offset any shortfall from targets has to be provided to Parliament. The government now also publishes its asset register annually, so permitting the calculation of a net asset position for the government. Its revenue account, though, does not account for capital consumption. Estimates of the revenue foregone through exemptions and concessions from standard tax rates are now also published annually, and the central government has made a first step towards accrual accounting by publishing the outstanding amounts of tax and non-tax revenue.

**4.1.2 Implementation of FRBM by States:** During 2005, 23 state governments introduced similar legislation and, by the middle of 2006, only three states West Bengal, Sikkim and Jharkhand had not introduced such laws, mandating a fiscal deficit of 3 percent of state GDP. To some extent, this move reflected the incentivisation process of the Finance Commission, a body established by the constitution to advise on the sharing of tax revenues between the centre and the states. Standardised and rapid accounting procedures are still lacking at the state level and are almost non-existent at the municipal level with most local authorities not even using a double-entry accounting system.

States have also reduced their fiscal deficits after the severe financial pressures that they faced at the beginning of this decade. These pressures were the result of a failure to adjust other expenditures after large centrally-determined pay and pension increases at the end of the 1990s. With increased outlays funded from borrowing that amounted to nearly 40 percent of income, outlays on wages, pensions and interest increased to almost 70 percent of current revenues on average in the period 2000-03. The process of consolidation started in 2004 and has continued since then with the states planning to almost eliminate (on average) their revenue deficit in 2006 and reduce their fiscal deficit of 2 percent of GDP. The increases in the states' own tax revenues has been helped by a significant increase in transfers from central government which came in the form of higher shared taxes, increased grants and write-offs of interest due to the central government.

The process of consolidation is far from uniform across the states. In 2005, the remaining revenue deficit of the states was concentrated in just four states (Jharkhand, Kerala, Uttaranchal and West Bengal) where the fiscal deficit still amounted to between 35 percent and 60 percent of state government revenues, with similarly large revenue deficits for three of them. Indeed, these four states accounted for the whole of the revenue deficits of states, small deficits elsewhere were offset by surpluses in a number of states. As a result, debt levels of these four states continued to increase, rising from 37 to 47 percent of state GDP between 2000 and 2005, a particularly high burden given that their total revenue from taxation and transfers from central government amounted to just 14 percent of their GDP.

**4.1.3 FRBM Act and Check on Public Debt:** The current FRBM targets have provided a marked check in the growth of public debt. The combined fiscal deficit of centre and states has been falling steadily since 2001-02. After achieving a high of 9.64 per cent in 2001-02, it is expected to fall to 4.95 in 2008-09 (Budget estimates). If deficit targets are met, slightly less than might be thought of, given that the both levels of government are aiming for a 3 percent deficit, it would help in fiscal discipline. The current consolidation compares favourably with the past. In the second half of the 1980s when the government had pursued expansionary fiscal policies to support growth from the demand side, the combined deficit of the centre and of states amounted to between 8-10 percent of GDP, and these high deficits contributed to the foreign exchange crisis in 1991 which then prompted economic reforms. The combined deficit then declined until 1996-97, but increased again in the following years and in 2001-02 it peaked at 9.64 percent of GDP.

The current consolidation is clearly positive for economic growth. In the past, increases in interest payments have crowded out other government spending including public investment which led to the built-up of infrastructure bottlenecks. In addition, the government was absorbing a large part of private saving for government consumption. As a result of consolidation, government interest payments are declining as a share of GDP and government investment is rising again. The reduction in government dis-saving also contributes to the increase in national savings.

### 4.2 Tax Structure Reforms at the Central Level

Since the early 1990s, India's tax system has undergone a landslide change from a highly interventionist system towards more neutrality. In the decades before, taxes were levied together with licenses and other regulations as the main tool, to allocate resources under the central economic planning towards priority sectors and at the same time redistribute income which accrued in the protected markets. As a result, effective tax rates varied widely across sectors and incomes created inefficiencies leading to large-scale tax evasion.

During the first three to four decades after Independence India's tax system was characterized by highly redistributive income tax rates, high import tariffs, a multitude of excises besides the sales tax and at the same time many exemptions and preferential treatments which aimed at channelling resources towards priority sectors. This system turned out to be inefficient and unfair and also led to widespread tax evasion.

Furthermore, during the 1990s, economic distortions stemming from indirect taxes were reduced by converting excise on manufactured products into a form of value-added tax while the tax base was gradually widened by the introduction of a service tax. In 2005, the cascading system of state sales tax on goods was also switched to a value-added tax. The reforms of tariffs and excises considerably lowered tax revenues from these sources but was partially offset by an increase in direct tax revenues as the tax base increased, perhaps linked to the reduction in direct tax rates. Overall, these reforms reversed the temporary increase in revenues that had occurred in the second half of the 1980s due to tariffication. By the second half of the 1990s, the combined tax ratio of the centre and the states was, at around 14 percent of GDP, a similar rate to that in the first half of the 1980s prior to reform, but with much lower marginal tax rates. After 2002, with the upswing in the economy and the introduction of the service tax, the tax-GDP ratio increased again, and is now exceeding the peaks reached in the late 1980s, even though all marginal tax rates are appreciably lower than in the second half of the 1980s.

Tax revenues in India are low compared with both OECD countries and a number of developing countries. Two factors have resulted in this low tax ratio. First is the absence of a system of social transfers (for health, pensions and unemployment) covering the whole population, given that the current system only covers employees of larger companies and government. The second was the ability of central and state governments to use borrowing to cover almost one-third of total spending in the 1990s, a policy that was financially possible only because interest rates were low relative to the growth of GDP. If social security contributions are excluded from the comparison, then India's tax level is similar to that of China, Japan, Korea, Mexico and not much lower than in the United States. Several forces are pushing towards an increase in the average tax burden, notably the need to reduce the deficit and the desire to introduce a basic social safety net.

Indirect taxation accounts for the bulk of government revenues. Indirect taxes are levied both by the central government and the states according to demarcation lines established in the Constitution. The Constitution allows the central government to impose taxes on the production of goods and the provision of services, but not on the sale of goods at later stages, with the exception of inter-state sales. State governments have the power to tax sales of goods within their state at all stages. Only the federal government is allowed to tax inter-state sales of goods and to impose tariffs on international trade. It also imposes a countervailing duty on imports designed to ensure that imports pay the same central VAT as domestically produced goods.

**4.2.1 Introduction of CENVAT:** The central government also taxes the production of goods through central excise taxes. This tax is known as the central VAT (or CENVAT). Within the goods-producing sector, there is no cascading effect as goods' producers can offset input tax against output tax. However, distributors cannot offset the tax against their payment of state VAT and so it effectively becomes an excise tax. The central government also levies a tax, known as a countervailing duty, on imports that is set at the same rate as the excise tax on domestic production. In addition, the centre levies a service tax (of 10 percent) on a growing number of services.

The emphasis on the taxation of consumption has to a large extent resulted from the difficulty of taxing income when there are a large number of potential tax payers with low incomes, with a large proportion not being literate. The collection costs are also likely to be lower for indirect taxes than for direct taxes given that, even though there is a large number of small shops and manufacturers, the total number of tax points is much lower than total employment. Thus, the parameters of the income tax system have always been set to ensure that the vast bulk of the population is kept outside the income tax system. For example, after the threshold for paying personal income tax was raised to almost four times the average yearly wage in 2005, the number of taxpayers fell to 12 million from 26 million (less than 2 percent of the population aged 15 and over).

More tellingly, the exemption limit is equal to the average salary of a male graduate working in an urban area. Perhaps surprisingly, in view of the many anecdotes on the difficulty of raising tax from the unorganised sector of the economy, the total yield of income tax from the self employed was greater than that from wage-earners in 2004. With the increasing computerisation of government records, cross-matching of data files is improving the extent of compliance and it would be less costly to include more workers in the personal income tax net.

Given the dominance of indirect taxes, the effective tax burden (as measured by tax revenues as a percent of an estimated macroeconomic tax base) is much higher on consumption than that on labour. The effective rate on consumption has been rising in recent years with the progressive introduction of the service tax and by 2004 had reached nearly 21 percent when measured on a tax-exclusive base. By contrast, the tax rate on labour income is low at less than 3 percent, while the tax rate on capital was higher, at above 13 percent in 2004. It is noticeable that there are large differences in the apparent tax rates on different types of capital. The corporate sector pays relatively high taxes on capital whereas the unorganised sector pays very low tax on capital employed. This results, because of the low level of capital employed per individual tax unit, keeping much of the capital in untaxed units. While the gap between the effective tax rate on consumption and labour incomes is larger than in OECD countries, it is similar to that in China, Korea Thailand and Sri Lanka. However, overall capital taxation appears to be similar to that in Korea and Thailand but markedly higher than in China.

**4.2.2 Exemptions Causing Distortions:** There are numerous deductions and exemptions that result in considerable distortions to economic activity. Such tax breaks are a significant remaining element of government intervention in the economy. They are very widespread and affect nearly all central government taxes. Significant tax breaks were also offered by states but these have diminished considerably with the introduction of the value added tax.

Revenues from both the personal and the corporate income tax have increased in recent years. The reason is that cuts in statutory rates have to some extent been accompanied by base broadening. Tax compliance also improved, eased by lower tax rates and reinforced by more efficient tax administration, in particular the increased scope of deduction at source. Nonetheless, both the personal and the corporate income tax yield relatively little revenues. While the revenue yield from corporate taxation is almost the same as in the median OECD country, the yield from income taxes is only one-fifth. With rising incomes of firms and individuals, revenues from corporate and personal income taxes should further increase in the future. However, the various exemptions and tax incentives as well as the large informal sector will continue to restrain revenues from these taxes.

Exemptions to income tax are most noticeable in the area of saving and capital incomes. The treatment of savings is so favourable that it is often exempted from taxation at all three stages: i.e. at the time of the initial saving, during the period when the funds are invested and finally when the investment is liquidated (so-called Exempt-Exempt-Exempt or EEE tax treatment). While the use of consumption as a base for taxation has a number of theoretical attractions, the Indian system goes well beyond a consumption tax base because there is no taxation of dis-saving. Thus, a deposit made in an approved financial instrument (such as a one-year post office deposit) could be made out of pre-tax income and on maturity be re-invested generating a new reduction in taxation. Few of the tax-favoured saving schemes are treated on the classical system of exemption of contributions and holding income and then taxation at withdrawal that approximates a consumption tax (EET). Moreover, there is little empirical evidence that similar, favourable, tax treatment results in increased saving in the OECD area.

There are a few other tax breaks that favour particular categories of taxpayers. Women and senior citizens are allowed higher exemption limits that together lowers the tax revenues. A further small tax break is extended to farmers. This source of income can only be taxed by state governments under the current constitutional arrangements but, in practice, they choose not to tax such incomes. In fact, given the current level of tax exemptions few farmers would have incomes sufficient to pay any income tax. However, this exemption does appear to result in some taxpayers deliberately misclassifying normal income as agricultural income, perhaps lowering the income tax yield by as much as 2 percent.

Despite the significant rate cuts during the reform period, the statutory tax rate for corporations is at the high end regards the international comparison. At the same time, there are many exemptions and special treatments that substantially lower the actual tax rate paid by corporations.

Over the complete lifetime of an investment project, there is very little difference between the statutory rate and the effective tax rate. This effective tax rate allows for factors which affect the tax base, in particular the difference between tax depreciation and economic depreciation. In the case of India, this rate is only slightly lower (at 31.7 percent) than the standard rate and is relatively high in comparison to other countries.

However, these calculations refer to standard model firms and do not consider the numerous exemptions and loopholes. In particular, significant tax breaks have been given to firms located in Special Economic Zones (or similar areas) where exports are subject to a lower than standard tax rate (or no tax at all).

The largest of these tax breaks has been given to firms located in firms that have developed the power and telecommunication infrastructure for these parks. In the new Special Economic Zones (SEZs), tax concessions similar to those in software parks have been introduced: a tax holiday for five years and a 50 percent reduction for the next ten years, followed by halving the tax rate on export sales for the next five years. While widening the tax breaks in SEZs, the 2007 Budget effectively lowered some of the concessions given to IT companies in software parks. It brought companies within the scope of the minimum alternative tax. A number of IT companies have unused foreign tax credits and so the impact may be limited.

The fiscal cost of these concessions is substantial, lowering tax yields by almost one half. Based on a random sample of firms, the Ministry of Finance estimates that, on a static basis (i.e. ignoring the fact that behaviour is altered by the tax concessions), the concessions reduce the corporate tax yield by 47 percent, lowering the average corporate tax rate in 2004 to 19 percent against a legislated tax rate of 36.59 percent in that year. However, companies are able to use these concessions to a varying extent, with the result that there is a large variation in the effective tax rate across companies, with only a small minority of companies paying the standard rate of taxation.

The cost of these concessions has been evaluated against the basic tax legislation but this may not be the appropriate base for evaluating tax expenditures. In the case of corporate taxation, depreciation allowances are not revalued to take into account inflation, so raising tax payments. There is also discrimination against groups of companies with subsidiaries. These structures are not allowed to file consolidated tax returns, so that it is possible that a group of companies can make a loss but continue to pay corporate taxes. In addition, the dividend withholding tax cannot be reclaimed on intra-group dividend payments, leading to cascading taxation.

**4.2.3 Tariff Reductions:** Reducing trade barriers was an important part of the policy reform agenda during the past 15 years. After the reforms of the second half of the 1980s, quantitative import restrictions and licensing were abandoned for capital goods and intermediate products but retained for consumer products, until negotiations with major trading partners led to their eventual abolition at the end of the decade. More importantly, import tariffs were progressively reduced to 35.5 percent (simple average) and 29.8 percent (import weighted basis) by 1999, but were still the third highest amongst the seventy countries for which data is available.

Moreover, the pattern of tariffs was such that, in effective terms, intermediate products were more protected than final products. Despite the major fall in tariffs, the ratio of import duties to total imports was still 22 percent by the end of the decade.

Tariff reductions were resumed in 2001 when the government committed to reducing tariffs to the level of ASEAN countries. The highest standard tariff rate was reduced from 35 percent in 2001 to 10 percent by 2007, bringing a commensurate fall in the ratio of tariff revenues to the total value of imports. Nonetheless, India continues to belong to the group of countries with relatively high level of Most Favoured Nation (MFN) import tariffs. As with other countries, there are numerous derogations from the standard tariff. These often take the form of regional tariff arrangements (as in Turkey and Mexico) but in the case of India the exemptions are mainly domestic. Taking account of these derogations, the ratio of import duties to the value of imports was well below the standard tariff (at 10 percent and half that once domestic taxes on imports are removed from the total) but was nonetheless still well above the levels seen in ASEAN countries. Detailed analysis of the tariff revenues shows that product, industry or end-use based exemptions lowered the yield of tariffs, in a static sense, by 62 percent in 2004. The extent of the subsidy varies considerably across products. The revenue shortfalls from current concessions and exemptions are estimated at 18.5 percent of import values. This shows that there is potential for cutting tariff rates further and at the same time reducing the dispersion of tariff rates which would increase economic efficiency and contain or prevent revenue losses.

The domestic indirect tax system has also been reformed significantly and has been made more neutral. Nonetheless, there remains considerable cascading of taxes and unequal tax treatment of different firms. It is discriminatory in design because of the separation of the taxation of goods from that of services which also makes taxation complex and facilitates tax avoidance. Taxation also cascades because the central VAT on goods becomes an excise tax once the taxed item leaves the production sector, though there is a mechanism, a the central level to set-off central taxes on inputs of goods and services against taxes on outputs. The central excise taxes are subject to numerous derogations both for particular goods but also for small industries and for firms in certain geographic areas. Overall, these exemptions lower the excise tax yield by one-quarter (1 percent of GDP). Despite the exemptions, the indirect tax burden on goods is much larger than on services, though the extent of service taxation is being continually widened. The central sales tax on cross-border sales favours the producers within a given state at the expense of other states. Moreover, there are physical border controls between states which are costly and are barriers to the creation of a uniform internal market, but necessary to prevent tax evasion through false reporting of intra-state sales as inter-state sales.

**4.2.4 Proposed National Goods and Services Tax (GST):** The government intends, in partnership with the states, to introduce a nation-wide goods and services (value-added) tax by 2010. A nation-wide GST would be a major step to creating a barrier-free common internal market. A first step in this direction has been taken with an agreement between state finance ministers and the central government to progressively phase out the central tax on interstate sales. A desirable second step would be for the central government to unify the three taxes that resemble a value added tax into one central goods and service tax. This would involve merging the countervailing duty on imports, the central VAT (CENVAT) and the services tax into one tax preferably with a unified rate. At the same time, the scope of the service tax would need to be widened. In addition, the nation-wide IT system that now covers 7,00,000 firms and is designed to ensure that income tax can be deducted at source should be broadened so that it can also handle VAT transactions.

There are various reform options which would allow the

elimination of controls at state borders so that taxation would no longer be a barrier to the development of a more dynamic internal market. Achieving this requires eliminating state entry taxes (and octroi which still exists in some municipalities) and also further reforming the VAT system as this currently also requires physical controls at state borders.

One option for further VAT reform is to tax goods and services without allowing any tax rebates for inter-state sales and collect the revenue centrally, but then redistribute the VAT yield using a formula. This system exists in most federal OECD member countries but suffers from two major drawbacks: first, agreeing on an adequate revenue distribution between the centre and states and between states is politically difficult. Second, as the VAT rate has to be set nationwide, states lose a major part of their tax autonomy, though in the case of India states have given this up by agreeing to set the same standard VAT rate of 12 percent (There are three other rates for certain products: 0 percent, 1 percent, 4 percent).

Another option would be to establish a dual VAT where both the central and the state level set their own rates on the same tax base. Individual states could then set different VAT rates (perhaps within limits).

Operating a dual VAT system with a unified federal rate and different rates across states and without border controls would be facilitated by a federal VAT that did not exempt interstate exports (i.e. in line with current treatment for the central government VAT on goods and the service tax). The states 'VAT would continue the current treatment of exempting interstate exports. This system ensures that the VAT chain is maintained for interstate trade (through the federal VAT) which would facilitate tax enforcement.

Among OECD countries, a dual VAT system where both the centre and the provinces levy VAT on the same tax base but with different rates exists in Canada in the province of Québec, which set its own VAT rate, on which the central VAT rate is added. However, in this system, sales between states, which only bear the federal VAT, are taxed less than sales within a state, which bear both the federal and the state VAT, there is still a risk of fraud with goods being declared as exports to other states although they are consumed within the originating state. The VAT chain is still intact, so efficient auditing is needed to limit such fraud. In the system used in Québec, fraud appears to be contained, but in the European Union, which uses a destination-based system for cross-border sales, fraud is a significant problem.

### 4.3 Modernisation of Public Pension System

The government has acted to ensure that the liabilities of the public pension system are contained. Public pension payments rose from 1.1 percent to 2.0 percent of GDP between 1990 and 2005. If such an increase had continued, payments might have reached 2.3 percent of GDP by 2009. As from 2004, however, the government closed the existing defined benefit scheme to new entrants who, instead, will contribute to a two-tier defined contribution system. This is beginning to help ease pressure on expenditure which may grow at a slower pace over the period till 2009 when pension outlays are expected to be only 1.7 percent of GDP. Contributors will be able to decide between three different investment strategies. The system separates management, record keeping and fund management into separate operations. Government employees will pay 10 percent of their salary to the tier one account and this will be matched by the government. They will also be able to contribute to a tier two account on a voluntary basis. Withdrawals can be made from this tier but it will not attract tax concessions. Three years after its announcement, the system has not yet been fully implemented due to delays in passing the bill for a pension fund regulator. Nonetheless, contributions have been accumulating and four fund managers will be appointed, but no private sector fund managers will be allowed. State governments have also followed these reforms with 19 states, covering 82 percent of the population, having adopted the system by January 2007. West Bengal and Kerala are the principal states that refuse to implement the scheme at the state level.

Once the record-keeping system has been put in place, private sector employees will be eligible to join the system. They can deposit funds in the first tier of the system but there will be no matching contribution from the government as will be the case for public employees. As for civil servants, at retirement, the individuals will have to use a fixed proportion of the funds in their accounts to purchase annuities with the remainder being taken as a cash sum. Once working, this system will provide the first universally available pension for private sector workers. Previously less than 3 percent of the private work force was eligible for pensions.

## 4.4 Introduction of VAT at the Level of States

Introduction of State level VAT is the most significant tax reform measure at State level. The State level VAT being implemented presently has replaced the erstwhile sales tax system of the States. Under Entry 54 of List II (State List) in the Seventh Schedule to the Constitution of India, "tax on sale or purchase of goods within a State" is a State subject. The decision to implement State level VAT was taken in the meeting of the Empowered Committee (EC) of State Finance Ministers held on June 18, 2004, where a broad consensus was arrived at amongst the States to introduce VAT from April 1, 2005. Accordingly, VAT has been introduced by all States/UTs by now. Uttar Pradesh is the latest State which has introduced VAT on January 1, 2008. Since sales tax/VAT is a State subject, the Central Government is playing the role of a facilitator for successful implementation of VAT. A compensation formula has also been finalized in consultation with the States, for providing compensation to them, during 2005-06, 2006-07 and 2007-08, for any loss on account of introduction of VAT and compensation is being released according to this formula. Technical and financial support has also been provided to the States for VAT computerization, publicity and awareness and other related aspects.

The Empowered Committee, through its deliberations over the years, finalized a design of VAT to be adopted by the States, which seeks to retain certain essential features commonly across States while, at the same time, providing a measure of flexibility to the States to enable them to meet their local requirements. The initial experience of implementation of VAT has been very encouraging. The new system has been received well by all the stakeholders. The transition to the new system has been quite smooth. The EC is constantly reviewing the progress of implementation of VAT. The revenue performance of VAT implementing States/UTs has been very encouraging so far.

### 4.5 Effectiveness and Transparency of Subsidies

The high subsidy outlays as a percent of GDP also biases the structure of total government spending. In India, around two-thirds of total government outlays (excluding interest but including loans) is on functions other than general administration and defence. One-half of this is spent on support to commercial undertakings and subsidies for food and the agricultural sector. Three-quarters of the transfers to enterprises go to electricity, gas, water and communication enterprises, either in the form of outright subsidies or as capital transfers to cover losses and/or finance expansion. A large part of the total sum spent on the enterprises is provided as loans. However, given that most of the state-owned utilities are loss-making, such loans do not represent a source of future income for the government but rather a source of future subsidy payments. Additional structural reforms are necessary to ensure that government-owned units can reduce losses while at the same time improving service delivery.

Aside from subsidies and transfers to public utilities, a considerable part of the subsidies on food, fertilizers and kerosene result in the waste of public money due to faulty delivery. Given the proportion of families living below the poverty line, the government has put into place a programme to ensure that low income families are able to purchase a number of basic products at subsidised prices through a network of fair price shops. Nationwide, over one-third of the grain distributed through the system is diverted either by the shopkeepers or through the existence of ghost ration cards. The beneficiaries of this diversion are officials in state governments and the Food Corporation of India and wholesale and retail dealers. In addition, one-fifth of the grain goes to people wrongly included in the programme, bringing the total loss to 58 percent. In two of the poorest states, Bihar and Uttar Pradesh, the loss rises to 98 percent and 80 percent respectively. For fertilizers, only 68 percent of the subsidy is estimated to accrue to farmers, with the bulk being paid to large farmers in irrigated areas.

The wide dispersion of performance across states in the efficiency of delivering food subsidies suggests a number of possibilities for reform. In particular, the two states with the highest delivery of subsidies to the targeted population have innovative schemes in place. In Andhra Pradesh, a coupon system has been introduced that allows rationed goods to be drawn in smaller quantities which reduces the probability of undrawn rations being diverted to the market, while in Tamil Nadu, target households are allowed to trade their excess rations against other rationed commodities (sugar and kerosene). Both of these schemes point to the possibility of establishing a food stamp system, especially if the beneficiaries can be publicly verified at the village level but the Tamil Nadu Government found that even food stamps, imposed transaction costs and so withdrew the scheme.

As mentioned above, in addition to the direct on-budget subsidies, the government also grants subsidies through fixing the prices of products of the public enterprises below shadow market prices (most often there is no market price and as a result the prices adopted are based on international parity-import or export, mostly of the former variety). This is particularly the case with liquefied petroleum gas (LPG) and kerosene. Kerosene is distributed through the public distribution system and it is estimated that about 38 percent of the total deliveries are diverted to the black market, where prices are three times higher. For LPG, while the market price is 45 percent higher than the subsidised price, the overall subsidy is larger and largely accrues to higher income urban residents. Finally, the budget has been deprived of higher profits from the state-owned marketing companies by the failure to allow regulated prices for gasoline and diesel to rise in line with world market prices and prevalent tariffs (at a cost of 0.5 percent of GDP); the budget was further hit by reductions in tariffs on oil imports that may have cost the exchequer 0.3 percent of GDP in 2005.

The employment guarantee programme, though, does represent a step to providing a form of social safety net for the rural population that could be effective, though costly, in terms of reducing poverty, if efficiently administered. Indeed, the objective of the programme is to provide a safety net rather than reduce poverty.

In general, the efficiency of government administration is reduced by the relatively small number of higher skilled staff. The structure of the bureaucracy is heavily skewed in favour of lower grades reflecting the legacy of the colonial era. The structure should be oriented to recruiting more skilled staff with competitive pay scales and markedly reducing the use of paper-based transactions. At present the central government has placed severe restrictions on recruitment of lower grade staff which could yield considerable savings going forward were it fused with a reengineering of business processes.

### 4.6 Summing Up

From the above description of the past reforms and current system, it is clear that the tax system has been modernised considerably. Nonetheless, there is still a large potential for making the system more efficient. Eliminating exemptions and loopholes for both direct and indirect taxes would level the playing field, reduce distortions and make the system simpler for both tax payers and the administration. For example, for tariffs, the direction should be to introduce a revenue-neutral reform that markedly reduces the dispersion of tariffs ideally aiming for one tariff rate, but certainly a limited number or rates on all non agricultural goods. For direct and indirect taxes (excluding tariffs) there are also various ways to make them more business-friendly without reducing tax revenues.

The internationally high statutory tax rates on corporations together with the existence of large tax expenditures suggest that there is scope for some further reduction in the corporate tax rate. Such a reform has started in the 2005-06 budget by the alignment of the depreciation rate for tax purposes with replacement life value. The goal could be to allow companies to unify the tax treatment of depreciation with the accounting treatment, making the tax base for corporate profits the same as profits declared in their accounts. This would remove discretion from the tax authorities and result in assets being valued at the company level. Just abolishing accelerated depreciation and various area and industry specific allowances would permit the tax rate to be lowered to just below 25 percent, and perhaps even lower if accounting depreciation were used for tax purposes. Reducing such special incentives and exemptions for firms, allowing group taxation (subject to single shareholding of group as well as individual units), and unifying the taxation of retained and distributed earnings would not only improve economic efficiency but also make the direct tax system fairer and simpler and thus easier to administer.

A major issue with tax exemptions is to what extent existing export-related tax allowances should be ended (covering the old type of special economic zones, export processing areas and most importantly software technology parks) and whether the generous tax holidays for companies established in the new special economic zones (SEZs) should continue. Given the relatively high effective average corporate tax rates for domestic and foreign firms that operate outside SEZs, and which do not have access to any special concessions, such tax holidays will certainly provide a big incentive for domestic firms to establish production facilities in SEZs when they wish to expand their export operations. They will also provide a considerable incentive.

Public expenditure is neither high in relation to GDP nor in relation to the needs of the economy and citizens for public services. However, there is ample evidence that spending could meet a number of the government's goals in a more efficient manner. The high proportion of expenditure that is devoted to the support of public sector enterprises is one area where considerable economies could be made through lessening the need for such transfers by making the recipient enterprises more efficient and improving governance.

Similarly, the use of subsidies appears to be excessive and costly in relation to the presumed goal of reducing poverty. These subsidies have other goals but these too need careful evaluation to ensure that money is being spent effectively. As yet, it is too early to evaluate the National Rural Employment Guarantee programme, but major efforts will be required to ensure that the problems seen by previous programmes do not re-occur. More broadly, there appears to be a need to improve the monitoring and control of public expenditure. The public distribution for food and fuels, in particular, seems to need considerable reform. Reform of spending has been undertaken in some areas. The move to a defined contribution retirement saving system is to be welcomed, even if it has been slow in implementation. It could form the basis of a much wider retirement security programme to cover people working in the private sector.

# 5

# Fundamentals of Fiscal Decentralization

## 5.1 Introduction

The reform of economic systems in developing countries during the 1980s focused largely on increasing the role of the market and improving the environment in which it operates. For some years, there was a preoccupation with the private sector, such that the potential role of the public sector in promoting development received little attention. [1] In recent years, there have been widespread attempts to both redefine the role of the public sector in developing countries and improve its performance. An increasingly important goal of these reforms is the decentralization of government functions.

During the 1990s, fiscal decentralization and local government reforms were among the most widespread trends in development. Many of these extensive and costly efforts, however, have made only modest progress toward meeting their stated goals. [2] Given this uneven performance, there has been considerable debate about the desirability of fiscal decentralization and how to approach it.

This chapter examines the origins, conceptual foundations, and practice of fiscal decentralization in developing countries. Several issues are covered. First, it has been briefly considered why fiscal centralization is historically prominent in developing countries and why the trend has been reversing. Second, attempt has been made to summarize conventional fiscal decentralization theory and consider its relevance for developing countries. Third, efforts have been made to review some popular claims made for and against fiscal decentralization and consider available empirical evidence. Fourth, the detail discussion on fiscal decentralisation and economic growth has been made. Finally, concluding observations on how to think about designing more appropriate and effective ways of fiscal decentralization in developing countries has been attempted.

## 5.2 Historical Basis of Fiscal Centralization

Although fiscal decentralization has emerged as a focus of public sector reform in many less-developed nations, the substantial body of theory and research on public finance in developing countries includes little substantive work on the fiscal role and performance of local government. Most analysis of this topic has been in the form of occasional case studies or chapters in studies of national tax systems, usually conducted by special commissions or international development agencies, such as the World Bank or the International Monetary Fund (IMF). Only a few attempts to conceptualize the issues broadly and/or to compare decentralization and local finance policies across a group of countries have been made (Ter-Minassian, 1997; Bird and Vaillancourt, 1998). Some of this literature predates the recent emphasis on decentralization, [3] and much of the rest focuses primarily on major urban areas [4] or non-fiscal aspects of decentralization (Manor, 1998; Blair, 2000).

This scarcity of research reflects the small fiscal role that local government have traditionally played in most developing countries. In the 1980s, just prior to the emerging fiscal decentralization trend, local governments in Organisation for Economic Co-operation and Development (OECD) countries accounted for, on average, 11 percent of total public employment, and in some countries as much as 25 percent. In contrast, local governments in developing countries accounted for an average of 4.5 percent of public employment, ranging from 2.5 percent in Africa to 8 percent in Asia (Cochrane, 1993). Public expenditure data from the late 1980s and early 1990s indicate that the local government share of total government spending averaged 32 percent in the industrialized countries versus 15 percent in the developing world (Bahl and Linn, 1992: Chapter 1).

In evaluating the suitability of fiscal decentralization, it is important to consider the historical basis for fiscal centralization and the factors that have been undermining it. Traditional systems in some parts of the world, particularly in Asia, have been highly centralized for centuries. Local governments were introduced in many developing countries through colonization and development assistance, often taking a form that neither met their intended purpose nor gained acceptance from the local people. Post-independence leaders, who were left with an institutional framework that was not consistent with their culture and needs, commonly used local governments for administrative and control purposes rather than to promote self-determination, democratization and economic development.

Early development economists also discouraged the development of local government by advising officials of developing countries that they could maximize growth by centralizing control over the economy. Development strategies were based on central planning, large-scale technology transfer, industrialization and spatial centralization to capture economies of scale and promote growth. [5] Thus, development responsibilities were concentrated at the centre, and local authorities were largely neglected.

In many developing countries, a general lack of managerial and technical expertise has precluded—or been used as an excuse to avoid—the formation of local government institutions and an effective working relationship between the central and local governments. [6] Given the limited pool of human resources and the scarcity of training and educational facilities, some central governments feared competition for qualified staff if decentralized governments were strengthened.

The most important reason local governments have been neglected in developing countries is that strong central governments often oppose decentralization. [7] Some reasons for this reluctance are legitimate, such as the need for nation building in ethnically fragmented societies and central macroeconomic control in fragile economies. Equally important, however, is the reality that the governing elite, who may be dominated by particular ethnic groups, fear the loss of power and wealth inherent in meaningful decentralization. In addition, central ministries and/or political parties that control substantial resources rarely want to share them with autonomous local governments.

### 5.3 Emerging Fiscal Decentralization Trends

Although many developing countries are likely to remain fairly centralized in the near term, a few emerging realities have collectively generated a growing interest in developing or reviving local government (World Bank, 2000: chapter 5).

First, economic planning by central governments has not been successful in promoting adequate development. Although there have been periods of strong economic performance in the developing world during the past few decades, particularly in Asia, many countries have faced a variety of economic problems that central governments have been unable to cope with.

Second, changing international economic conditions and structural adjustment programmes designed to improve public sector performance have created serious fiscal difficulties for developing countries. Growing service demands and underperforming economies resulted in large budget deficits, which were financed primarily by external borrowing. Over time, interest payments claimed an increasing share of public resources, and a vicious cycle of borrowing and overspending ensued. In response, central governments are trying to reduce their role in managing development and to rely more on local governments, which are often underutilized and may have considerable untapped revenue potential.

Third, changing political climates also encourage the development of local governments in developing countries.

As people become more educated, better informed through improved communications and more aware of the problems of central bureaucracies, they desire to bring the control of government functions closer to themselves. In numerous developing countries, there has been movement toward greater democracy as military regimes and dictatorships are forced to relinquish power and institute political reforms. [8] This sets an example for other countries and emboldens people to push for further changes, including efforts to decentralize.

The new focus on a greater fiscal role for local government has been increasingly supported by international development agencies. The World Development Report 1988/1989 devotes an entire chapter to local government, and a widely cited World Bank report states that an effective public sector in a modern developing country "depends on the ability of the central government to harness the resources of lower levels of government" (Cochrane, 1983). The World Development Report 1999/2000 opined, "Entering the 21st Century places considerable emphasis on decentralization and urban development". More generally, donors are increasingly assisting efforts to decentralize and strengthen local governments. [9]

## 5.4 Conventional Fiscal Decentralization Theory

Mainstream economists have traditionally defined a suitable role for local government in the industrialized countries using the basic theory of fiscal decentralization known as fiscal federalism. [10] Drawing on the standard Musgrave model of public sector responsibility for stabilization, distribution and allocation (Musgrave, 1959), the decentralization theory provides direction for sharing these functions among different levels of government.

**5.4.1 Primary Responsibility of Stabilization:** Primary responsibility for the stabilization function has conventionally been assigned to the central government, partly because of the obvious problems that would result if sub national jurisdictions had independent control over their own money supplies. In addition, local economies were considered highly open, so that the effects of local fiscal policy would be dissipated into other areas. Finally, deficit finance policies at the local level have not been considered desirable because of concern that repayment would involve substantial real income transfers to creditors external to debtor jurisdictions. On the revenue side, the types of revenues considered most appropriate for local governments tend to be income inelastic, constraining the ability of local governments to pursue appropriate fiscal policy.

Although the international macroeconomic environment has changed in ways that raise questions about the conventional case for fiscal decentralization, and there is increasing recognition that decentralized levels of government can play a more important stabilization role in industrialized economies than was formerly believed, it is not difficult to justify stabilization as primarily a central function in developing countries. First, macroeconomic fluctuations can be particularly severe in emerging economies, especially in agricultural countries subject to substantial and unpredictable climate variations and countries heavily dependent externally for basic production inputs, manufactured goods and credit. Under such conditions, stabilization policies must be planned and coordinated centrally by well-trained and experienced people. A second important consideration is that, as noted earlier, local governments in developing countries often have only a minor role in the economy relative to industrialized nations, frequently accounting for modest percentages of public sector employment and spending. Moreover, they are typically very dependent on central governments for resources and regulated by central agencies, even under relatively decentralized regimes. The impact of their fiscal behaviour is, therefore, extremely limited.

Finally, the local revenue situation in developing

countries can be even more problematic than in industrialized countries. In some cases, local governments are more dependent on taxes related to economic activity (agricultural, business and market) than on more stable wealth-based taxes (land and property) and charges (for example, water and sewerage). These dominant taxes are often structured such that they are inelastic during growth, but the fragility of the local economy can result in dramatic yield reductions during contractions, undermining local ability to behave counter cyclically.

**5.4.2 Redistributive Function:** The fiscal federalism theory also places principal responsibility for distribution with the central government.

First, only the central government is in a position to redistribute resources from wealthier to poorer jurisdictions.

Second, differential local redistribution programmes would be expected to create problems if factors of production were mobile. Wealthy residents and businesses might move out of a jurisdiction practicing redistribution, while poor individuals eligible for benefits would try to move in, thereby undermining the redistributive base.

Third, local governments tend to have access to revenue sources that are not easily levied in a way that is progressive with respect to income.

Although there have been challenges to the conventional recommendation that distribution be centralized, it is still generally accepted that decentralized governments are typically more constrained than the central government in altering the distribution of income. They may play a role in intra-jurisdictional redistribution, but they clearly control what happens across jurisdictions. [11] Constraints on intra-jurisdictional redistribution may not be as problematic in developing countries as in industrialized countries. Domestic mobility of the rich may be less significant in developing countries because there are few cities that provide high levels of public services and wealth-responsive amenities.

Thus, the wealthy have little choice about where to live if they wish to enjoy the standard of living of a major urban centre. They are unlikely to flee the few major cities in large numbers, even as these cities grow rapidly from high birth rates and the in-migration of rural peasants unable to make an acceptable living from agriculture. Despite the possibility of fewer mobility problems in less-developed countries, there is no strong case to be made for assigning substantial distribution responsibility to local governments. Local resource bases are often limited, as are the expenditure role of local authorities and their capacity to administer major redistributional programmes. Finally, prominent local residents with substantial influence might undermine the development of significant local redistributional policies.

**5.4.3 Allocation Function:** The prescribed role of decentralized levels of government in the allocation function is substantial because demand for many public services is not likely to be uniform across space.

Welfare gains would thus be enhanced through decentralization because residents in different jurisdictions could choose the mix of public goods and taxes that best conforms to their preferences. In the absence of a market and competitive pricing for public services, community-wide demand would be articulated through the collective decision-making process, that is, voting. In this framework, decentralization is desirable not only because of preference differentiation, but also because expenditure decisions are tied more closely to real resource costs in smaller jurisdictions. In addition, when there are a large number of decentralized governments, there is likely to be greater experimentation and innovation in the provision of local public goods, potentially leading to improvements in overall resource productivity.

Extensions of the logic of preference variation suggest that in a system where there are opportunities for mobility, people will move to an area where a local government provides their preferred mix of public services. This produces a market-like solution to the local service provision problem. [12] Equilibrium occurs when people distribute themselves across differentiated communities in such a way that there is no incentive for anyone to move; everyone is satisfied with the services being provided in the jurisdiction in which they reside. [13]

There are important exceptions to the general rule of decentralizing to maximize allocative efficiency. Certain capital-intensive services, such as electric utilities and transportation systems, may exhibit economies of scale in production. In these cases, it is more efficient to provide services on a larger scale and over a wider area. In addition, the provision of some services, such as water and roads, may generate inter jurisdictional externalities. In such cases, resource allocation is more efficient when the service provision area is drawn such that externalities are internalized. Defining an efficient decentralized structure is a complex process because optimal service area may vary greatly for different public goods and may in few or no case correspond exactly to the boundaries of existing political jurisdictions. The welfare gains from establishing new levels of government with efficient boundaries for providing a particular public good must be weighed against the institutional and transaction costs involved in having a larger number of jurisdictions.

It is often more practical to pursue alternative policies that have the same overall effect, such as the formation of co-operative agreements among existing decentralized political jurisdictions; or provision, subsidy, or regulation of services by a more centralized level of government.

On the revenue side, four basic guidelines are suggested as a starting point for defining or evaluating a revenue system (Oates, 1972). First, local taxes should be as neutral as possible in terms of their effect on economic behaviour. Second, the benefits and costs of local taxes should be clear to those for whom services are to be provided. Third, the pattern of incidence of local taxes should meet basic equity standards.

Fourth, administration and compliance costs should be minimized by avoiding the assignment of complex taxes to local governments.

In addition to these four basic guidelines, three other broad issues regarding local revenue systems emerge from the local finance literature. First, the spatial dimension of local government actions requires that interdependence and competition across jurisdictions be explicitly considered and that mobile tax bases be avoided. Second, central governments have national goals regarding public service provision and inter-jurisdictional equity that justify inter-governmental transfers and service standards. Third, the optimal criteria for assigning revenue sources to local authorities will generally differ from the perspectives of central and local governments. [14] These differences in perspective and their potential effects must be recognized when designing local revenue systems.

## 5.5 Relevance for Developing Countries

Theories by definition involve simplification and generalization. The type of abstraction that theorizing requires is problematic with respect to considering fiscal decentralization in developing countries. Although context should never be ignored in public policy analysis, there are some relatively established practices and standard institutions that must be considered in assessing macroeconomic structure and performance, international trade management and many other economic functions. The rules of the game for considering fiscal decentralization in complex and varied contexts are much less clearly defined, and there is much less "good practice" experience for policy makers to draw on.

It has already been commented above on the relatively straightforward case for centralization of the stabilization and distribution functions in developing countries. The issues surrounding assignment of responsibility for both the expenditure and revenue dimensions of the allocation function in developing countries are considerably more complex. First, a number of explicit and implicit assumptions underlying public finance theory in general, and fiscal federalism in particular, may be violated in some developing countries. Among the potential concerns are: the relevance of individual preferences as the principal basis for defining demand; the potential role of mobility in generating an efficient spatial pattern service provision; the applicability of conventional models of public choice; and the existence of an adequate legal basis for an effective intergovernmental system. To the extent that such mechanisms and assumptions are not valid, some of the standard policy prescriptions of the theory may have to be discarded or adapted.

Second, even if basic principles are essentially valid, local conditions that are fairly common in developing countries can substantially affect the way they should be interpreted. Widespread poverty, for example, may make preferences more homogeneous across local jurisdictions, justifying greater centralization of some functions. This could be offset, however, by substantial spatial diversity in local environments and economic bases, and/or by the existence of widely dispersed and poorly linked settlements, both of which might suggest the need for greater decentralization. In addition, a wide variety of cultural, political and institutional conditions can also influence the need and prospects for fiscal decentralization. Since these factors can vary across countries and can move the system in different directions, their relative importance must be understood in analyzing a specific case.

The greatest challenge for analysts is that the structure and characteristics of decentralized institutions are so diverse across countries. Systems of government are basically of two types: unitary and federal. The overwhelming majority of developing countries are unitary states in which local governments are the creation of the centre. True federal states exist by virtue of a voluntary union of decentralized units, which agree to surrender certain powers to the central government. Most of the few developing countries with semi-autonomous state governments, such as Argentina, Brazil, Mexico and Nigeria, are really quasi-federal in that the state structure was at least partially imposed from above.

Unitary governments display a wide variety of decentralization practices. Some have no local governments, although there may be decentralized administrative units of the central government. Under the field or local administration system, local governments operate as extensions of the state bureaucracy with few autonomous powers, as in former French colonies. In extreme cases, the central government may appoint the members of local government councils rather than permit their election by popular vote. In contrast, a system of semi-autonomous local government was established in some developing countries, such as those colonized by the British. Local authorities under this system are legal entities, which can sue and be sued as well as enter into independent contracts. Significant central control is often retained, but local authorities are usually governed with some degree of independence by locally elected councils. In either the local administration or local government system, there are several dimensions along which governments can vary.

First, systems differ in the number of levels of government that exist and the constitutionally and legislatively mandated relationships among them.

Second, local authorities differ in their degree of political decentralization and grassroots legitimacy. Some have significant political power and are popularly elected, while others are appointed councils that follow the directives of a more centralized level of government.

Third, local authorities differ in their degree of autonomy in revenue-raising and expenditure decision making. Some have significant autonomy in both, others in one area, and still others have little autonomy of any sort.

Fourth, local authority systems differ in the average

degree of fiscal capacity relative to service responsibilities. Local authorities in some developing countries can more or less finance their designated services, while others raise only a small percentage of the resources they spend. In some cases, the central government steps in with financial assistance, while in others there are few or no grant systems and the revenue shortfalls remain.

Thus, there are enormous differences in the way public sectors are structured and the way they share functions and resources across levels of government.

The difficulties of comparison are further complicated by the lack of adequate data, particularly for smaller and least-developed countries and crisis states. [15] There are large differences across countries in the way fiscal data are classified, so that even if data were available, it could be difficult to compare them. An attempt to collect comparative intergovernmental fiscal data from IMF sources for a sample of 12 developing countries left so many holes that it was impossible to make more than a limited number of comparisons, usually with different subsets of countries for each type of comparison. [16]

The point of making these detailed selective comparisons is to demonstrate the significant differences among developing countries in intergovernmental fiscal structure and the broader environment in which local governments function, even across a few neighbouring countries in one region of the world. Even with good data, no single framework could take full account of all of the highly complex issues involved in assessing an appropriate fiscal role for local governments. The great variations in the internal context of developing countries along many dimensions can significantly influence the "optimal" assignment of public service responsibilities and revenue-generating powers among levels of government, as well as the types of reforms required to deal with existing system deficiencies. Traditional economic concerns must, therefore, be balanced with careful consideration of the unique economic, cultural, institutional and political environment in a particular case and an understanding of how this affects the desirability of and possibilities for meeting the normative prescriptions of public finance theory.

## 5.6 Decentralization and Economic Development

Having briefly reviewed the relevance of conventional fiscal decentralization theory for developing countries, we now turn to whether there is clear empirical justification for pursuing fiscal decentralization in developing countries. Unfortunately, evidence is scant and mixed. This section considers several common propositions about the desirability of fiscal decentralization, including that it: retards economic development and has undesirable macroeconomic effects; negatively impacts distribution; improves local service delivery; and enhances government accountability to local citizens.

Some analysts have long maintained that the more pronounced role of decentralized governments in industrialized countries suggests that decentralization may stimulate development and that local authorities have an important role to play in the management of development. [17] Some recent empirical evidence suggests, on the contrary, a negative effect of fiscal decentralization on growth. [18] These studies typically use regression analysis that relates income levels or growth rates to fiscal decentralization. In addition to the static nature and limited time frame of some of these models, there is a problem with the key independent variable: fiscal decentralization is typically defined as the sub national share of total government expenditure.

At one level, this is the obvious choice of variable, but it problematically abstracts from political and institutional context, the importance of which was discussed above. An example drawn from two countries will help to illustrate the potential problems involved. As noted above, decentralized governments in Kenya are responsible for only 4-5 percent of total government expenditure, but they do provide some level of many basic local services, they receive virtually no intergovernmental transfers and their elected councils conduct their fiscal affairs with an unusual level of autonomy for a developing country. And while Indonesian sub national governments account for a substantially larger share of total public expenditure, many local services are not their formal responsibility, they are heavily dependent on intergovernmental transfers and they have little autonomy in making decisions about how to spend their resources. [19] In this case, the positive attributes of decentralization promoted by its proponents are more clearly embodied in the Kenya situation, but the empirical models would consider Indonesia to be more fiscally decentralized.

The implication, for example, is that any growth-inhibiting fiscal decisions attributed to the "fiscally decentralized" Indonesian local governments would in fact be determined largely by central government decrees.

Such anecdotal evidence does not disprove the case of the "fiscal decentralization harms national growth" analysts, but it does raise questions about the interpretation of their results.

Until there are more sophisticated analyses that can control for critically important contextual variations across countries, definitive generalizations should not be made on this issue.

There is also a small literature that examines the impact of public infrastructure provision on local economic development. Most of this literature, which focuses on industrialized countries, suggests a positive and significant effect, including when infrastructure is a local responsibility. The topic, however, has not been widely studied in developing countries. [20]

## 5.7 Macroeconomic Effects of Decentralization

A number of analysts have gone beyond broad analysis of

the aggregate impact of decentralization on economic growth to suggest specific ways in which fiscal decentralization harms macro-economic stability. [21] The list of alleged problems is long, but a number of propositions are particularly prominent and tend to recur in attacks on the desirability of fiscal decentralization.

First, critics argue that local governments in many countries tend to run deficits, and they draw on the central government budget to cover their shortfalls.

Second, the anti-decentralization camp argues that strictly defined arrangements for sharing central resources with local governments take control from the centre over how to use public resources.

Third, some analysts charge that local governments fail to repay loans from the central government, again forcing the latter to dip into its general funds, often to repay loans to international development organizations, such as the World Bank.

Fourth, it is alleged that local governments extract resources from the centre because they have political power over it.

Fifth, there is an argument that local governments tend to be more corrupt than central governments, leading to bad spending decisions and misuse of public resources.

Sixth, anti-decentralization analysts worry about the extent to which decentralized units of government compete with the centre for tax bases, or compete with each other by undertaking policies that may affect business costs and free domestic trade. Collectively, these and a variety of other problems are said to undermine macroeconomic stability.

Such arguments are both difficult and easy to counter. They are difficult to counter because most people with applied public finance experience would agree that at least some of these problems exist in a significant number of developing countries. They are easy to counter, or at least question, for four reasons.

First, these conditions certainly do not exist in all developing countries, and some of the most prominent generalizations in the literature are drawn from non representative cases.

Second, the impact of a number of these potentially problematic types of behaviour is not likely to be significant in the context of the "typical" developing country.

Third, the elaboration of these problems is myopically focused on potential short-term macroeconomic concerns. Even if these concerns are real, it is important to consider whether they are eventually offset by the potential microeconomic gains that are the primary justification for decentralization in the fiscal federalism model and its derivative literature.

Finally, and most importantly, many of these problems, where they exist, are empirical manifestations of undisciplined fiscal behaviour that is potentially correctable. Not a single one of them establishes fiscal decentralization as an inherent and unavoidable danger to macroeconomic stability.

The empirical evidence on the macroeconomic dangers of fiscal decentralization is mixed and anecdotal. Some of the literature cited above does provide examples in which the alleged problems exist and are substantial. Many of the highly publicized stories about dramatic negative effects of decentralization, however, have occurred in countries where decentralized entities are unusually significant and substantially autonomous. Thus, critics of fiscal decentralization often cite the clearly documented, negative post-decentralization macroeconomic effects resulting from the behaviour of lower tiers of government in such countries as Argentina, Brazil and Russia. As noted above, local governments in many developing countries, even post-decentralization, remain relatively modest players in the overall public sector fiscal scene.

Few countries decentralize substantially enough or allow

uncontrolled access to capital markets, particularly in early stages, to give local governments anywhere near the level of power and influence that, for example, state governments in Brazil had during the fiscal crisis of the mid-1990s. Although there are a few cases such as Ethiopia and Uganda in which fiscal or political crisis led to plans for excessive fiscal decentralization, there were "natural" constraints on the situation getting out of hand. In Ethiopia, the planned level of decentralization never materialized due to capacity constraints, and in Uganda the government has backtracked in response to weak local performance.

There are also cases in which exactly the opposite conditions of those alleged by the anti-decentralization camp are said to prevail. [22] For example, several analysts see corruption as a much greater problem at the central level than the local level, particularly in countries where adequate accountability has been established through the development of local democracy.

Similarly, it is believed that many knowledgeable analysts of decentralization would also argue that the central government typically has a lot more control over local governments than the local governments have over the centre (Paul Smoke, 2007). This includes the power of the central government to quickly stop local attempts to compete in a serious way with the central tax base.

Second, the effects of some of the alleged pitfalls of decentralization may be greatly overstated. Consider, for example, the debate about whether local governments can compete with each other in undesirable ways that undermine development. There may, of course, be some inter jurisdictional tax competition among local governments in fiscally decentralized countries, but it is generally unlikely to be a major problem. The absolute levels of most local taxes in many developing countries are fairly low, and they are of little significance compared to national taxes that all firms must pay (Bahl and Linn, 1992). In addition, research in industrialized countries indicate that local tax differentials often have only a marginal influence on behaviour—other relevant considerations, particularly access to inputs and amenities, tend to be more significant in business and household location decisions. There is little research in developing countries, but the effects are likely to be similar or even less important than in industrialized countries.

Third, the concerns are focused on the immediate negative macroeconomic effects of fiscal decentralization. Even if these exist, it is important to consider whether the potential microeconomic gains of fiscal decentralization (discussed below) may eventually offset short-term macro problems. [23] This raises an important policy question that has received virtually no serious attention in the literature. Are any negative effects on the central budget acceptable to lay the foundation for attaining the potential microeconomic gains of decentralization that should also eventually yield macroeconomic benefits? If so, what is an appropriate limit. In addition, a few specific dimensions of the micro-macro "trade-off" require special attention. For example, giving local governments a fixed share of central revenues does undermine central budgetary flexibility to some extent, but it also provides local governments with a predictable source of revenue that allows them to undertake regularized activities that support local economic growth. More empirical evidence is needed to understand the dynamic relationship between micro and macro impacts as well as the potential effects of particular tensions and trade-offs.

Finally, although some of the anti-decentralization charges are real, they are not inherent flaws of fiscal decentralization; rather, they are empirical problems that ought to be the target of sensible fiscal decentralization programmes. For example, local governments in some countries do impose taxes that might impede free economic activity, such as the infamous octroi on inter jurisdictional trade prominent in South Asia. [24] Economists berate such taxes, but they often remain in force because they are so productive for local governments with few other reliable sources. The existence of such problematic taxes is a weak excuse for not decentralizing; rather, the policy conclusion should be that the decentralized fiscal system ought to be structured in a way that both prohibits such potentially growth-constraining local taxation and provides local governments with viable alternatives for raising revenue. More generally, many "problems" of fiscal decentralization, particularly those related to local governments' large and pervasive budget deficits and their failure to repay debts, exist not because local governments are naturally irresponsible; rather, they are a function of poorly designed inter-governmental fiscal institutions and rules and a lack of capacity and incentives at both the local and central level to make the system work properly. To say that such problems require the maintenance of fiscal centralization is equivalent to saying that it would be best to keep a dictator in power rather than attempt to develop democracy in countries where people are not adequately educated and familiar with democratic concepts.

## 5.8 Growth-retarding Effects of Fiscal Decentralization

Most of the evidence, however, is anecdotal, relevant only under particular uncommon circumstances or focused on correctable rather than inherent problems. The reality is that the appropriate degree of fiscal decentralization will vary with the context of particular countries, and some steps can be taken in most countries to neutralize potential macroeconomic dangers. Simply decentralizing is not going to bring development, and failing to decentralize is not necessarily going to undermine it. The challenge is to devise an appropriately structured system that mandates and provides incentives for responsible local government fiscal behaviour and enables the creation of a climate conducive to private investment. It is also critical to develop the skills of local government employees to meet the requirements of the system and the abilities of central government officials to assist local governments in the process of their evolution to greater autonomy. This issue is part of the broader problem of decentralization strategy—what to decentralize and when and how to do it—to which we will return later.

## 5.9 Fiscal Decentralization and Distribution

The impact of decentralization on income distribution is not well studied in developing countries. For the reasons discussed above, it is clear that interregional redistribution cannot be effected in a highly decentralized system with substantial disparities in fiscal capacity across local governments. The burden for such redistribution should always be placed on the central government, which could affect the desired results through appropriate national tax policies, intergovernmental transfers, and expenditure programmes that target the poorest local governments. There is some evidence that appropriately designed transfer programmes can effect meaningful interregional redistribution, but there is not a great deal of empirical research on this topic, and some of it shows that redistributional transfers can be offset by other types of transfer programmes and government activities. There is also some evidence that decentralized federal countries (of which there are few), such as Brazil, have been more successful at redistribution than more centralized federations, such as Mexico, India and Pakistan.

How decentralization would affect the interpersonal and inter-area inequalities within local government jurisdictions is particularly unclear. Although a major redistributive role for local government is not likely, it is possible for local authorities in developing countries to be reasonably progressive internally in the way they finance local services. In some countries, for example, most local taxes are raised from relatively well-off local businessmen in the form of property taxes, trading license fees and charges for urban services (Crane, 1992; Smoke, 1994).

This revenue may be used to help provide basic services for the general population, including the urban poor and rural peasants, who pay little to no local tax. If such a system were standardized throughout the country, there would be scant opportunity for avoiding local taxes by moving to another location. Thus, some redistribution can take place at the local level without necessarily inducing undesirable spatial efficiency effects. Much more research is needed on this topic, however, before any definitive recommendations can be made.

## 5.10 Fiscal Decentralization and Revenue Generation

Many alleged benefits of decentralization have been claimed in the literature, most of which relate to improvements in the level and quality of local services and revenue sources, better matching of local services to the preferences of local constituencies, and greater accountability. [25] The evidence on service delivery is limited and mixed. Given that claims of service improvements are so central to the arguments of decentralization advocates, it is somewhat surprising that so little research has been conducted to see if decentralization indeed increases the level of services delivered and their quality. A fairly recent study of 10 developing countries found that decentralization does increase total and sub-national expenditures on public infrastructure (Estache and Sinha, 1995).

Leaving aside the issue of whether increases in spending improve services, such increases do not seem to be related directly to increases in transfers, so that concerns about local overspending from the national budget do not seem to be realized. Other anecdotal evidence suggests that particularly in countries where few services were being provided at the local level—decentralization seems to lead to a genuine addition to the types and levels of services being provided to local government constituents. The major constraint on further expansion of local services under decentralization appears to be a lack of balance between the revenue sources (including transfers) allowed to local governments and the increases in service functions assigned to them.

Data on whether decentralization improves the quality of services is even more scant. One major study develops a set of objective indicators on this question for three services traditionally provided by the public sector—roads, electricity and water—in a large sample (a minimum of 75 countries per sector) of developing countries. The results are neither highly encouraging nor discouraging. The only negative impact was for one measure in the electricity sector, while there was an increase in at least one indicator in each sector studied. For many indicators, however, decentralization had no statistically perceptible impact. In some cases, there was evidence of a functional split, such that facilities are better provided centrally, but operation is less expensive and more effective when decentralized. Country studies are rare, but a recent study of Kenya found that public water infrastructure services provided by local authorities are more accessible and reliable than those provided by the centre (B.D. Lewis, 1998).

Three important points emerge from this discussion. First, whether decentralization has positive effects on service delivery is a somewhat country and sector-specific issue. There are surely some types of local-impact, low capital-intensive services that are more likely to be efficiently decentralized, but variations in available technologies, institutional structures, and local capacities will influence the desirability of decentralization of a specific function in a particular country. Second, existing "objective" studies of service quality focus primarily on productive efficiency—for example, whether more of a service is being provided at a lower cost. Questions regarding allocative efficiency—whether people are getting the level and quality of a service they want and are willing to pay for—are not often deeply considered, although some evidence on this is discussed below. Third, there is little attention given to the often substantial initial transaction costs of undertaking decentralization programmes and how these relate to expected benefits. There is obviously a need for much more research on the impact of fiscal decentralization on service delivery—in terms of quantity, breadth of coverage and level of sophistication.

## 5.11 Fiscal Decentralization and Accountability of Local Participation

By this time, it will come as no surprise to the reader that the evidence on the extent to which decentralization improves accountability is mixed. There is certainly evidence that participation, in terms of elections and interaction between elections and local government officials, can be substantially enhanced by decentralization. There is also some modest evidence that democratic decentralization can enhance the speed, quantity and quality of responsive actions from local governments. [26] The quality and distribution of participation, however, varies, and it does not always result in improved accountability of the local government to local residents. Several issues seem to matter here.

First, the extent of genuine autonomy is a critical concern. Local governments, fuelled by local participation, might make decisions that represent the interests of their constituents. If there is insufficient local autonomy, central authorities could overturn such decisions, angering local residents who might blame the local government. This is not to say that some degree of central control is inappropriate; on the contrary, in developing decentralized systems, there are some national priorities that should take precedence, and some types of supply-side standards may be appropriate for certain services and activities. Even so, it is critical that decision rules are clearly specified and adhered to, and any standards for particular services should be disseminated in advance of the decision-making process.

Second, it is well known that local elites can dominate local decision-making processes in developing countries. Where this is the case, other local people may become alienated from the local government and withdraw from participatory opportunities. Such a situation reduces the local government to an institution that is accountable to a small, powerful group with little connection to the broader community.

Third, the quality of participation may vary with the development of local experience with social decision-making. In some cases, there may be considerable experience with local decision making, such that residents are able to articulate their demands clearly and forcefully to local governments after decentralization. In other cases, local people do not clearly understand the choices they have or the basic rights and responsibilities of citizenship. They may automatically elect the person who would have been chosen as the local leader according to traditional rules, even if they do not believe that person will fairly represent their interests in making decisions.

Fourth, it must be recognized that the development of genuine local participation and accountability is a process, not an administrative action. Local governments themselves are often quite used to heavy subsidization from central governments, and they are not accustomed to feeling particularly accountable to anyone. Local government constituents may be accustomed neither to paying for services nor to expecting much responsiveness from local governments. [27] The mind-sets and patterns of behaviour that have developed under such circumstances will require years to change. In some cases, higher levels of government can help to build the awareness amongst people about the types of demands they can legitimately place with their local governments. [28]

Finally, it is important to keep in mind that there is a

difference between responsiveness in terms of process and responsiveness in terms of outcomes. Residents may be genuinely satisfied with the mechanism that local governments develop to consult them about decisions. For many people, simply being consulted will seem like such an achievement that they may, at least initially, worry more about this process than the actual results., Ultimately, however, accountability requires that local governments develop both the processes whereby residents feel their opinion is being solicited, and provide outcome that make residents feel that their public service needs are being met.

Thus, decentralization guarantees neither local participation nor accountability of local governments to their residents, and neither of these things comes about immediately or automatically as a result of decentralization. This is a critical point for two reasons. First, some of the alleged benefits of decentralization can be realized only if local governments are able to develop—even if gradually—a genuine accountability to their constituents. Second, bringing about accountability should not be expected to occur rapidly—it will typically require a strategic, gradually implemented process for building trust between local government officials and their constituents.

## 5.12 Elements of a Good Fiscal Decentralization Programme

Having considered whether the broad benefits and disadvantages commonly attributed to fiscal decentralization are genuine, the discussion turns to a consideration of the key elements that should be included in a good fiscal decentralization programme. These include (a) an adequate enabling environment, (b) assignment of an appropriate set of functions to local governments, (c) assignment of an appropriate set of local own-source revenues to local governments, (d) the establishment of an adequate intergovernmental fiscal transfer system and (e) the establishment of adequate access of local governments to development capital. Each of these is discussed in turn, first outlining principles, and then turning to commonly encountered problems and possible ways to mitigate them.

**5.12.1 Adequate Enabling Environment:** An enabling environment for fiscal decentralization can begin with constitutional or legal mandates for some minimum level of autonomy, rights and responsibilities for local governments. This provides a foundation on which to build decentralization, but it does not by any means guarantee successful fiscal decentralization. There are many countries with constitutional clauses and laws on local government that have not managed to decentralize successfully. A good example is Indonesia, which became more fiscally centralized after a major decentralization law was passed in 1974 (Smoke and Lewis, 1996). A number of elements appear to be critical in establishing a sustainable enabling environment for fiscal decentralization.

It was opined by (Smoke, 2007) whereby he illustrated Ethiopia and Uganda, two often-cited cases of recent good performance. [29] First, in both countries, emerging political conditions have led to a strong national will to decentralize. Ethiopia and Uganda adopted decentralization in response to a perceived need to surrender certain powers to their regions as a way of holding their ethnically fragmented nations together. This domestic political interest has taken the initiative away from the international donor community, which has driven recent decentralization efforts in many developing countries. In Ethiopia and Uganda, donor agencies were invited to assist only after the respective governments laboriously determined the general direction in which they intended to move.

Second, both countries have recently developed unusually robust and clearly defined constitutional and legal provisions to support decentralization and the strengthening of decentralized levels of government. The 1995 Ethiopian Constitution provides for a federal system, with different service provision and revenue responsibilities for the federal and regional governments. [30] In Uganda, the Local Governments Statute of 1993, the 1995 Ugandan Constitution and the Local Governments Act of 1997 provide considerable details about the service and revenue powers of local governments.

Third, fiscal decentralization programmes in many developing countries are under the direction of fairly bureaucratized, often competing, and poorly coordinated central agencies with a direct stake (loss of power) in decentralization. These include broad-purpose ministries, such as Local Government, Home Affairs, Finance and Planning, as well as various sectoral ministries (Smoke, 2000a). In contrast, both Ethiopia and Uganda have developed special-purpose, somewhat more "neutral", and high-level mechanisms to oversee and co-ordinate decentralization and local government reform. In Ethiopia, the Regional Affairs Department in the Office of the Prime Minister has substantial overall responsibility in this regard, and a Decentralization Secretariat was set up for similar purposes in Uganda. Although the Secretariat reports to the Permanent Secretary for Local Government, staff members are not civil servants, and they are in principle detached from the normal government bureaucracy. In addition, the Local Government Finance Commission, a broad-based, constitutionally mandated, independent body that reports directly to the President, has considerable control over local revenue and intergovernmental transfer design.

Fourth, function off-loading and local revenue inadequacy are major concerns in many developing countries. Both Ethiopia and Uganda recognize that effective local governments must have adequate resources to meet their responsibilities under decentralization. Accordingly, both countries have developed significant transfer programmes that account for substantial proportions of total central revenues (around 30 percent in Uganda and more than 40 percent in

Ethiopia).

Although both Ethiopia and Uganda have strong enabling environments for decentralization, their perceived political imperative to decentralize has led to some of the other common problems of decentralization discussed below, including attempts to move forward more rapidly and less strategically than a complex process like decentralization merits. Thus, the basic policy frameworks for the decentralization programmes in Ethiopia and Uganda can, at least in some respects, serve as models for other countries, but care must be taken to learn from their mistakes in implementation.

There are also other countries in which a solid enabling environment is laying or likely to lay a strong foundation for fiscal decentralization. The 74th Amendment (1994) to the Indian Constitution, for example, lays a constitutional base and process for proceeding with decentralization to municipalities. Bolivia passed the often-cited Law on Popular Participation (1994), defining a strong legal and institutional framework in which to pursue decentralization.

The South African Constitution (1996) sets out an important role for local governments, which the central government is now struggling to deliver on. In other cases, such as Cambodia and Indonesia, there are new efforts under way to develop legislation that gives local governments a solid foundation of autonomy and responsibility before moving ahead with additional reforms. Such experiences merit comparative analysis to see how they might serve as examples for other countries in transition to a more decentralized system, with the caveat that a strong enabling framework is clearly not a sufficient condition for effective fiscal decentralization.

**5.12.2 Assignment of Appropriate Functions to Local Governments:** The principles for assignment of services to local governments as developed in the fiscal federalism literature summarized above are fairly clear, and there is no need to elaborate on them further here. Many countries do in fact follow these principles in a broad way (Bahl and Linn, 1992; Shah, 1994). The problems with fiscal decentralization on the expenditure side appear to be related more to a lack of attention to implementation than to decentralizing inappropriate services. Two aspects are particularly worth noting.

First, no matter what a constitution or law says, central government agencies rarely have a desire to decentralize services they have been providing, particularly if decentralization involves a loss of prestige and resources to these agencies and they perceive each other as competitors. Thus, they almost invariably try to slow the process. Second, if too many sectors are decentralized too rapidly and local governments do not have the capacity to handle these new responsibilities, they will perform poorly, as in the Ethiopia and Uganda cases. If this happens, central agencies hostile to decentralization can use poor local performance as an excuse for keeping the services centralized.

This common scenario is directly linked to the earlier discussion on the effects of local government fiscal behaviour on macroeconomic variables and central government deficits. Although poor fiscal performance of local governments is often a genuine problem, this does not necessarily prove that fiscal decentralization is inappropriate. It may simply mean that the fiscal decentralization or local government reform programme is giving local governments too much functional responsibility too rapidly and without appropriate capacity building and local governance development support from the central government.

Some recent experiments with approaching intergovernmental fiscal reform demonstrate possible ways to get around this problem. Kenya, for example, has a long history of local government, but its system was weakened by the centre in the post-independence period, primarily in the name of national unity. [31] Various efforts made during the

1980s and 1990s were purportedly designed to re-decentralize and re-strengthen local governments, but most were donor driven and undermined by national authorities. As a result, the performance of many local governments in terms of service delivery deteriorated considerably. In recent years, however, fuelled by political and economic pressures to reform, some genuine attempts to strengthen local governments have been undertaken.

Given the number of local governments, the magnitude of their problems and the ineffectiveness of earlier efforts, the government realized that not all required reforms could be undertaken at the same time or in all places. Recognition of the need for a clear, gradual, pragmatic strategy was manifested in the design of the first of a new generation of reform programmes, the Small Towns Development Project (STDP). This Ministry of Local Government-based project, which started in the mid-1980s with Kenyan and German funding, has thus far involved experimentation with about 15 smaller towns.

Under this project, there have been some broad common reform goals for the local authorities participating in the programme, but the exact steps each local authority took and the pace at which they took them differed depending on their capacity and willingness to accept new responsibilities and to undertake needed reforms. In addition, a mobile technical assistance team periodically worked on-site with the local governments to implement the negotiated reforms gradually and, as necessary, to modify them. Citizen participation mechanisms were required to develop local governance and improve accountability, and some training opportunities were provided for local officials and community groups. Local governments that met the goals they agreed to, were rewarded in various ways, such as increased funding and reduced central interference in expenditure decisions. Performance in most of the participating local governments has improved considerably. [32]

The Kenyan government, with substantial World Bank funding and technical assistance, is now defining a much broader programme of reform—the Kenya Local Government Reform Program—largely based on the successful experiences of the STDP and lessons learned from past donor efforts. The gradual, tailored approach to fiscal decentralization and capacity building is increasingly becoming a common element in reform, albeit to various degrees and in different ways. Some other countries—including Cambodia, Ethiopia, India, Indonesia, South Africa and Uganda—are beginning to struggle with how to take incremental, realistic steps toward service decentralization to local governments.

**5.12.3 Assignment of Appropriate Revenues to Local Governments:** The fiscal federalism principles for assignment of revenues to local governments, like the service assignment principles discussed above, are well defined and generally appropriate. Many developing countries basically follow these principles, with a few prominent exceptions, such as the infamous South Asian octroi noted above (Bahl and Linn, 1992; Shah, 1994). Thus, central governments generally attempt to assign local governments revenue bases that are relatively immobile and should therefore not lead to serious spatial efficiency effects, that do not compete seriously with central tax bases and so on.

Four particularly problematic concerns remain on the revenue side. First, assigned revenues are almost never adequate to meet local expenditure requirements. This means that central government transfer programmes are inevitably required. Second, local governments often use too many unproductive revenue sources that barely cover the costs of collecting them. Third, the same lack of attention to implementation discussed above in relation to service decentralization also plagues the revenue side. Fourth, individual local revenue sources suffer from some serious design problems, such as static bases, overly complex structures and ineffective collection mechanisms. Issues related to transfers are discussed below, focusing on local own-source revenue design and implementation strategy.

One of the most critical international lessons of local tax reform is that local governments should focus their energies on a few local sources of revenue that can provide substantial yields and pay less attention to the many minor taxes that they typically have access to (Bahl and Linn, 1992; Shah, 1994). The concentration here is on property taxes and user charges, two significant sources of revenue that local governments might use more effectively in developing countries.

The property tax is known to suffer from a variety of obstacles, inequities and inefficiencies, particularly in developing countries.

First, there can be serious local political problems with adopting and enforcing it. Although the property tax is an appropriate local tax, it is also very visible, not hidden in deductions from income or in prices of goods consumed, and is notoriously difficult to administer. Local residents may be particularly reluctant to pay if they do not feel they are getting adequate or desired local services. In addition, powerful leaders often own a large proportion of property, leaving not much middle-class housing to tax. Better local services, improved local political mechanisms and more broadly based participation can help remove political obstacles to more effective use of the property tax.

Second, there has been a tendency in some countries to overtax business property through higher assessments and higher rates. This could lead to relocation or shifting of the tax burden in the form of higher prices to the very residents the differential property taxation is trying to protect. There is an increasing trend in property tax reform toward reducing or eliminating differentials in property tax rates on different classes of property. Thus, residential classifications, special exemptions, plot subdivision and other forms of tax avoidance and evasion are minimized.

Third, valuation procedures tend to be too complex and too infrequently applied, such that the tax base stagnates for long periods. Simplified assessment procedures that use standardized land and building classifications have been employed in successful property tax reforms throughout the world, improving yields and reducing administration costs. Provisions to revalue at regular intervals and to index between valuations can improve the buoyancy of the tax revenues.

Fourth, collection is a major concern in most countries and it often receives less attention than valuation reform. The successful property tax reform in Indonesia in the late 1980s and early 1990s was among the first to replace a valuation-led strategy with a collection-led reform. The logic was that improved valuation without improved collection could not bring about significant gains in yields. Some key elements of collection-led reforms include legal provisions that broadly define liability and allow renters to deduct property tax payments from rent; steps to make it easier for taxpayers to meet their obligations, such as more convenient payment points and simpler payment procedures; and measures to enhance enforcement, such as stiff penalties for non-payment and seizure of properties in default.

Finally, strategic implementation, as on the expenditure side, is critical for successful property tax reform. Simple and more acceptable reforms should be undertaken before more complex and contentious ones. New systems should be tested in pilot areas, allowing the government to improve them before widespread application. Better linkages should also be created between the tax policy and tax administration officials. This would improve the ability to respond in a timely manner to unworkable rules and problems that develop during implementation. In addition, contentious reforms should be phased in, for example by gradually increasing assessment ratios and negotiating with taxpayers. Property tax reforms that have worked in some countries may not be applicable everywhere, but the general strategies and principles involved can often strengthen a local tax that has considerable potential to support fiscal decentralization.

A second type of local government own-source revenue with considerable potential is user charges. There is agreement among local finance experts that user fees are underutilized, and that they could be implemented to some degree for many services, even those that are routinely subsidized. [33]

There are powerful arguments for charging for services, including the potential benefits of creating a close connection between consumption and cost; ease of collection due to the direct nature of charges; and for excluding non-payers. There are also, however, serious problems with instituting and increasing user charges for public services. These include political sensitivity; the difficulty of choosing among marginal cost, average cost and hybrid pricing schemes that have different implications for cost recovery and efficient resource use; a reluctance to raise charges over time, such that revenues may fall below costs in times of inflation; and equity concerns about the effects of charges on the poor.

While it is difficult to make specific recommendations regarding user charges without referring to the context of specific sectors and countries, successful reforms in a number of countries suggest several principles.

First, it is most appropriate and easiest to charge for services that have some private characteristics—particularly where benefits vary among individuals and non-payers can be excluded from consumption.

Second, even for more "public" goods, some level of charges can be appropriate to establish a link between consumption and costs and to discipline use of scarce resources. There is increasing evidence from many countries that people are willing to pay something for services if adequate quality and reliability are maintained.

Third, equity must remain a key concern in setting charges; even so, cost recovery may still be possible if demand elasticities vary such that price discrimination can occur across users, which allows cross-subsidization of target groups.

Fourth, public education and consultation schemes are normally required to get people to accept new and increased user charges.

Fifth, user charges invariably need to be phased in over time to prevent harsh equity effects, undesirable changes in patterns of service use, administrative and political resistance and so on. If care is taken to follow these basic principles, user charges have great potential in many countries to provide substantial resources to support fiscal decentralization programmes in an efficient way.

**5.12.4 Appropriate Inter-governmental Transfer System:** Because local own-source revenues generally do not cover local government expenditure responsibilities, virtually all governments have intergovernmental transfer programmes. These serve multiple, often interrelated purposes, three of which are particularly important.

First, they help to cover local government fiscal imbalances, supplementing inadequate local own-source revenues to improve the ability of local governments to meet their expenditure responsibilities.

Second, they can be used to meet national redistribution objectives as discussed above, helping to offset fiscal capacity differences among local governments.

Third, they can be used to encourage local expenditures on particular goods and services that exhibit positive externalities or are considered to be basic needs that should be distributed less unequally than the ability to pay for them. Most transfer systems, even in developing countries, are intended, at least officially, to meet these objectives.

There are several typical issues and problems involved in designing transfer programmes.

First, it is important to recognize explicitly that different types of transfers are appropriate in different circumstances. Unconditional grants, for example, are best for income redistribution purposes, while conditional grants are a cheaper way of encouraging expenditures on particular types of target services. If designed properly, both types can help to encourage local resource mobilization and to ensure over time the provision of a basic minimum of services in all local governments regardless of fiscal capacity.

Second, fiscal equalization grants are often considered important, but they are very difficult to design because of the technical and political complexities involved in defining an "optimal" distribution of income across decentralized jurisdictions and in determining a fair way to raise the revenues to be redistributed. Equal resources do not guarantee equal results, and there are often inequalities within recipient jurisdictions that may not be lessened by transfers. In spite of these problems, redistributive grants can generally be designed to improve on the status quo.

Third, macroeconomic problems can be created, as highlighted by the anti-fiscal decentralization camp discussed earlier, if too large a percentage of central resources are guaranteed to local governments each year. The potential dangers, however, must be weighed against the value of providing local governments a stable revenue base and the potential microeconomic gains of decentralized service delivery. The most likely solution is to start a fiscal decentralization effort with modest transfer programmes that involve substantial central control and monitoring. The significance of transfers can be increased as local governments develop the capacity to deliver services and to behave in a fiscally responsible way. Some flexibility in determining the size of the transfer pool during crisis situations can give central governments the fiscal power they need to meet macroeconomic challenges.

Fourth, transfer programmes may have conflicting objectives or unintended results that must be recognized. For example, an equalizing grant may be offset by types of categorical grants that go to wealthier areas. Careful research prior to transfer system design can help to understand and minimize, as appropriate, such effects. Grants may also substitute for rather than stimulate local tax effort, thereby failing to increase public spending as much as expected. Including a simple local tax effort variable in a transfer allocation formula can alleviate, but not eliminate, this problem. Finally, multiple transfer programmes with different allocation criteria for a particular sector can confuse local officials and provide incentives for unproductive competition and strategic behaviour. Consolidation and simplification can reduce such problems.

Fifth, many transfer systems by design or by manipulation—are allocated with a degree of subjectivity that undermines basic economic objectives. Given the political nature of transfers, it would be unreasonable to expect any system to be fully rationalized in terms of achieving basic efficiency and equity goals. More objective and transparent distribution formulas, however, can help move the system in the right direction.

In the final analysis, it is difficult to make generalized prescriptions for the appropriate structure of an intergovernmental transfer system, which should be expected to vary across countries depending on national objectives, the extent of service and revenue functions assigned to local governments, the fiscal capacity of local governments, the extent of inequalities across local governments and so forth. In a very basic system, such as the one under development in Cambodia, local governments need not be given specific mandatory responsibilities initially, only modest resources to provide local services that are considered important by the community and are not provided by the central government. This approach can make local people better off and help to develop governance and capacity. Because the local governments will be responsible for such a small portion of public expenditures in a country with one of the lowest aggregate tax rates in the world, there is no conceivable threat to macroeconomic stability from the local public sector in this case.

In advanced systems where local governments have significant service responsibilities and in-adequate sources of revenue, such as South Africa, a more substantial and sophisticated system of transfers is being developed. This system includes redistributive grants designed to alleviate fiscal inequalities and conditional grants designed to cover priority investment needs. In this case, local government revenues and local autonomy over certain taxes are being enhanced at the same time that transfer programmes are being reformed (Reschovsky and Smoke, 1999).

Under such conditions—in which local governments have significant expenditure responsibilities and increasing control over major revenue sources, and intergovernmental transfers are significant and growing—the National Department of Finance is justified in keeping watch over the size and performance of the local fiscal system (Republic of South Africa, 1998; Reschovsky and Smoke, 1999).

**5.12.5 Adequate Local Access to Investment Capital:** Local governments in many developing countries get most of their capital budget from intergovernmental transfers, but some decentralized governments, typically states, provinces and large cities, are able to borrow. In some cases, such as Brazil and Colombia, there is direct and significant access to commercial banks and the bond market. In other cases, such as India and Poland, access is limited, but some decentralized governments borrow and there are efforts to improve access to loans. In still other countries, such as Kenya and Indonesia, virtually all borrowing occurs through special government accounts or lending institutions along the lines of a municipal development bank.

The issue of local government borrowing cannot be separated from the broader question of investment finance, including the role of intergovernmental grants. In many countries, local government investment has been financed largely by grants, which have often been allocated through complex, fragmented programmes that leave significant discretion to central and state officials and often fail to meet basic economic goals. Where local borrowing occurs, often through some type of municipal credit institution, it is normally subsidized, and repayment is often inadequate.

Substantial dependence on grants and subsidized loans developed during a period when funds for infrastructure were abundant and developing countries faced fewer internal or external pressures for good fiscal performance than at present. Moreover, many analysts long believed that subsidization would improve equity in service delivery, a key objective of donors and governments. The recent economic and fiscal changes discussed above, however, as well as increasing evidence that subsidization does not primarily benefit those in need, have pushed many countries into reforms. On the grant side, as noted above, fragmented programmes are being consolidated and standardized formulas developed. On the loan front, countries are adopting objective appraisal techniques, charging near-market interest rates and enforcing repayment, often through municipal development funds or banks assisted by the major donors. Some central governments—particularly in Latin America, but also in India and South Africa-are trying to develop a municipal bond market.

The real challenge for fiscal decentralization is to develop a spectrum of options to finance capital investment—from grants and subsidized loans for poorer local governments and non-self-financing projects, to various types of loans and bonds for fiscally sound local governments and self-financing projects. As with grants, the approach that a central government takes toward enhancing local government access to loans depends on the fiscal context, as does the extent to which these efforts pose any danger to macroeconomic stability. In cases like Brazil or Argentina, where decentralized levels of government are relatively strong, efforts to develop direct access to capital markets make sense. As the Brazilian debt crisis discussed above demonstrates, however, it is critical in such cases that the central government regulate municipal bond markets, develop and enforce credit limits and stop bailing out local governments that default on their debt.

In more typical cases, in which local government investment responsibilities are smaller and they are fiscally weak, some type of municipal development bank will generally be the correct approach. Municipal credit institutions are initially regulated or managed and substantially capitalized by central governments, either with their own resources or donor loans. This approach gives central fiscal authorities considerable control over borrowing activities of local governments, although this power must be structured to minimize abuse. In addition, such institutions are likely to be increasingly privatized as local governments develop greater creditworthiness, which will help limit the extension of nonviable loans. Thus, serious impacts of local debt on the broader economy can generally be avoided if municipal credit institutions are properly structured, managed and developed over time (Peterson, 2000).

Central government involvement in municipal credit institutions also creates a rarely used opportunity to improve the overall effectiveness of fiscal decentralization programmes by creating an explicit relationship between the grant and loan systems. In most developing countries, grant and loan reforms have been independent of one another, except to the extent that grant allocations are sometimes reduced if local governments fail to make loan repayments. Most countries—except a few in Latin America and Southern Africa—and the Indian state of Tamil Nadu have not used grants and loans together in an integrated package. [34] The failure to link grants and loans when investment decisions are made can create conflicting signals for local fiscal behaviour. Most importantly, local governments have no incentive to borrow from a development bank if they have access to grants or highly subsidized loans from other central or state agencies. If wealthy municipalities use grants for self-financing projects, they divert scarce resources from projects with weak revenue potential and from poorer local governments unable to borrow.

A direct grant-loan linkage has the potential to improve resource use considerably in some cases. In adopting such an approach, all infrastructure projects that seek central government financing assistance, at least those with significant self-financing potential, could be evaluated as if they were to be financed by loans. If loan repayments were to cause an unacceptable burden on project beneficiaries, grants would be provided to cover all or part of capital financing. Affordability would have to be measured according to clear rules, and a grant would be approved only if operating expenses fell within an acceptable range and tariff collection efficiency meets specified standards. Such rules ensure that local governments are not subsidized, even if deserving on affordability grounds, unless they meet minimum performance standards, which would require technical assistance to some local governments. [35]

If this type of system were adopted, municipalities making a new investment would have a greater incentive to operate more efficiently and to recover costs from service users. Equity objectives would also be better served because well-off local governments and revenue-generating projects would rely more heavily on loans, while poorer local governments and important projects that could not recover costs would be subsidized with grants. Such a system could help to prevent the type of local government debt crisis feared by opponents of fiscal decentralization.

## Notes

1. Overseas Development Institute (1989); Perkins (1991:11–53); Roemer and Radelet (1991:55–80); and World Bank (2000:chapters 1–3).

2. Mawhood (1983); Olowu (1987:48–59 and 1988); World Bank (1989); Stren (1991:9–22); Wallis (1991:121–129); Olowu and Smoke (1992:1–17); Smoke (1993:901–923); K.-H. Kim (1993); Dillinger (1995); Tendler (1997); Rondinelli (1997); Bird and Vaillancourt (1998); Litvack et al. (1998); Manor (1998); Cohen and Peterson (1999); and Blair (2000:21–40).
3. For example, Hicks (1961 and 1978) and Hicks et al. (1961).
4. Bahl (1979 and 1981); Bahl et al. (1981, 1983 and 1984:215–230); Bahl and Miller (1982); Davey (1983 and 1989); Cochrane (1983); Bahl and Linn (1992 and 1983); Mawhood (1983); and Campbell et al. (1991).
5. W.A. Lewis (1954); Hirschman (1958); Brenner (1966); Alonso (1971); and Richardson (1973 and 1977). For a more recent look at this topic, see Henderson (2000:65–68) and Mills (2000:69–73).
6. Cochrane (1983); Rondinelli et al. (1983); Rondinelli and Nellis (1986:3–23); and World Bank (1989).
7. Cochrane (1983); Rondinelli et al. (1983); Rondinelli et al. (1989:57–87); Rondinelli (1990); Wunsch and Olowu (1990); and Olowu and Smoke (1992).
8. Huntington (1991); Diamond (1997); and Manor (1998).
9. World Bank (1989, 1991 and 1996) and UNDP (1992 and 1997
10. The theory of fiscal federalism is set forth in detail in Oates (1972).
11. The case for centralization of the distribution function is set forth in Oates (1972), but it has been challenged by a number of analysts on both theoretical and empirical grounds. Pauly (1973:33–58) suggests that income redistribution may increase the utility of higher income people and that taxpayers would try to raise the incomes of the poor primarily in their own local area, where poverty most directly affects them. Gramlich (1987) argues that, in recent years, state governments in the United States have been playing a more substantial role in redistribution than was previously believed possible. Crane (1992:84–98) demonstrates that the effects of local redistribution policies on social welfare are not nearly as unambiguous as conventional wisdom holds.
12. This theory was set forth by Tiebout (1956:416–424) during the early development of public finance theory and prior to the advancement of the fiscal federalism theory. However, it fits

neatly under efficiency in resource allocation and so is considered under the umbrella of fiscal federalism.

13. This "voting-with-the-feet" theory is based on strict and unrealistic assumptions: no externalities; perfect mobility of consumer-voters; perfect information about public goods and services in a very large number of heterogeneous communities; zero government fixed costs; and constant costs of production. Nevertheless, it is useful conceptually, and the results of relaxing the strict assumptions can be analysed. There has been a variety of theoretical writing and empirical research on the fiscal federalism and Tiebout theories. Much of this work is summarized, critiqued and analysed in King (1984). Bennett (1990) supplies a set of more interdisciplinary readings on related issues.
14. Bahl and Linn (1992) argue that from the central point of view, the most important criteria are to: (a) limit local competition for key national tax bases; (b) limit local taxes whose burden is exportable to residents of other jurisdictions; (c) provide local authorities with buoyant revenues to limit demands on central government resources; (d) minimize local reliance on regressive taxes; (e) encourage the use of taxes that can be easily administered at the local level; and (f) encourage the use of taxes that closely reflect the costs of infrastructure and congestion. Local governments are likely to agree more or less with criteria (c) through (f), and will be particularly concerned with having taxes that are buoyant and easily administered. However, local authorities will have the opposite priorities from those reflected in criteria (a) and (b). They would prefer a share of productive national tax bases and, as noted earlier, it is in their interest to rely on exportable taxes.
15. The IMF standardizes data classifications, but data for decentralized levels of government are not as fully collected as central government data.
16. Data for Argentina, Brazil, Cambodia, India, Indonesia, Kenya, Mexico, the Philippines, Poland, South Africa, Uganda, Venezuela and Viet Nam were collected from the IMF Government Finance Statistics Yearbook.
17. A number of analysts have found a positive correlation between decentralization and the level of development, as measured by income levels or urbanization, which is itself positively

correlated with income. These include Kee (1977:79–97) and Bahl and Linn (1992). Correlation, of course, is not causation, so the direction of influence is unclear, and these findings do not imply that a country must achieve a certain level of income before decentralizing. A more interdisciplinary approach to this issue is elaborated in Bennett (1990).

18. Two recent examples of empirical analysis suggesting that fiscal decentralization has a negative effect on economic growth are Zhang and Zou (1998:221–240) and Davoodi and Zou (1998:244–257). One recent study that found a positive effect using a similar model is S. Kim (1995). The results of another study (Huther and Shah, 1996) using a different approach suggested a positive relationship between fiscal decentralization and growth. A detailed review of the studies on fiscal decentralization and economic growth and an attempt to replicate the dominant models can be found in Shankar (2000).
19. The situation in Indonesia will change as the new government moves to implement two new laws on decentralization passed in 1999. One of these laws focuses on fiscal decentralization.
20. See B.D. Lewis (1998), which reviews the broader literature and develops a model that finds a positive impact of local roads and water infrastructure on municipal economic development in Kenya.
21. Tanzi (1995); Prud'homme (1995); and Ter-Minassian (1997).
22. See, for example, Walsh (1992); Sewell (1995); Shah (1997a); and Huther and Shah (1996).
23. There is, of course, a relationship between macroeconomic and microeconomic concerns, but it has been little explored in the literature on fiscal decentralization.
24. This was a major topic of conversation at a workshop on the implementation of the 74th Amendment to the Indian Constitution on decentralization to the municipal level, sponsored by the Ministry of Urban Affairs and Employment and the World Bank and held in Hyderabad in March 1996.
25. There is a substantial and diverse literature that focuses on the benefits of decentralization and its role in rural and urban development. See, for example, Hicks (1961); Montgomery (1972); Oyugi (1978); Rondinelli (1978, 1981, 1982 and 1990); Esman and Montgomery (1982); Cheema and Rondinelli (1983); Davey (1983); Mawhood (1983); Rondinelli et al. (1983); Evans

(1986); Mawhood (1987); Baker (1990); B.D. Lewis (1991:147–153); Evans (1992:640–667); and Gaile (1992:131–148).

26. 51 See, for example, Crook and Manor (1994); Panganiban (1994); de los Reyes and Jopillo (1995); Slater (1994); Souza (1994); Brillantes (1994:576–586); World Bank (1995); Rajas and Verdesoto (1997); Shah (1997a); Manor (1998); Porter and Onyach-Olaa (1999:56–67); UNCDF (1999); Blair (2000); and UNDP (2000).
27. A recent study in South Africa found that citizens considered local governments to be the least responsive level of government and the people did not want to pay for local services even if they were improved. See Taylor and Mattes (1998).
28. See, for example, the cases analysed in Tendler (1997).
29. There are several good references on Ethiopian and Ugandan decentralization policy, including Cohen (1995); Bahl (1997); and World Bank (1999).
30. This builds on Proclamation 41 of 1993, which provides more information on a number of issues related to regional government functions, detailing on a bureau-by-bureau basis certain fairly specific responsibilities. Revenue bases and provisions for their administration are defined in greater detail in Proclamation 33 of 1992.
31. The history of Kenyan local government and current reform efforts are detailed in Smoke (1993, 1994 and 1999b).
32. It is important to note that the STDP project developed slowly (over a period of more than five years), in very close consultation with Ministry of Local Government officials; it is now in its twelfth year of operation. Thus, the project gradually developed very strong credibility with local counterparts, which is an extremely important factor in helping to get project ideas on limited, gradual, negotiated, individually tailored reforms accepted by Kenyan government officials and policy makers. It is also important to note that the STDP did not start from scratch—it built on other, more modest donor efforts, primarily a USAID market towns project that started in the early 1980s. By the mid-1980s, when the STDP came on the scene, USAID had already begun to focus more on financial and managerial capacity building than on simply producing infrastructure projects.
33. Good discussions of local government user charges and

willingness to pay are found in Mushkin (1972); Jimenez (1987 and 1990); Gertler (1987:67–88); Anderson (1989:525–542); Gertler and van der Gaag (1990); Bahl and Linn (1992); Whittington et al. (1991:179–198); Crane (1994); and Beede and Bloom (1995:113–150).

34. The South Africa proposal is discussed in a speech by Deputy Minister of Finance Alexander Erwin to the South African Infrastructure Investment Conference, March 1996. The Tamil Nadu experience is examined in Allaudin and Rajaraman (1996).
35. For more detailed discussion of grant-loan linkages, see Smoke (1999a).

# 6

# Fiscal Decentralization and Economic Growth

## 6.1 Introduction

Traditionally, the theory and practice of fiscal decentralization has given little attention to the objective of economic growth. Only quite recently have normative discussions of fiscal decentralization added economic growth to the traditional list of public finance objectives of efficiency in the allocation of resources, horizontal fiscal imbalances, and economic stabilization. [1]

Instead the traditional argument for fiscal decentralization is that it may provide great economic efficiency in the allocation of resources in the public sector. Under the assumption that public officials respond to the desires of their constituents, sub-national governments are better able to match differing preferences across jurisdictions. Gains in efficiency are enhanced if taxpayers are mobile because they can migrate or sort themselves out among the jurisdictions that best match their preferred tax-expenditure package, as first discussed by Tiebout (1956).

In short, if preferences for public goods differ across regions or individuals, the level of welfare achieved through a uniform provision of public goods by a central government is inferior to that which can be attained by a decentralized provision which allows for differences across jurisdictions. [2]

Efficiency is one of the three objectives, the other two being income redistribution and macroeconomic stability, initially stated by Musgrave (1959) and widely accepted as guides to government policy. But if decentralized governments can play an important role in efficiency, there is some agreement that the objectives of income redistribution and macroeconomic stability may be better pursued by the central or federal governments. Even though sub national governments may differ in their preferences for income redistribution, the mobility of households and businesses will tend to make differences in redistribution policies self-defeating because the rich would move out of and the poor would move into the jurisdiction.

Attempts to implement macroeconomic stabilization by sub-national governments are also believed to be ineffective because of the considerable economic leakages associated with local expenditures. [3] Overall, the lack of direct concern with the objective of economic growth in the theory and practice of fiscal decentralization has its roots in the lack of attention given to this objective in public sector economics. However, public sector economics has paid indirect attention to the objective of economic growth by focusing on issues such as how taxation may distort economic incentives toward savings and investment, how to evaluate the relative worthiness of public investment projects (as for example in the theory of cost-benefit analysis), or how to improve the performance of private markets through spending on education and health systems or investments in basic infrastructure. The general implicit assumption in public sector economics has been that economic growth is fuelled by the growth in the quantity and quality of economic inputs (labour, capital, and natural resources) and by technological change in the private sector. The role of the public sector is to facilitate, or not to impede, this process.

A significant feature of the current state of the fiscal decentralization literature is the paucity of empirical information regarding the effects of decentralization, not only on economic growth, but also on the traditional objectives of economic efficiency, income redistribution, and macroeconomic stability. As we discuss below, the analysis of the direct role of the public sector in economic growth is a relatively new area of study, with the contribution of fiscal decentralization to economic growth only emerging in the last decade. In the following paragraphs we discuss the existing empirical evidence on the potential relationship between fiscal decentralization and growth.

Even though there has been little research on the causation line from decentralization to growth, interestingly, there has been extensive empirical analysis of the reverse question: to what extent is the level of decentralization a function of the level of economic development. It is well documented that most measures of fiscal decentralization across countries, such as share of expenditures or revenues of sub-national governments in the general government budget, are positively correlated with the level of economic development, generally measured by per capita income. There is less agreement in the literature about how to interpret the fact that decentralization is a more common and deeper phenomenon in industrialized countries. One possible explanation is that decentralization is like a superior good. It is only at relatively high levels of per capita income that decentralization is demanded or becomes attractive to taxpayers in the sense that its benefits can be more fully exploited without the problems or disadvantages that tend to be more present in countries at lower levels of development (Bahl and Linn, 1992). This correlation between economic development and the depth of decentralization may also be due to the fact that many developing countries inherited highly centralized systems at the time of their independence from their colonial powers. However, there appears to be wide agreement with Oates' (1993) assessment that the empirical correlation between the level of development and the presence of fiscal decentralization should not be interpreted to say that there is a monotonic relationship between the two such that decentralization intensifies without bound with per capita income, or that a decentralized system of public finances will not offer advantages to countries at lower levels of economic development.

## 6.2 Decentralized Government Expenditure and Growth

While several recent studies have attempted to quantify the role of government expenditures on economic growth, the question of what impact decentralized government expenditures have on economic growth remains largely unaddressed. Aschauer (1989) and Barro (1990) find that an increasing share of central government consumption in GDP is negatively associated with growth in per capita income. In an earlier study, Ram (1986) found a positive relationship between central government consumption in GDP and growth in per capita income. Devarajan, Swaroop, and Zou (1996) examine the impact of the composition of public expenditures on economic growth and find that while an increase in the share of current central government expenditure has a positive and statistically significant effect on growth, the capital component of public expenditure has a negative impact on per capita growth. They conjecture that developing country governments may have been allocating too many resources to capital investments at the cost of more productive current expenditures.

On the other hand, other researchers have found that public infrastructure spending has a positive significant impact on growth (Aschauer, 1989 and Easterly and Rebelo, 1993). There is also some evidence that the efficiency of public expenditures can differ considerably across countries. Gupta, Honjo, and Verhoeven (1997) assess the efficiency of government expenditures on education and health in 38 countries in Africa and find that, on average, countries in Africa are less efficient than countries in Asia and the Western Hemisphere. They do suggest that the observed inefficiencies may be a result of relatively high government wages and the intra-sectoral allocation of government resources. None of the studies above is concerned with the potential impact of the degree of decentralization (or intergovernmental composition of public expenditure or revenue assignment) on economic growth.

An emerging line of research has attempted to test the presence of a direct link between fiscal decentralization and economic growth with mixed results. Zhang and Zou (1997) find that different measures of fiscal decentralization seem to have a positive and sometimes significant effect on regional economic growth in India. Lin and Liu (2000) conclude that fiscal decentralization positively and significantly influenced economic growth in China. This contrasts with the opposite general finding that fiscal decentralization is associated with slower growth for the case of China by Zhang and Zou (1998), for the United States by Davoodi, Xie, and Zou (1995), and for a full sample of both developing and developed countries by Davoodi and Zou (1998). However, Woller and Phillips (1998) fail to find a growth for a panel of developing countries. [4]

Although the theoretical underpinnings of this literature still need to be further developed, as discussed below, these studies have not only provided the first empirical estimates of the potential effect of decentralization on economic growth but have also provided insights into different aspects of this relationship. For example, if fiscal decentralization could be measured, as is done in this literature, in a single dimension (for example the share of expenditures or revenues of sub national governments in the general government) then we should not expect a monotonic relationship between decentralization and growth (Davoodi and Zou, 1998). That is, it is not necessarily true that the more decentralized a country's fiscal system becomes, the faster its economy will grow, but rather, we should expect that there exists an optimal degree of fiscal decentralization which is less than full decentralization (sub national governments' share of expenditures (revenues) is 100 percent). Of course, the bounds are imposed by the fact that there are some public goods, those with nation-wide benefits that can be more efficiently provided at the national level.

However, within the context of more complex, multi-dimensional definitions of decentralization (for example, an index encompassing tax autonomy and budgetary discretion), it may be possible to obtain multiple optima, and even a monotonic relationship between decentralization and economic growth. The recent literature on the empirical relationship between decentralization and growth also raises several estimation issues for future work, which we address next.

### 6.3 Estimation of Relationship between Decentralization and Growth

Several estimation issues will need to be addressed in the future to strengthen our confidence in the empirical results on the role of fiscal decentralization in economic growth. First, there is the issue of possible misspecification of the empirical estimation models. The literature on economic growth suggests that long-term growth may be a function of many variables such as economic freedom and basic legal structure, savings rates, investment behaviour, and general capital accumulation, human capital, technological development and change, and so on. Excluding some of the necessary control variables across countries or over time may result in omitted variable bias leading to the false conclusion that a statistically significant relationship exists between growth and fiscal decentralization. In short, there is a need to verify that the estimated relationships between decentralization and growth are robust under alternative specifications of the estimation model. Levine and Renelt (1992) note the general lack of robustness in the empirical growth literature that has tried to identify the impact of diverse government policies on growth. Using cross-country time series data, they conclude that the significant correlation between measures of economic policy and economic growth found in many previous studies are fragile.

In particular, they find that the statistical significance for those economic policy variables is lost by the inclusion of other explanatory variables in the estimation equation. This is the fate of a wide array of fiscal-expenditure variables, monetary policy indicators, and political stability indices. The only robust correlations they find are for the share of investment in GDP and for the share of international trade in GDP and economic growth. To date, the majority of the studies directly linking fiscal decentralization and economic growth employ Barro's (1990) endogenous growth model, where the production function for the economy has multiple inputs including private capital and multiple public spending by the three levels of government. [5] While Davoodi and Zou (1998) use the Levine-Renelt conditioning variables (investment, population growth, human capital) to test the fragility of the estimate for fiscal decentralization, they do not control for the impact of the external sector. [6] Many of the other studies of the relationship between fiscal decentralization and economic growth also fail to properly condition their estimates. Second, the measurement of fiscal decentralization used by the majority of empirical studies as an explanatory variable is, at least, problematic. The issue is that there is no single or best measure of decentralization.

The empirical literature has evolved significantly in the precision with which the explanatory variable for fiscal decentralization is measured. Initially public expenditures were disaggregated into recurrent or consumption and capital expenditures, later into different levels of government, and finally into types of expenditures by sector at different levels of government. However, all these measures of fiscal decentralization are defined on the basis of a single dimension of decentralization, expenditures going through the sub national budgets or revenues raised by sub national governments. We are sure to misrepresent decentralization when we use a single dimension, no matter how detailed or disaggregated. Clearly, fiscal decentralization is multi-dimensional. There are many aspects of a country's fiscal affairs that can be more or less decentralized.

Even if one country has a greater share for sub-national governments in general expenditures or tax revenues, it can be the case that a second country may be more decentralized overall because its sub national governments have more significant autonomous sources of revenue or discretion over tax rates, or greater freedom in how to make expenditure decisions on education, health or other services provided at the sub national level. Even worse, a country may have a high share of general government expenditure going through sub-national budgets, but *de facto* the level of decentralization may be small because regional and/or local officials are not democratically elected and are only accountable to central government authorities. It would be desirable in future empirical research to attempt to capture the multi-dimensionality of fiscal decentralization in estimating the impact of fiscal decentralization on economic growth. A possible point of departure could come from quantifying the minimum conditions for effective fiscal decentralization such as discretion in the margin to raise own revenues or the use of democratic elections, as suggested in the literature.

Given that our understanding of how decentralization may affect growth is not well developed, there is a danger of accepting too willingly the product of spurious correlations.

This is a difficult problem to control, but a serious one given that decentralization and growth are broad concepts which themselves are correlated with many other variables. Consider the following: Mauro (1995, 1996) finds that corruption lowers investment, thereby lowering economic growth. But Mauro also finds that corruption is highly correlated with ethno linguistic fractionalization (which measures the probability that two persons drawn at random in the country will not belong to the same ethno linguistic group). [7] In general, we should expect decentralization to be highly correlated with ethno linguistic fractionalization because the tensions associated with diversity in population are often addressed through more decentralization. In these circumstances it would not be the case that decentralization slows growth, but that there may be more corruption with fractionalization and, therefore, less growth. The problem of spurious correlation can only be controlled with better data and careful specification of the estimating equations.

The review of the empirical literature shows clearly that we may be far from understanding and therefore properly testing the relationship between decentralization and economic growth? The empirical work on the potential impact of fiscal decentralization on economic growth has offered thus far little detailed discussion of why we should expect this relationship to exist. Answering this basic question should allow us to construct better and more discerning empirical tests. The lack of a theoretical framework has also hampered the statistical work. There is also wide agreement on the desirability of developing such a theoretical framework. 28 In this section we examine in some detail the avenues through which fiscal decentralization may affect economic growth. This may provide the basis for the development of a theoretical framework in the future.

## 6.4 Direct and Indirect Linkages between Decentralization and Growth

The first question that arises is whether we can expect a direct linkage to exist between decentralization and growth. Oates (1993) argues that, intuitively, the static proposition that fiscal decentralization enhances economic efficiency should have a parallel in the dynamic setting of economic growth. Thus, expenditures for infrastructure and the social sector that respond to regional or local differences are likely to be more effective in enhancing economic development than central policies which may ignore those differences. [8] However, Oates is not very explicit about what this means. The basic question is why, for example, US$ 1 million spent on roads or education at the sub national level should be more growth-enhancing than the same amount of money spent at the national level. The direct effect, pointed out here would mean that in a dynamic sense, sub-national government expenditures would be more growth enhancing. On a closer look, this argument would seem to need further development.

*Indirect linkages between fiscal decentralization and economic growth*: Even if there is no direct linkage between fiscal decentralization and growth derived from Oates' (1993) argument, there would appear to be several potential indirect linkages between fiscal decentralization and economic growth.

What is well accepted in the theory and practice of fiscal decentralization is that, given certain conditions, sub-national governments can be more efficient. This can mean two things.

First, the same amount of funds spent at the sub-national level rather than at the national level can result in increased individual welfare. This can be true for some services since local and regional governments are better at discerning the preferences and needs of their constituencies and can more easily adapt their expenditure policies to fulfil them. This increase in welfare through decentralized expenditures can be termed the greater consumer or allocative efficiency of decentralized expenditures.

Second, it is also possible, but by no means a foregone conclusion, that spending the funds through sub national governments can lead to greater producer efficiency, i.e. the same services or infrastructure can be put in place at a lower cost, or a particular budget can yield larger quantities or better quality of services and infrastructure when the funds are spent at the sub national level.

In general, there would be little dispute with the contention that fiscal decentralization can result in greater consumer efficiency. The lack of disagreement is not because there have Oates, indicates that if sub national governments have an advantage in making public expenditures more efficient (by better satisfying the needs and preferences of local taxpayers based on better knowledge of these preferences), then this static advantage can also be present been measurements of these effects. In fact, tests of this nature have been few and far between. [9]

This is because of a priori belief that a decentralized

system can be more responsive to differences in demands among taxpayers and to their basic needs. It can be argued tnat differences in preferences are not likely to be that important in developing and transitional economies (Prud'homme, 1995) but, in fact, sub-national governments can be more efficient than the central government even if all individuals have identical preferences or if they lack mobility.

Central governments may have a greater tendency to spend funds, for example, on national defence when the priorities of taxpayers may be better reflected, for example, by greater expenditures on education and sanitation.

The assertion that fiscal decentralization can result in greater producer efficiency would be disputed by many. What kind of evidence is there on differences in producer efficiency? The question put forward by Prud'homme (1995), Tanzi (1996), and others is whether or not local governments operate on the same production frontier as the central government and whether or not this question would receive the same answer in developed and developing and transitional economies. [10] On the other hand, Shah (1999) argues that the institutional environment in developing countries necessitates a greater degree of decentralization because of the high transaction and administrative costs implied by centralized systems. In addition, decentralization may lead to greater producer efficiency in that it fosters experimentation and innovation in the provision of goods and services. [11] In practice, sub-national governments in many countries have been in the vanguard of privatization of public services (World Bank, 1999). But on the whole, there is little empirical evidence, one way or another, about whether local governments are more or less producer-efficient than central governments.

For the sake of argument, let us assume that at least in some cases decentralization leads to greater consumer and producer efficiency. It is very significant that neither of these two potential effects of decentralization, greater consumer efficiency and greater producer efficiency, are recorded in the national income accounts.

If fiscal decentralization leads to greater producer-efficiency, then the indirect link, greater consumer-efficiency translates into greater individual welfare but no independent measures of this exist. Public expenditures with different levels of consumer efficiency are identically recorded in the income accounts: by the level of expenditures at the national or sub-national level. Similarly, equal expenditure programs with very different levels of producer efficiency will provide the same reading in the national income and product accounts. If the greater efficiency associated with fiscal decentralization is not directly accounted for in the conventional measures of output and economic growth, how is it that greater efficiency may affect measured growth.

## 6.5 Linkage between Efficiency and Measured Growth

Linkage between fiscal decentralization and growth is somewhat intuitive. National accounts measure public output by the level of expenditures, regardless of which level of government spends the funds. But if decentralized governments can produce more output (or better quality output) than the central government, with the same level of expenditures, then greater producer efficiency at the sub national level is occurring. Eventually the higher quantity or quality of the locally-provided public services, the true output, would result in increased income and, therefore, in measured growth.

In the case of consumer efficiency, the relationship is less intuitive. Several complex elements are at play. On the positive side, by better matching the preferences of citizens and increasing their individual welfare, there may be secondary effects on work effort, savings, and private investment, all of which would have a positive impact on measured economic growth at a later date. It is also possible that if public resources are more efficiently spent at the sub-national level, this would mean, for example, that a better educated and healthier labour force or faster, less costly, transportation will result in greater (measured) economic growth in the future.

In this sense, tighter empirical tests of the impact of decentralization on economic growth should focus on whether or not fiscal decentralization, other things being equal (such as expenditure levels, per capita income, and so on), results in improved test scores or other measures of education, or better health status indices. This means that we should test for the presence of direct impacts of fiscal decentralization on the basic components of the growth equation (better quantity and quality of inputs) rather than just directly on economic growth per se. However, the intermediate effect of decentralization on the quantity or quality of some public services, such as roads built by sub-national governments, is likely to be more difficult to quantify.

On the negative side, it is conceivable that the mix of recurrent and capital expenditures and the sectoral composition of these expenditures (into roads, education, parks, and so on) that maximize the welfare of local residents may not be the mix that maximizes measured economic growth over time. The issue is whether or not there are other mixes of public expenditures that will have a greater positive impact on measured economic growth and whether some of these mixes may be more easily achieved through a centralized system of public finances The underlying premise of socialist planned economies and central management and planning in many market economies in past decades was that centralized systems were superior in this respect. The poor performance of centralized systems has put into question their alleged superiority. However, in general, there is no reason to expect that the allocation of resources that maximizes voters' welfare through a fiscally decentralized and a democratically representative process is the one that maximizes growth of measured output. In practical terms this means that it would be empirically possible to find that decentralization and measured economic growth are not positively correlated.

The theory of design of fiscal decentralization emphasizes a number of tradeoffs between efficiency and other objectives such as balanced distribution of resources across regions or macroeconomic stability (Guess, Loehr, and Martinez-Vazquez, 1997). The issue is whether or not changes in income distribution and in macroeconomic stability resulting from fiscal decentralization will also have an indirect but measurable impact on economic growth. [12]

Empirically, estimating the indirect impact of fiscal decentralization through horizontal fiscal imbalances and macroeconomic stability will require two sets of estimations. First, is fiscal decentralization actually associated with, or does it result in, a more unequal distribution of resources across regions and a more unstable macroeconomic environment. Second, what are the quantitative tradeoffs between macroeconomic stability (assuming that it comes from decentralization) and economic growth. That is, how much does macroeconomic instability retard economic growth. And, how much does the unequal distribution of income across regions affect the rate of economic growth. Let us take first the issue of macroeconomic stability. There is considerable controversy in the fiscal decentralization literature as to whether or not fiscal decentralization works against macroeconomic stability. As pointed out above, Prud'homme (1995) and Tanzi (1996) are among those that have issued warnings on these negative potential effects of decentralization but McLure (1995), Sewell (1996), and Spahn (1997), among others, have questioned the validity of this link. So far, there has been no empirical test of the link between decentralization and macroeconomic stability. [13]

But even if there is no inexorable link between fiscal decentralization and macroeconomic instability, there is wide consensus that poorly designed systems (for example, allowing sub national governments to borrow without controls with central governments covering any defaults) lead to instability.

In these cases, fiscal decentralization could lead to less growth because there is some evidence that macroeconomic instability retards growth (Fischer, 1993). But curiously, what most researchers point to as an example of decentralization gone awry, the crises in Argentina and Brazil during the late 1980s and early 1990s, may not be attributable, at least entirely, to decentralization policies. Easterly (2000) finds that, in general, economic and fiscal policies improved during this period for the countries in this region and that economic shocks, not poor policies, were to blame for the debt crises and recessions of this period.

Let us now take on the issue of the distribution of public resources across sub-national governments. The first issue is whether or not decentralization causes a more unequal distribution of public resources. Again, there has been no empirical test of this proposition. However, a priori, there may be some agreement with Prud'homme's (1995) argument that, all else being equal, unfettered fiscal decentralization is likely to lead to a concentration of resources in a few geographical locations and thus increase fiscal disparities across sub national governments. The accompanying presumption is that more centralized public sectors will attempt to produce a geographically more balanced distribution by channelling resources from richer areas to poorer ones. Conversely, centralized systems could create inequitable distributions of public resources by favouring politically important jurisdictions over jurisdictions with greater needs but of less political importance. But again, neither of these two propositions, that unfettered decentralization leads to the geographical concentration of resources and that centralized public sectors yield more geographically balanced distributions, have been empirically tested. There is also little evidence regarding how inequality across regions affects long-term economic growth. [14] This is an another area that awaits testing.

A different issue is how the distribution of resources

among sub national jurisdictions actually affects economic growth. Economists have given considerable attention to understanding the links between income distribution and economic growth. However, this research has concentrated on income inequality across the population and not with income disparities across regions. Whether or not lower levels of income inequality across the population translate into increased economic growth is still a matter of debate, with more recent studies suggesting that increased inequality retards economic growth. However, while the findings of these studies suggest that policies to reduce inequality will positively influence economic growth, caution must be used when interpreting these results. Significant problems do exist when attempting to compare income inequality across countries and across time. First, two different measures of inequality are typically used in the analysis: those measures based upon income distribution and those measures based on the distribution of consumption. For the class of countries with income-based measures of inequality, differences exist between those countries that measure inequality on the basis of gross income versus those that measure inequality on the basis of net income. Finally, while some countries use the household as the unit of measurement, other countries measure inequality using the individual as the unit of measurement.

## 6.6 Sub-national Governments, Competition and Development

A quite different perspective on the impact of fiscal decentralization on economic growth is that fiscal decentralization for better or worse can provide sub-national officials with the ability to actively pursue economic development policies. Often, sub-national governments' development policies include several forms of competition among regional and local governments. These may include granting tax privileges and offering other forms of assistance to businesses willing to locate in a particular jurisdiction. This is an issue surrounded by considerable controversy in North

America and in Western Europe. [15] Less research and discussion has been addressed to these issues in developing and transitional countries, but it would appear that similar policies are at play there as well. At stake is whether inter jurisdictional competition can actually help promote economic growth in a country or whether it is actually a zero-sum or even a negative-sum game among local and regional governments for a fixed set of resources or economic activity. On the positive side, there is the possibility that inter jurisdictional competition (of whatever form) forces government officials to deliver services at minimum feasible cost, thus enhancing producer efficiency at the sub-national level. The lack of competition at the central government level may mean that costs of public services are higher than they ought to be. On the negative side, competition may lead sub-national governments to under provide public services and basic infrastructure (Break, 1967; Strumph, 1999). This, of course, would retard growth.

## 6.7 Corruption and Fiscal Decentralization

Does fiscal decentralization result in increased corruption or the capture of local governments, and, if so, how does it affect economic growth. Some researchers have suggested that corruption is likely to increase when central government authority declines or fails and that corruption is more prevalent in federal systems. [16] Corruption is likely to be more prevalent at the local level because there is more opportunity and pressure by local interests, and local officials may have more discretion and fewer obstacles because of the often blurred distinction between politicians and bureaucrats. Treisman (1999, 2000) argues that federal states may be perceived to be more corrupt than unitary states due to three factors: federal states are typically larger than unitary states, implying diminishing returns to reducing corruption; the existence of separate police forces at multiple levels of government; and a higher likelihood of having a bicameral legislature where the upper house is regionally elected and possesses veto power. However, these results appear to be sensitive to the inclusion of other variables and may also suffer from omitted variable bias (Gurgur and Shah, 2000). In some developing countries there is a widespread belief that corruption is deeply ingrained in local government institutions. [17]

Corrupt behaviour on the part of local officials, of course, reduces the potential benefits of fiscal decentralization. Corrupt behaviour would also reduce private incomes (as citizens must pay bribes to receive public services for which they have already paid taxes) and increase income inequality (as the tax structure is modified to favour those who have sufficient resources to influence government officials). But several counter arguments have been made to this proposition. Decentralization may reduce opportunities for corruption since local policymakers are more visible to their constituents and thus corrupt behaviour is more likely to be noticed than at the central level of government. Corruption is enhanced by the presence of monopoly powers and discretion, and is diminished by the presence of accountability (Klitgaard, 1988). If decentralized governance limits monopoly political power and makes government more accountable to the local constituencies, then decentralization may help reduce corruption. In addition, the potential for the realization of economic rents may be larger in the case of central government policies such as import quotas or tax privileges. The damage inflicted by corruption at the central level can be several orders of magnitude greater than what can be inflicted at the local level due to increased access to resources and capital markets. Local officials have limited powers and budgets. Thus, the return to rent-seeking behaviour at the local level of government may be small, relative to the centre.

While the relationship between fiscal decentralization and corruption has been the subject of increased attention in the literature, there has only been limited empirical analysis of this issue. Huther and Shah (1998), in the first empirical study of this issue, found a negative correlation between fiscal decentralization and corruption. Fisman and Gatti (2000) also found empirical evidence to support the argument of a negative relationship but Treisman (2000) finds that corruption is more prevalent in federal states. More recently, Shah (2000), using a cross-section of developed and developing countries, found that decentralization negatively influences corruption and enhances accountability in the public sector. Decentralization, in this study, appears to have a more significant, negative influence on corruption in unitary rather than in federal countries. Further empirical study will be required on the topic of decentralization and corruption and how it may impact economic growth.

Another potential effect of fiscal decentralization, which may affect expenditure efficiency and ultimately affect economic growth, is that local officials, even if they are popularly elected, may be subservient to the needs of the local elites. Local capture creates a series of problems including overstatement of the cost of provision of local public goods, corruption, and diversion of local public goods to non-intended groups. The local elite may also wish to understate the demand for local public goods in order to lower revenue requirements and taxes. If the preferences of the local elites differ significantly from those of the majority of voters, decentralization reduces local expenditure efficiency and eventually retards economic growth. This, of course, assumes that centralized systems can be more responsive to the tastes and preferences of local voters. However, if the central government is itself controlled by a cadre of national elites, then it is possible, as population heterogeneity increases, that decentralization might still deliver a more efficient allocation of resources, especially if local preferences differ significantly from those at the centre. In addition, competition among regional interest groups may lower the return to capture by elites at the sub-national level relative to the central level of government. [18]

In practice, democratic governance, including frequent and open elections, a free press and mass media, and rule of law may serve to prevent local (and national) capture of public resources by the minority elite. Case studies of democratic decentralization in developing and transitional countries suggest that many new constituencies gain representation through public office (Blair, 1998). This suggests that the concern over local elite capturing the allocative efficiency gains may be overstated. In summary, it is not clear whether capture by local elites and divergence from local preferences will be more pronounced under decentralized or centralized systems and therefore how fiscal decentralization may indirectly affect economic growth. These questions await empirical research.

## 6.8 Summing Up

The impact of fiscal decentralization on growth is more than an academic question. Whether decentralization affects economic growth has become an important policy issue for developing and transitional countries. This is an issue of importance both for large countries like China and India and also for small countries like the Baltic Countries or those in Central America.

In general, our knowledge of how decentralization affects economic growth is too limited at the present time to allow us to proffer advice. We have seen that the empirical evidence of the correlation between the extent of decentralization and economic growth is mixed and that this empirical evidence may not be entirely reliable because of several potential problems with the methodological approaches followed to derive those tests. On a theoretical level we have also seen that the overall impact of fiscal decentralization on economic growth may be uncertain. In terms of a direct impact, if Oates' (1993) argument is correct, we should expect higher growth associated with decentralization. But this dynamic superiority of decentralized over centralized public expenditures is by no means obvious. We have also seen that there are potentially a multiplicity of indirect effects of decentralization on growth including those through consumer efficiency, producer efficiency, the geographical distribution of resources, macroeconomic stability, corruption, and capture by elites. Through these indirect effects there are forces at work that will link decentralization to higher economic growth but there are others that work in the opposite direction. At the present time, we are not even in a position to capitalize on what we know with more certainty is a significant determinant of economic growth, i.e. capital spending.

Currently, we have no knowledge about whether or not decentralized fiscal systems dedicate fewer resources to public investment than centralized ones; nor do we know about differences in the effectiveness or quality of public investment undertaken by different levels of government. [19] In light of the lack of consistent knowledge on the impact of decentralization on growth, it would seem safe to argue that policy advice and international aid must still focus on improving the design of fiscal decentralization in developing and the transitional economies. Even if we were to find at some later date that decentralization retards economic growth, this effect would need to be weighed against the positive impact of decentralization on the efficient allocation of economic resources and other possible benefits such as democratic governance and enhanced accountability. A contribution of this review, we hope, is to begin to outline a research agenda which may allow us a better understanding of the direct and indirect effects of fiscal decentralization.

## Notes

1. See, for example, Bird and Vaillancourt (1997). The lack of preoccupation with economic growth in the fiscal decentralization literature is evidenced by the fact that there is no discussion of this objective in textbooks on the subject; for example, Fisher (1993).

2. A number of researchers have questioned whether developing and transitional countries have the preference revelation mechanisms (voting and geographical mobility) or the institutional capacity to realize the full gains resulting from fiscal decentralization. See Bahl and Nath (1986), Conyers (1990), Prud'homme (1991, 1995), Tanzi (1996, 2000), Litvack, Ahmad, and Bird (1998), and Dethier (1999, 2000).
3. Macroeconomic stability in decentralized systems may be more easily attained if shocks to the economy are not symmetrically distributed (Gramlich 1993 and Spahn 1997) or if decentralization results in a more transparent assignment of responsibilities across levels of government (Shah 1999).
4. These studies use different levels of disaggregation of expenditures and revenues at different levels of government. For example, Davoodi, Xie and Zou (1995), Davoodi and Zou (1998), and Woller and Phillips (1998) concentrate on the role of aggregate spending of different levels of government while Zhang and Zou (1997, 1998) carry this analysis further by looking at the impact of the sectoral composition of public expenditures at different levels of government on economic growth. Lin and Liu (2000) use the marginal revenue retention rate as a measure of fiscal decentralization. statistically significant and robust relationship between fiscal decentralization and economic growth.
5. Recently, Lin and Liu (2000) follow Mankiw, Romer, and Weil (1992) and specify a Solow (1956) model of economic growth that assumes decreasing returns to all forms of reproducible capital.
6. Feder (1992) and McNab and Moore (1998) show that increases in exports are significantly and robustly associated with economic growth. This may be an important omission especially for developing and transitional countries, where external trade plays a critical role.
7. Mauro (1995, 1996) conjectures that more fractionalization may lead to more corruption because bureaucrats may favour members of their same group. Shleifer and Vishny (1993) also suggest that more heterogeneous societies may be subject to more corruption than homogeneous societies.
8. Of course, the direct linkage between decentralization and growth can be derailed if fiscal decentralization does not

function effectively The same is true for the greater efficiency of decentralization in a static sense. Oates (1993) and others have questioned whether or not voting mechanisms, mobility, or competition, for example, function well enough in developing and transitional economies to allow the realization of efficiency gains associated with decentralization.

9. The public finance literature has concentrated on testing how well local budgets may satisfy the demand for public services from representative taxpayers based on statistical tests and surveys. There are no quantitative studies comparing the relative (consumer) efficiency of decentralized versus centralized fiscal systems.
10. Prud'homme (1995) argues that there are reasons, such as better paying jobs and career prospects, to believe that central government bureaucracies are likely to operate closer to the technical production frontier, even though both central and local bureaucracies probably operate quite far from this frontier. For dissenting views see Sewell (1996), who argues that well-functioning sub national bureaucracies exist in many countries and Bardhan (1997) who notes that putting decision-making authority in the hands of those who have information on local tastes and preferences provides strong incentives for the more efficient provision of local public goods.
11. Gramlich (1987) and Salmon (1987) are among those who argue that decentralization results in increased competition among sub national governments and fosters innovation in the provision of public goods. See Strumph (1999) for a dissenting view to this line of reasoning.
12. See Shah (1999) for a review of the literature on the relationship between fiscal decentralization and macroeconomic stability. Little cross-country research has been undertaken on the relationship between fiscal decentralization and horizontal fiscal imbalances across sub-national governments.
13. Burki, Perry, and Dillinger (1999), using a panel data set of 32 countries, found that there is an almost 1-to-1 correspondence between increases in sub-national deficits and central government expenditures and deficits in the subsequent period. They failed, however, to examine whether this translated into greater macroeconomic instability.
14. Prud'homme (1995) cites a number of studies showing that

regional disparities do not disappear with economic development. On the other hand, there is evidence of a substantial narrowing of regional income differentials in the long run in the United States (See Barro and Sala-i-Martin,1992).

15. In the United States early research found that this type of competition would appear to have little effect on business location. However, more recent research (for example, Bartik 1985, and Wasylenko and McGuire, 1985) finds that there is some effect.
16. While not specifically addressing the question of whether fiscal decentralization results in increased corruption, Schleifer and Vishny (1993) argued that rent-seeking activities increase when the role of the central government in society declines.
17. Corruption, in fact, takes many forms, from the formal inclusion of exemptions in the tax structure that favour certain segments of society to bribes to tax assessors, kickbacks or other side payments in the awarding of contracts.
18. See Shleifer (1997), for an examination of the effects of capture on economic development in Russia relative to Poland since the beginning of transition.
19. To complicate things further, it is not entirely clear that greater public investment/expenditures (as opposed to public consumption expenditures) lead to higher economic growth (Devarajan et al., 1996).

# 7

# Fiscal Decentralization in India

## 7.1 The Indian Polity

India became an independent democratic nation in August 1947 and a constitutional republic in January 1950. The constitution explicitly incorporated a federal structure, with states as sub national entities that were assigned specified political and fiscal authorities. However, these states were not treated as independent sovereigns voluntarily joining a federation. In particular, the states' boundaries were not inviolate, but have been repeatedly redrawn by central action (though often in response to sub national pressure), as allowed by the constitution. India is now comprised of 28 States, 6 Union Territories (UTs), and a National Capital Territory (NCT), Delhi. In general, the constitution was structured to give the central government residual authority and considerable sovereign discretion over the states, creating a relatively centralized federation. In particular, the assignment of residual political and fiscal authorities to the centre, either explicitly or through escape clauses, represents the polar opposite of then principle of subsidiarity, found, for example, in United States and European federal institutions.

The primary expression of statutory constitutional authority in India comes through directly elected parliamentary style governments at the national and state levels, as well as (relatively new) directly elected government bodies at various local levels. The national parliament has two chambers, one (the *Lok Sabha* or peoples' assembly) directly elected in single member, first-past-the post constituencies, the other (the *Rajya Sabha*, or states' council) indirectly elected by state legislators. The Prime Minister and council of ministers serve as the executive branch, rather than the largely ceremonial President of the republic. The states, plus the NCT and the UT of Pondicherry, mostly have single chamber, directly-elected legislatures, with Chief Ministers in the executive role. The other UTs are governed by central government appointees. Each state also has a Governor, nominally appointed by the President, but effectively an agent of the Prime Minister. Overlapping political authorities at the central and state levels have been dealt with through intra-party bargaining, and, more recently, through explicit bargaining and discussion.

## 7.2 Distribution of Powers between the Centre and the States

India has a three tier structure of Government. The Central government, State governments, and local bodies i.e. panchayats and municipalities. The constitutional changes in 1992 (73rd and 74th Amendments) now envisage the panchayats (rural local bodies) and municipalities (urban local bodies) as institutions of self-government. These rural and local institutions have been in existence even before the constitutional amendments. But now, with these Amendments it has become mandatory for the States to hold regular elections for these bodies under the supervision of State Election Commissions. Besides, detailed provisions have been made under which state legislature, by law, may entrust the local bodies with such powers, functions and responsibilities to enable them to function as institutions of self government. Before a review of recent developments and issues a look at the main features of the Indian system may be of use.

The concept of decentralization, the purposes and the institutional system for the same is not new to India. It was under the Directive Principles of the Constitution that Article 40 requires that "the State shall take steps to organize village panchayats and endow them with such power and authority as may be necessary to enable them to function as units of self government". Many State governments over the period attempted to translate this Directive Principle into practice by enacting necessary legislation and creating Panchayat Raj Institutions (PRIs). However, such efforts were confined to a few states only. Also, repeat efforts and emphasis on decentralized planning in different five years plans had very little success.

The constitution gives the centre considerable powers over states in certain exceptional situations. The union parliament has the power (with qualified majority) to redraw the boundaries of a state (though this requires the consent of the States concerned) and to create new states. The powers have been exercised three times in the past two decades. The union also has the power to take over the administration of a state under certain circumstances and promulgate President's Rule (Article 356), although judicial rulings in recent years and differences in the party composition of the lower- and upper-house have made it more difficult to exercise such powers recently. Moreover, a deliberate choice was made at the time of Independence that the recruitment and initial training of the senior civil and police employees should be undertaken by the central government which also has joint control with the states over their subsequent careers. Such personnel rotate rapidly through state and central government postings typically at any point of time. More than 50 percent of staff members have been in their current post for less than one year and less than 20 percent for more than two years (Singh and Bhandarkar, 1994 and Mishra, 1997).

The Constitution splits the powers of jurisdiction to legislate into three sectors: areas reserved to centre, areas reserved to states and areas of joint jurisdiction (the concurrent list), with any unspecified areas assigned to the centre or states. Areas with large externalities like defence, foreign affairs, international trade and macroeconomic management are the responsibility of the centre, while law and order, public health, sanitation, schools, irrigation, agriculture, fisheries, industries, land rights, local government and others with state-wide effects are assigned to the states.

In practice, however, the centre has often intervened in areas of states' responsibility. Functions which create benefits across States and with significant effect on development (such as economic planning, energy, parts of education, health and family welfare) are undertaken concurrently with states. Supervision of a number of major economic activities (including national highways and airways) are assigned exclusively to the union. A number of activities are assigned to urban local governments, some of them concurrently with the state government (such as secondary and adult education, housing and land use, electricity distribution and industrial and commercial estates). As well as assigning duties, and hence expenditure, to the centre and to the states, the Constitution also gives the right to levy specific taxes to either the central or state governments, while any unspecified taxes can be levied by the central government.

Furthermore, the constitutionally mandated quinquennial Finance Commission *de jure* decides on the arrangements for sharing revenue between the centre and the states.

## 7.3 Centrally Biased Constitution

Concentration of powers in the hands of the central government did not create serious conflicts in the early years of the functioning of the constitution since the same political party, the Indian National Congress (INC), ruled at the centre and in the states. Many potential interstate or centre-state conflicts were resolved within the party. The INC was essentially an umbrella organization that had pursued a campaign of independence from colonial rule, and this nationalist history contributed to its initial near monopoly of political power. India's relative political centralization was also reflected in bureaucratic and judicial institutions. The national Indian bureaucracy is provided constitutional recognition, and there are provisions for independent bureaucracies in each state. The key component of the bureaucracy is the Indian Administrative Service (IAS), whose members are chosen by a centralized process and trained together. They are initially assigned to particular states, and serve varying proportions of their careers at the state and national levels.

The judiciary is a constitutionally distinct branch of government at both national and state levels, though the legislative/executive branch exerts influence through appointments and budget allocations. The Supreme Court has broad powers of original and appellate jurisdiction, and the right to rule on the constitutionality of laws passed by Parliament. In specific issues of centre-state relations concerning taxation and property rights, the basic centralizing features of the Constitution have tilted the Court's interpretations towards the centre. More recently, in the 1990s, it has made decisions, checking the centre's ability to override sub-national political authority by such means, including dismissing the state legislatures. At the state level, the High Courts superintend the work of all courts within their jurisdictions, including district and other subordinate courts.

At inception, the Indian Constitution clearly laid out the areas of responsibility of the central and state governments, with respect to expenditure authority, revenue raising instruments, and legislation needed to implement either. Expenditure responsibilities are specified in separate Union and State Lists, with a Concurrent List covering areas of joint authority. Unspecified residual expenditure responsibilities are explicitly assigned to the centre. Tax powers of the two levels of government are specified in various individual Articles. Legislative procedures for each level, particularly with respect to budgets and appropriations, are also spelled out in the constitution. Powers of legislation for the centre and states follow the responsibilities assigned in the three constitutional lists, but there are several broad "escape clauses," which gives the national parliament the ability to override the states' authority in special circumstances, with a role for the Supreme Court as arbiter in some cases.

The power to amend the Constitution also resides with the national parliament, with a weak requirement that half or more of the states ratify the amendment for it to take effect. The constitutionally assigned expenditure responsibilities of the central government are those required to maintain macroeconomic stability (e.g. all monetary and financial issues), international trade and relations, and those having implications for more than one state, due to economies of scale or spillovers (e.g. defence, transport and communications, atomic energy, space, oil and major minerals, inter-state trade and commerce, and inter-state rivers).

The major subjects assigned to the states comprise public order, public health, agriculture, irrigation, land rights, fisheries and industries and minor minerals. The Concurrent list includes major areas such as education and transportation, social security and social insurance.

The initial constitutional assignment of tax powers in India was based on a principle of separation, with tax categories being exclusively assigned either to the centre or to the states. The centre was also assigned all unspecified residual tax powers.

Most broad-based taxes were assigned to the centre, including taxes on income and wealth from non-agricultural sources, corporation tax, taxes on production (excluding those on alcoholic liquors) and customs duty. These were often taxes where the tax revenue potential was greater, as a result of relatively lower collection costs, and higher elasticities with respect to growth.

At the sub-national level, a long list of taxes was constitutionally assigned to the states, but only the tax on the sale of goods has turned out to be significant for state revenues. This outcome is largely a result of political economy factors (e.g. rural landed interests were initially quite powerful in government at the state level) that have eroded or precluded the use of taxes on agricultural land or incomes (and even user charges for public irrigation and electricity) by state governments. Inefficiencies arose in indirect taxes because, while in a legal sense taxes on production (central manufacturing excises) and sale (state sales taxes) are separate, they tax the same base, causing overlapping and cascading, and effectively leaving the states less room to choose indirect tax rates.

The framers of the Constitution were aware of the need for a common market, but included another broad escape clause. An early amendment to the Constitution added clauses that enable the central government to levy taxes on inter-state transactions. Furthermore, sales taxes have been levied by exporting states on the inter-state sale of goods, making these taxes origin-based and relatively more distortionary in practice. Finally, adding to internal impediments to trade, states and localities have been permitted to impose various entry taxes, under a separate (and somewhat inconsistent) constitutional provision.

### 7.4 Extent of Fiscal Devolution to State Governments

The overall pattern of finance shows that state governments receive a much higher proportion of total tax revenues than in federal countries in the OECD area. The share of taxes assigned exclusively to state governments is larger than in other federal countries and this is accentuated both by the tax sharing arrangements and the extent of grants. However, this does not necessarily reflect a greater degree of autonomy of Indian states relative to states or provinces in other federations. In particular, the comparison is biased by the very low level of social insurance taxation and expenditure in India. In nearly all OECD federal countries, social insurance taxation is a significant portion of total taxation and is nearly always raised by the federal government, thereby reducing the share of the tax revenue flowing to states.

States in India are not very efficient in creating non-tax revenues with many of their commercial enterprises returning a loss, in contrast to central government enterprises. As a result, the states have a significantly lower share of spending than their share of the total tax revenue of central and state governments. Overall, the states share of spending is about 10 percentage points lower than their share in tax revenues.

### 7.5 Mechanism of Transfer of Resources from the Centre to the States

The flow of funds from the centre to the states occurs through three channels. First, the Finance Commission recommends the proportion of central government taxes that should be transferred to states. These recommendations are generally followed and these transfers represent the bulk of financial flows to states. Second, the Planning Commission grants central assistance to either projects or schemes that are included in state planning documents that it has to approve. Finally, The Planning Commission also administers more than 200 schemes for selected areas of government expenditure that were originally designed by ministries. Moreover, it is often the case that funds allocated for these schemes by the Planning Commission are not fully utilised by a large number of states due to problems of the delivery system at the state level. Central government ministries administer these schemes, which are designed to ensure that state governments follow the policy directions of central government.

Transfers through the Finance Commission have increased, and the share of earmarked grants has also increased, which may lower the efficiency. The latest Thirteenth Finance Commission has enhanced the states' share from 30.5 to 32.0 percent for 2010-11 to 2014-15. Twelfth Finance Commission had raised transfers to states for the period 2006 to 2010, with the states' share of central taxes being increased from 29.5 percent to 30.5 percent, while earmarked grants jumped by 143 percent (on average compared with the previous five-year period). It also recommended that central government should stop lending to states. Shifting from central loans to transfers is a welcome move. The growth of earmarked grants within the transfer system runs counter to the experience in a number of OECD countries where block grants were found to be more efficient than earmarked grants.

The system of grants and tax sharing essentially provides for horizontal redistribution of income between states. The amounts which are distributed to states in the form of tax sharing and grants (in both the Finance Commission and the Planning Commission routes) are determined by formulae that differ. In deciding on the distribution of shared taxes, the Finance Commission places most weight on income redistribution and less weight on the size of the state œ whether measured by population or area. In the case of the Planning Commission, the weights are almost exactly reversed, with the added twist that the population structure is always based on the 1971 Census, so as not to reward states that failed to implement effective family planning programmes. The Planning Commission distributes only part of its grants according to its distribution formula; the states classified as general category states receive less than half of their grants from the Planning Commission according to the formula while the special category states receive only 10 percent according to the formula and 90 percent as discretionary grants; special category states, with two exceptions, are physically isolated areas in either the north-eastern or north-western borders of India with strategic importance as well as poor infrastructure.

Within the general category of states, the distribution of the totality of central grants is highly redistributive. Before redistribution, poorer states have a slightly lower own tax revenue relative to state GDP than higher income states. After redistribution, there is a strong negative correlation between tax and grant revenues of states relative to state GDP and the income level of the states. Part of this lower own tax revenue might be the result of disincentive effects with poorer states making less efforts to create own revenues as they rely heavily on central transfers. Indeed, for the special category states, such disincentives may be significant as their tax effort is markedly lower than average while their total grant income represents, on average, 40 percent of state GDP, though it is possible that the tax base of these states is lower than the average, relative to state GDP.

Despite the high degree of redistribution of tax revenues, there remains a marked difference in total current revenues across states. Although the current mechanism has reduced the coefficient of variation of tax revenues by a factor of almost two, the extent of inequality in revenues still remains more than double that in a number of OECD federal countries. However, given the scale of income differentials and the size of the poorer states, equalisation of per capita revenue would be difficult to achieve and would also create additional disincentives for creating own revenues. For example, moving to a degree of equality similar to that seen in Canada would require implausibly large transfers to a number of states (Bihar, Jharkhand, Madhya Pradesh, Rajasthan, Uttar Pradesh and West Bengal), that would be equivalent to half of the income currently remaining for the central government after grants and transfers. Nonetheless, within the group of low income states, the transfers received by Bihar and Uttar Pradesh are relatively low as compared to the transfers to the special category states.

Part of the redistributive impact of central transfers may have been counter-balanced in the past by other elements of fiscal policy, but these offsets are now coming to an end. Horizontal redistribution was partially offset by exporting part of the tax burden from richer states to poorer states through the origin nature of inter-state sales tax with taxes accruing to the (richer) exporting states while being paid by citizens in poorer importing states (Rao, Shand and Kalirajan, 1999). The progressive ending of the interstate trade tax will eliminate this tax export. Furthermore, vertical redistribution from the centre to states was lessened by the high interest rates charged by the Planning Commission for loans that largely offset the grant element of such transfers in the past. This policy ended in 2006 and states are now allowed to borrow from the market where interest rates tend to be lower than borrowing from the central government. Some states have been unable to access the market and continue to rely on the National Small Savings Fund.

Some studies have suggested that political economy factors, such as proportion of ruling party members coming from a particular state, have also affected the distribution not only of earmarked grants but also (with a lag) of the formulae-based Finance Commission transfers (Rao and Singh, 2002; Biswas and Marjit, 2000). Nonetheless, despite such influences, there is a significant progressive redistribution mechanism at work, even if these fiscal transfers have been unable to prevent a further widening of income inequalities across states in the past decade.

### 7.6 Controlling Debt of States by Central Government

Formally, the centre has the power to limit states' borrowing as states have to obtain the permission of central government for any borrowing; only if a state were not indebted to the centre, which has never been the case, could it borrow in the market without facing central government controls. India's legal arrangements for the control of state-level borrowing differ from those in a number of other federal systems. In India, there is no national legal restriction on the ability of states to borrow to finance consumption expenditure, nor is there any nationally set ceiling on the overall debt of the states. The absence of such constraints is compounded by the absence of national laws that explicitly limit the central government guarantee of state borrowing and forbid the bailout of states that default on debt. Moreover, the law does not forbid states from guaranteeing loans. On the other hand, nearly all states have now introduced Fiscal Responsibility Acts that aims to eliminate revenue deficits, broadly equivalent to not using borrowing to finance consumption.

Despite its general power to limit states' debt, the central government does not appear to have used this power to a significant degree. Furthermore, in the past, numerous factors underlined below, have softened states' budget constraint:

- The centre provided large loans to states to finance their deficits and sometimes these loans were later converted into grants.
- Furthermore, states were obliged to borrow most of the savings which are accumulated in the postal national savings fund (the Small Savings Scheme), a regulation that undermined fiscal consolidation and was particularly expensive for states. They are now required to borrow only 80 percent of the funds raised by this scheme in their state.
- In addition, states also borrow from public enterprises and have also received overdrafts from the Reserve Bank of India.
- Past fiscal slippages by the central government also had a negative signalling effect on fiscal discipline of states and local authorities (contagion effect).
- Some features of the transfer system have weakened fiscal discipline as transfers by the Finance Commission were partly based on (initial or projected) expenditure-revenue gaps of individual states (gap-filling grants) rather than on normative indicators, thus rewarding states with relative poor fiscal management.
- Infrastructure projects are also often financed by newly created corporations which borrow from the market with State guarantees, thus creating contingent liabilities. Contingent liabilities also emerge through other State guarantees as well as through unfunded pension liabilities, although the recent pension reform is limiting the growth of these liabilities and will eventually eliminate them.

Given the factors that have contributed to a weakening of the budget constraint at the level of the states, their debt rose from 22 percent to 33 percent of GDP between 1990 and 2003, with the ratio of debt to total current revenue of the states rising from 1.8 to 2.9 during the same period and interest payments increasing from 13 percent to 26 percent of revenue. The main reason for this relatively modest increase was the fact that, in the 1990s, nominal GDP growth was higher than nominal interest rates, which compensated for the effect of the primary deficit on the debt ratio and resulted in a stable debt ratio between 1990 and 1998 (Rangarajan and Srivastava, 2003). However, the dangers of relying on such a combination were seen between 1999 and 2003 when the interest rate-growth differential moved against the states and debt rose sharply.

The central government has now obliged the states to go to the market for new borrowing. It has stopped acting as a direct intermediary for borrowing by the states and has ended the requirements that central grants covering state investment projects should only cover 30 percent of total outlays with the rest covered by state borrowing. This absence of lending to states only covers expenditure through the Consolidated Fund of the government. The central government continues to lend to states through the Public Account which manages the postal savings system.

### 7.7 Significant Role Played by Postal Savings System

The postal savings system has played a key role in financing public sector deficits and, as designed, needs a significant reform. The states have privileged access to these funds through the National Small Savings Fund (NSSF) where all postal savings are held. Since 1999, each state government is obliged to borrow all of the cash raised in its geographic area and all pay the same interest rate which is set administratively. These postal savings attract significant tax concessions and also benefit from the administrative setting of interest rates above market rates and also from the backing by the full faith of the union government. States are charged a rate of 9.5 percent against their average market borrowing rate of 7.9 percent. Loans are unconditional and so can permit continued borrowing when access to markets might be difficult. Indeed, West Bengal, with a high debt burden, expects to finance its deficit entirely through this form of funding. States in this position are then vulnerable to any slowdown in the growth of deposit in their area. Indeed, such a slowdown is partly the cause of the recent fiscal problems in Kerala.

The obligation to borrow from the National Small Savings Fund (NSSF) also places a burden on fiscally responsible states. In 2005, for states such as Tamil Nadu, Karnataka, Haryana, Punjab and the National Capital Territory of Delhi, almost one-third of the inflow of funds from the NSSF was in excess of their overall borrowing requirements. So these states were obliged to increase balances held with the central government by a similar amount. As the rate on the balances with the central government is well below that on the NSSF loans, the states make a significant loss on the transaction and are locked into a 25-year loan from the NSSF. A reform of the NSSF mechanism is required to install greater fiscal discipline at the level of states. The increase in postal savings has amounted to 2.7 percent of GDP on average between 2002 and 2005 and represented one-quarter of the total acquisition of financial assets by the household sector. Even with the current FRBM targets for states, postal savings provide almost total finance for their deficits. This goes against another one of the desirable reforms of the FRBM Act, namely that the central government should cease lending to the state governments and instead oblige them to borrow on financial markets. In any case, if, over the medium-term, government borrowing were to be used only to finance net capital formation, then the flow of funds from postal savings would exceed the requirements of states.

The latest Finance Commission has lessened the extent of moral hazard in its grants and transfers. It recommended that states should introduce Fiscal Responsibility legislation that would involve balancing their revenue budgets and limit their overall fiscal deficit to 3 percent of state GDP. It further recommended that states that achieve specified targets for the reduction of revenue deficits should receive grants in the form of debt relief. Perhaps unfortunately, it tied the amount of the grant to the amount of maturing debt due to central government in a given period, thus tending to reward the highly-indebted states, *i.e.* the worst performers in the past more than the good performers.

Nonetheless, it is unclear at this stage, if poorer states which face particularly serious fiscal strains and also have high infrastructure needs will be able to meet these fiscal targets. The Finance Commission has also reduced the extent of the grants for states deemed to be in need of assistance (where the moral hazard problem appears to be most prominent). This form of grant is now very small, accounting for less than 7 percent of tax sharing transfers.

Moreover, from 2007 onwards no general category state will be receiving this form of grant which will be made only to the north-eastern and north-western special category states. However, the obligation of states to borrow 80 percent of the proceeds of the Small Savings Fund was not removed and continues to undermine the intended hardening of state's budget constraint as well as the flow of savings to private investment.

A further weakness in the control of state borrowing is the difficulty of obtaining consistent and timely data on the overall fiscal performance of state governments. The states do not use accrual accounting, nor is there a standardised form of accounts across states, with the result that states are able to switch expenditure between current and capital expenditure, notably for the payment of subsidies to loss-making state enterprises. Overall data for the budgets of all states are only available with a nine month delay, with the result that nationwide data for actual spending in a given fiscal year is not available until 21 months after the end of that fiscal year when they are presented by the Reserve Bank of India.

## 7.8 Constitutional and Legal Framework for Local Bodies

The 73rd and 74th amendments of the Constitution in 1992 have been a major step towards strengthening of local governments and operationalising the decentralization process. Provisions were made relating to (a) constitution and composition of the panchayats and municipalities (b) functional and fiscal powers of the Panchayats and Municipalities and (c) institutional arrangements for planning for economic and social development.

For the constitution of the Panchayats and Municipalities, the Constitution provides that: "there shall be constituted in every State, Panchayats at the village, intermediate and district levels in accordance with the provisions of this Part. Panchayats at the intermediate level may not be constituted in a State having a population not exceeding 20 lakh" (Article 243 B).

"There shall be constituted in every State:

- a Nagar Panchayat for a transitional area, that is to say, an area in transition from a rural area to an urban area;
- a Municipal Council for a smaller urban area, and
- a Municipal Corporation for a larger urban area" (Article 243Q).

Regarding functional and fiscal powers, now the Constitution contains two schedules, viz. Schedule XI (243G) and Schedule XII (Article 243W) which comprises a list of functions considered appropriate for devolution to Panchayats and Municipalities. The list of functions is illustrative in nature. The Constitution, thus, maintains the prerogative of the State in respect of determining the functional/spending responsibilities of the Panchayats and Municipalities. The Constitution has provided for the setting up of a finance commission in every State, for the propose of reviewing the financial position of the Panchayats and Municipalities, and making recommendations to the Governor as to the principles which would govern:

- The distribution between the State and Panchayats, and the

State and Municipalities of the net proceeds of the taxes, duties, toll and fees leviable by the State;

- The determination of the taxes, duties, tolls and fees which may be assigned to, or appropriated by, the Panchayats and Municipalities.
- The grants-in-aid to the Panchayats and Municipalities from the Consolidated Fund of the State, and
- Any other measure that would improve the finances of the Panchayats and Municipalities.

For institutional arrangements the Constitution now provides for the constitution of District Planning Committee (DPCs) and Metropolitan Planning Committees (MPCs). Articles providing for the constitution of such Committees are a significant step in the direction of initiating a process of planning from below. The DPCs are to be responsible for the consolidation of plans prepared by the Panchayats and the Municipalities, and preparation of a draft development plan for the district. The MPCs are to be responsible for the reparation of draft development plans for the metropolitan areas. The composition and functions of DPCs and MPCs are to be determined by the legislature of the States.

### 7.9 Local Bodies Remain Underdeveloped

While the basic principles of the vertical and horizontal distribution between the central government and states appear to work reasonably well, there is inadequate account taken of the needs of local government. This is a particularly important deficiency in a country where the median population of a general category state was 62 million in 2005. The Constitution recognised only in 1992 the existence of local government [Districts, Taluks (Blocks), villages in rural areas (Panchayats) and municipal corporations in urban areas] and specified a number of services that should be in the domain of local authorities and also assigned taxes. More than a decade later, progress in developing an effective third tier of local government has been very limited. This is particularly the case in rural areas where there was no history of functioning institutions to build on, in contrast to urban areas where there has been a long history of municipal corporations. Even to the extent that they do function, the rural authorities have little autonomy and their own tax revenue is almost non-existent. Municipal authorities scarcely do better, raising less than one-sixth of the level of own taxation seen in federal countries in the OECD area.

Moreover, the autonomy of municipalities to set their own tax rates is often strictly limited while the value of the property tax base is often adversely impacted by state-level rent control laws. There is somewhat less of a difference in total local revenues from taxes and grants as a percent of state and central taxes with some other federal OECD countries. Nonetheless, the overall tax and grant income of local bodies is only around 1 percent of GDP, which is about one-third of that seen in the federal OECD countries.

The low level of municipal taxation is clearly associated with a low level of provision of basic local services. The provision of a piped water supply, a sewage disposal system and effective waste disposal are three key municipal services to which could be added an adequate road network and street lighting. Access to the first three basic services in urban areas varies enormously across different states in India. The average access across all states is 24 percent but the coefficient of variation is 50 percent with the range of individual indicators being from zero (provision of sewage disposal in urban areas in Bihar) to 79 percent (provision of piped water in Rajasthan). The variation of access to provision of basic services across municipalities is closely related to the average income of municipal authorities which shows considerable variation across states. In part this variation is due to the municipal income per capita being related positively to average incomes of the state in which they are located. This suggests that part of the problem of low income for municipal authorities is the failure of lower income states, which receive large transfers, to treat local authorities in their jurisdiction in the same way as they are treated by central government.

Indeed, it would appear that the mechanism put in place to ensure revenue sharing at the state level, at the time when the constitution was amended to formalise the role of local authorities, has never functioned in the way that was envisaged. In part this reflects poor availability of basic accounting data. Few municipalities have kept double-entry accounts and even fewer use them on an accrual basis. But the problem appears deeper. The Constitution envisages that each state should create a finance commission to regulate revenue sharing. They appear to be viewed as a constitutional formality, with recommendations often being ignored. According to the Twelfth Finance Commission, the delays in their constitution, frequent reconstitution, delays in reporting and action taken and the qualifications of those serving on the commissions have in many cases defeated the very purpose of the institution.

### 7.10 Assessment of Effectiveness of Local Bodies

The third tier of government in India consisting of panchayats for rural areas and municipalities for urban areas together exceed 250 thousand in number with different layers and compositions depending upon such factors as population, area, density etc.

Developments in decentralization process particularly during 1990s have shown a highly diversified experience in terms of its effectiveness to achieve the objectives being pursued. Given the dimensions of the developments in terms of implementation of the mandatory provisions in the constitutional amendments like periodic holding of elections, legislative amendments at state level, constitution of various committees at different levels, delegation and devolution from Centre and States to the local bodies — it is much beyond the scope of this study even to summarize the major changes over the period. For the same reasons (dimensional aspects) any generalizations on progress or performance of the local bodies could only be misleading. While experiences and developments with decentralization in Kerala State are reportedly exemplary in terms of success story at one extreme, some field survey reports on the other extreme, point out disastrous failure of local bodies in the state of Uttar Pradesh and absolute systemic failure of the process in the state of Bihar where even the mandatory process of decentralization has not been completed.

The Expenditure Finance Commission while analyzing the process of implementation of the 73rd and 74th Amendments has come across several problem areas which need to be looked into, to make decentralization process effective.

Notwithstanding the fact that all the States (except Arunachal Pradesh) have either enacted a new Panchayat/Municipal Act or have brought the existing legislation in conformity with the 73rd and 74th Amendments there remain significant gaps in administrative measures taken, uncertainties of role assigned to the local bodies, and deviations from true spirit of amendments.

The EFC found that the schemes relating to the subjects included in the Eleventh and Twelfth Schedules have not yet been transferred by the States to the local bodies. States' legislation merely enumerate the subjects indicated in the two schedules but do not specify the schemes that have to be implemented by these bodies as contemplated in articles 243G and 243W. Thus, the funds and functionaries relating to these schemes remain under the control of the departments of the State governments.The District Planning Committees (DPCs) have not become operational in most States; Metropolitan Planning Committees have not been constituted in any State. On the other hand, in some States, DPCs have been entrusted with executive functions, by which they overshadow the local bodies.

Provisions of the Central Act 1992, had excluded out of its purview Fifth Schedule areas falling in some 9 States. After the Parliament had passed an Extension Act in 1996 these

States were to amend their existing Acts in consonance with the Extension Act within a year (by December 24, 1997). Except Bihar all other States have amended their Acts. However, it has been noticed that these States have kept provisions in such a way so as to make the extension to scheduled areas meaningless because the powers have been retained by the state governments themselves. (Mahi Pal, May 2000). Further, the Parliament is yet to pass the extension act for the sixth schedule areas.

A hierarchical structure of Panchayats has been contemplated in the States' legislation with the intermediate level panchayats supervising the village level panchayats and the district level panchayats supervising, advising and coordinating the activities of village level and intermediate level panchayats.

However, the role of the three tiers of the panchayats has not been clearly delineated in the State legislation and the matter has usually been left to be decided by way of executive instructions.

The financing gap for the rural local bodies is not yet significant. This could be primarily because the rural local bodies spend only what is made available to them by the State government. In any case these institutions would not have many sources of tax and non-tax revenue at the local level.

The finance gap with the urban local bodies on the other hand is significant. This is mainly because while these institutions have the sole responsibility of providing core services in the urban areas they are administratively weak in realizing cost related user charges of these services. Also these institutions, thus increasingly depend on funds provided by the State government which in most cases remain under severe financial constraint.

The Eleventh Finance Commission did the whole exercise of analyzing the developments on fiscal decentralization for local bodies because for the first time, a finance commission, in its terms of references, was required to make recommendations on the measures needed to augment the consolidated funds of the States to supplement the resources of the local bodies on the basis of the recommendations of the Sate Finance Commission (SFC). Also, the EFC was required to make its own assessment wherever SFCs have not reported or even constituted. It is in this process of assessment and recommending the measures that the EFC has found significant problems and issues confronting the smooth functioning of the fiscal decentralization from states to local bodies. State Finance Commission mechanism could be found of not much help to the EFC.

Study reports sponsored by the EFC to two research institutions could not provide usable estimates of financial requirements of local bodies. Perhaps the most intriguing fact is that States' memoranda to EFC did not even give the position in regard to transfer of powers, authority and responsibility or the financial powers devolved on the local bodies to raise resources. The powers of taxation mentioned in the legislation have been made subject not only to the rules, notifications and orders to be issued by the State governments, but also to the procedures and limits to be prescribed. Finally, in quite a few States action is yet to be taken. Some of the important problem areas in fiscal decentralization as identified by the EFC are as follows:

SFCs mechanism is not working well. The fact that EFC could not utilize the outcomes of SFC mechanism is an indication enough of a systemic failure. The EFC found that:

- There is no synchronization of the periods covered by the SFCs with that of the Finance Commission.
- Many SFC reports have not addressed the specific terms listed in Articles 243I and 243Y, nor have they provided a clear idea of the powers, authority and responsibilities actually entrusted to the local bodies.
- In some States, the action taken report (ATR) on the recommendations of the SFC is yet to be submitted to the state legislature, despite the fact that the reports have been

available for about two to three years.

- Several important recommendations of the SFC, relating to sharing/transfer of resources, are often reported to be under consideration for months or even years.
- In some states, serving government officers are appointed as chairperson and members of the SFCs and that too in ex-officio capacities. This puts limitation on the ability of the SFC to act as an autonomous body to make recommendations in a free and independent manner, as has been envisaged in the Constitution.

There is no significant change in the functional domain of Panchayats post 73rd Amendment. The study entrusted by the EFC to National Institute of Rural Development (NIRD) revealed that few States have been serious in vesting the panchayats with the necessary powers, funds and staff to enable them to perform the functions assigned to them under the statutes. Further, the States' legislation provide for levy and collection of certain taxes, fees and tolls but the rules relating to fixation of rate structure are not periodically done and reviewed.

Local bodies are merely performing agency functions. The Central sector and Centrally sponsored schemes are mostly implemented through special agencies created at the district level. In some cases, the local bodies have been associated but they have no decisive role clearly assigned to them in the preparation and implementation of these schemes.

In consideration of the slow and half hearted implementation of the 73rd and 74th Amendments in the Constitution for creating local bodies as self government, the EFC has made wide ranging recommendations both for administrative and legal changes as well as for proper utilization, accounting and audit of the expenditure of these bodies. In the ultimate sense, however, it will all depend on the sincerity of purpose with the State governments to see that the local bodies do function as the self-government in its real effective form.

## 7.11 Summing Up

A major achievement of India's federal system is that it has preserved the political cohesion between the states, which is a main challenge in a country of this size and with its ethnic, religious, linguistic and economic diversities. Nonetheless, there remains much room for improving the operation of India's fiscal federalism. Given the various weaknesses of the current system there is much agreement that reforms are needed and a reform path seems clear.

The first stage would be to set clear objectives for the system, which are lacking at the moment. The current tax sharing arrangements and transfer systems appear to be rather complex and not very transparent. However, designing an efficient system is notoriously difficult given the tradeoffs between the efficiency and equity objectives, and the need to make political compromises. Nonetheless, making the different functions of the transfer systems explicit, such as reducing fiscal imbalances between the different levels of government (vertical equity), supporting the financing of spending with positive externalities (efficiency) and redistributing resources in favour of poorer states and regions (horizontal equity), would increase transparency and help to improve the system. The multiplicity of channels for directing funds to states could also be simplified in order to give an overall view of the extent of redistribution.

There are large differences in state government revenues and, on this basis, it could be argued that the transfer system should be more redistributive. Here, an explicit redistribution objective might help, such as those adopted in Canada and Australia. However, relying on redistributive transfers alone will not be sufficient to achieve economic catching-up of poorer states. They will also need to implement structural reforms that improve framework conditions for the private sector, which is the main driver for growth in all OECD countries as well as in the more successful Indian states.

Future reforms should also aim in particular at eliminating

those elements of the fiscal system which undermine economic developments and spending efficiency and create problems of moral hazard. Experiences in federal OECD countries show that it is possible to provide states with relatively high tax autonomy, including indirect taxes, without creating barriers to inter-state trade. The move to reduce the central sales tax on inter-state trade is thus welcome. International experience also shows that appropriate safeguards are needed to achieve fiscal discipline at all levels of government. In India, recent reform efforts are aimed at hardening the budget constraints for the centre and the states, but more needs to be done. In particular, States should be freed from the obligation to absorb private savings which are accumulated under the Small Savings Scheme.

Reforming the system of fiscal federalism along these lines remains a major political challenge. But the benefits of such reforms could be huge. A more efficient indirect tax system would help to create an internal market for goods and services within the country and improve the efficiency of public spending, while more fiscal discipline would help to sustain high growth. This would be beneficial if accompanied by market-oriented structural reforms to further raise living standards in India as a whole, as well as in poorer regions, and would thus, help to achieve the government's objective of sustainable and inclusive economic growth.

# 8

# Progress, Prospects and Challenges of Indian Economy

## 8.1 India's Development Experience: Pre-reforms Period

Some hold the view that India was a poor country for most part of the human history though there were pockets of prosperity and islands of riches. However, accounts of others, especially global travellers and those who invaded India indicate that India was a prosperous country at least till the 17th Century. According to an OECD publication, in 1700 AD, broadly defined, India's gross domestic product (GDP) at US$ 90.8 billion was 24.4 percent of world GDP (Maddison Angus, "The World Economy: A Millennium Perspective", OECD, 2001). Lord Meghnad Desai, while delivering the first P.R. Brahmananda Memorial Lecture in Mumbai in September 2004, noted that the story of the 19th century for India is not one of gloom and doom. He added that during the second half of the 19th century, where the data are best available, India was an open economy enjoying an export led growth but there was a drain of the export surplus to pay Home Charges. During the forty year period from 1860 to 1900, the per capita income growth ranged from 0.5 to 1 percent.

According to Lord Desai, the first fifty years of the 20th Century were much less favourable for the Indian economy than the last forty years of the 19th century. Further, in a book titled "The National Income of India in the Twentieth Century", Professor Sivasubramonian observed that in the first five decades of the 20th century (1900-01 to 1946-47), before we got our Independence in 1947, the per capita GDP in India was stagnant, as the trend growth in GDP during this period was 0.9 percent with population growing by 0.8 percent (Sivasubramonian, S., Oxford University Press, 2000). As compared with near stagnant growth in the first 50 years of the 20th century, the annual growth averaging around 3.5 percent during the period 1950 to 1980 was comparatively better, while per capita growth broke out of the long period of inertia and averaged 1.1 percent until around 1980. Whereas the average growth rate has been around 6 percent since the 1980s, embarking on a higher average growth path of 8.6 percent in the last four years could be a paradigm shift.

The Indian experience clearly suggests that the mixed-economy model and planned development strategy in the first phase during the 1950s and 1960s, improved growth rate dramatically relative to previous five decades, and also provided the essential building blocks and laid the strong foundations of an indigenous industrial base, vibrant entrepreneurial class, knowledge economy, with considerable improvement in vertical, social and economic mobility. However, the inward looking import substitution strategy pursued during the initial decades of the planning period resulted in declining productivity and high cost economy.

Economic performance in the first decades after Independence was impressive. Since Independence in 1947, India's economic policies have followed a number of distinct paths. Initially, policies were based on socialist planning and a philosophy of self-sufficiency through large-scale state intervention in industrial production, price setting and foreign trade. Most imports were strictly controlled by government and purchases of most foreign capital goods were banned. Government also extended the scope of the commercial public sector well outside the area of transport and utilities and controlled the expansion of the remaining private sector domain. Certain areas of economic activity were reserved for small enterprises and credit flows were directed towards priority sectors.

Larger firms were subjected to highly restrictive labour laws. These policies led to excessive bureaucracy (the so-called license-Raj system) and failed to achieve the desired outcome of raising growth. As a result, poverty remained high and government policies, from the mid-1960s onwards, were oriented towards redistributing income and providing food and energy subsidies to the poor (OECD, 2007).

Realizing this, significant changes in policy were initiated in the early 1980s, taking account of oil shocks in the 1970s and early 1980s. These policy measures took India into a higher growth trajectory in the 1980s but in its wake created some macroeconomic imbalances leading to a crisis in 1991 that triggered more comprehensive and sustainable reforms. The policies since 1991 provided ample opportunities to build on the strong foundations in economic, political and social sphere, laid during the pre-reform period of planned development.

## 8.2 Economic Policies in the 1980s

The precise date when economic policy changed course is difficult to determine. From the late1970s onwards, reforms were undertaken in a piecemeal fashion. In the late1970s, there were only 79 products, all capital goods, which could be imported without a license. Following a major reform push in the mid-1980s, the number of items on the list increased enormously, rising almost twenty fold during the1980s and outright bans on imports were replaced by a combination of import quotas and tariff rates. Furthermore, the extent of the state-trading import monopoly fell markedly (Panagariya, 2004). As a result of this liberalisation, importers' rents were reduced and revenue from tariffs rose by almost one percentage point of GDP in the second half of the decade, doubling the revenue from tariffs relative to the value of imports.

While such a reform was a step forward, the import-weighted tariff was 87 percent and quantitative restrictions were rampant — 92 percent of internationally tradable domestic production was sheltered behind quantitative import restrictions in the late 1980s. Moreover, for most products the permitted volume of imports was extremely low in most areas—84 percent of possible five-digit SITC products accounted for only 10 percent of total imports. However, from the mid-1980s, government began to reduce the extent to which domestic firms required permission to expand their activities or enter new product areas, freeing 31 industries of restrictions and raising the asset ceiling over which government permission for investment was required from US$ 12 million to US$ 600 million.

The1980s can thus be seen as a period of transition and the beginning of the move away from a dirigiste economic model. Reforms during this period were essentially oriented towards improving the position of domestic producers rather than increasing competition through a generalised opening of the economy. The policy environment, though, moved away from distributional concerns towards improving productivity; but progress was limited. For example, as reductions in energy and food subsidies in the mid-1980s proved unpopular, the government sharply increased subsidies to agricultural inputs (power, fertiliser and irrigation), which quadrupled during the decade to reach 2.4 percent of GDP.

Reforms to public sector enterprises were limited to raising performance through setting efficiency targets for management. In sum, reforms during the1980s were hesitant and unsystematic and have often been characterised as reform "by stealth".

## 8.3 Initiation of Economic Reforms in Early 1990s

Economic performance in India has improved appreciably over the past two decades, bringing a marked increase in real incomes and reductions in poverty levels. This constant improvement stands in stark contrast to the outcome of the first four decades after Independence when growth was relatively low. India's catching-up over the past two decades has more than exceeded the performance of nearly all other emerging economies. The opening of the market from the constraints and opportunities of the global economy have been at the origin of this change. This reorientation of policy started in the mid-1980s and was strengthened at the beginning of the 1990s, with reforms in the area of foreign trade, foreign direct investment and the financial sector. After an intervening period of relatively low key changes in policies, reform efforts were renewed this decade with further trade liberalisation, a marked effort to reduce budget deficits, improvements to the tax system and efforts to improve infrastructure. These reforms transformed the Indian economy into a more open and market-based economy and played a key role in enhancing growth. Nonetheless, a number of factors continue to restrain growth and prevent India from catching-up even faster. After a discussion of India's economic reforms, this chapter examines the main sources of India's improved growth performance.

The policy reforms in the 1980s provided impetus for high growth and enhanced competitiveness but the growth process turned unsustainable. It manifested in the growing macroeconomic imbalances over the decade in the form of high fiscal deficit, high levels of current account deficit, and increasing levels of short term external debt, besides a repressive and weakened financial system. The immediate provocation for the crisis in 1991 was also a combination of external events that generated liquidity problems on the external front.

The Gulf Crisis of 1991 not only affected India's oil imports due to soaring oil prices but also eroded export markets in West Asia, and caused a setback to inward remittances and tourist earnings. The deterioration in exports to Eastern Europe, with the break-up of erstwhile USSR, accentuated the crisis. Around the same time, India's credit rating was lowered, which restricted its access to commercial borrowings and there was unwillingness on the part of normal banking channels to renew short-term credit to Indian banks abroad. Exceptional financing measures became inevitable, and the overall deficit in 1990-91 was financed almost equally by recourse to IMF and drawdown of reserves. The severity of the balance of payments crisis in the early 1990s could be gauged from the fact that India's foreign currency assets depleted rapidly from US$ 3.1 billion in August 1990 to US$ 975 million on July 12, 1991.

Therefore, rapid economic growth in the second half of the 1980s, driven in large part by expansionary fiscal policies, proved unsustainable. The resulting foreign exchange crisis in 1991, led to the introduction of a more far-reaching set of economic reforms, covering a broader number of areas. The industrial licensing system was changed from a system under which positive approval was required for any investment in all but a few selected industries, to a system where, by the end of the decade, approval was only required for certain items like alcohol, tobacco and defence-related industries. The sectors reserved for public sector enterprises were reduced to just railways, mining and petroleum refining, defence equipment and atomic energy. In contrast, little progress was made during the 1990s in reducing the number of industries reserved for small enterprises or "small-scale industries" (SSIs): only 17 industries were removed from the list leaving 821 areas still restricted to SSIs despite there being no import restrictions in these areas by the end of the 1990s. Hence, foreign large scale firms were allowed to compete in these areas but large domestic companies were forbidden. This anomaly was tackled only after 2002 when industry reservations for SSIs were progressively reduced.

Reducing trade barriers was the second plank of policy reforms in the first half of the 1990s. After the reforms of the second half of the 1980s, quantitative import restrictions and licensing were abandoned for capital goods and intermediate products but retained for consumer products, until negotiations with major trading partners led to their eventual abolition at the end of the decade. More importantly, import tariffs were progressively reduced to 35.5 percent (simple average) and 29.8 percent (import weighted basis) by 1999, but were still the third highest amongst the seventy countries for which data is available (Government of India, 2001). Moreover, the pattern of tariffs was such that, in effective terms, intermediate products were more protected than final products. Despite the major fall in tariffs, the ratio of import duties to total imports was still 22 percent by the end of the decade.

Tariff reductions were resumed in 2001 when the government committed to reducing tariffs to the level of ASEAN countries. The highest standard tariff rate was reduced from 35 percent in 2001 to 10 percent by 2007, bringing a commensurate fall in the ratio of tariff revenues to the total value of imports. Nonetheless, India continues to belong to the group of countries with relatively high level of Most Favoured Nation (MFN) import tariffs. As with other countries, there are numerous derogations from the standard tariff. In other countries, for example Turkey and Mexico, these often take the form of regional tariff arrangements but in the case of India the exemptions are mainly domestic. Taking account of these derogations, the ratio of import duties to the value of imports was well below the standard tariff (at 10 percent and half that once domestic taxes on imports are removed from the total) but was nonetheless still well above the levels seen in ASEAN countries.

At the beginning of the 1990s, fundamental reforms were also undertaken in the area of taxation in a manner that enhanced the efficiency of the economy. Marginal tax rates for individuals and companies were reduced significantly, building on the cuts that had been introduced in the previous decade. Furthermore, during the 1990s, economic distortions stemming from indirect taxes were reduced by converting excises on manufactured products into a form of value added tax while the tax base was gradually widened by the introduction of a service tax. In 2005, the cascading system of state sales tax on goods was also switched to a value added tax. The reforms in tariffs and excise considerably lowered tax revenues from these sources but was partially offset by an increase in direct tax revenues as the tax base increased, perhaps linked to the reduction in direct tax rates.

Overall, these reforms reversed the temporary increase in revenues that had occurred in the second half of the 1980s due to tariffication. By the second half of the 1990s, the combined tax ratio of the centre and the states was, at around 14 percent of GDP, a similar rate to that in the first half of the 1980s prior to reform, but with much lower marginal tax rates. After 2002, with the upswing in the economy and the introduction of the service tax, the tax-GDP ratio increased again, exceeding the peaks reached in the late1980s, even though all marginal tax rates remain appreciably lower than in the second half of the1980s. Financial market liberalisation was another area of reform that started after 1991, although the pace of reform was slower than in product markets and taxes, in part because product market reforms had revealed significant problems in banks' asset portfolios.

Financial market reform started from a position in which state-owned banks controlled 90 percent of bank deposits and channelled an extremely high proportion of funds to the government; interest rates were determined administratively; credit was allocated on the basis of government policy and approval from the Reserve Bank of India was required for individual loans above a certain threshold. Bank interest rates were deregulated as part of the reform process and were only subject to control in four remaining areas: saving deposit accounts, small loans in priority areas, export credits and non-resident transferable rupee deposits. The deposit rate in the government small saving system remained administratively determined. The government bond market was also liberalised. Although some broad restrictions on the areas in which banks can lend remained in force, the share of bank deposits that must be lent to the government, through the mechanism of the Statutory Liquidity Ratio, was reduced to 25 percent while the proportion of deposits that must be deposited with the Reserve Bank through the Cash Reserve Ratio was held at 6.5 percent.

Competition in the banking system was also increased by allowing new private banks, including foreign ones, to enter the market.

The financial regulatory system was considerably strengthened. A Board of Financial Supervision was created within the Reserve Bank to focus on supervision, and the rules governing the recognition of bad loans were substantially tightened. By the early 1990s, capital requirements were also strengthened by the establishment of a system under which banks were required to promptly undertake specified changes to their portfolios and management when various trigger points are reached. In addition, bank capital was considerably strengthened. Government funds were used to recapitalise banks, although the recapitalisation of rural co-operative banks still did not taken place. By 2004, new laws and institutions were functioning that allowed banks to foreclose on secured loans that were in default, thereby removing one of the major hurdles to the development of credit.

## 8.4 Fiscal Consolidation in the Indian Economy

During the period of reforms, fiscal policy was managed in a discretionary fashion and eventually became unsustainable at the beginning of the 2000. The central and state governments ran large fiscal deficits initially, averaging together 8 percent of GDP during the period 1985 to 1991. The deficit then declined until fiscal year 1996-97, but increased again in the following years. Until the end of the 1990s, these deficits did not result in an increase in debt to GDP ratio, as the gap between interest rates and the growth of nominal GDP exceeded the primary deficit. Nonetheless, increase in interest payments forced a reduction in non-interest outlays, particularly public investment, which led to a build-up of large infrastructure bottlenecks and was problematic from a development viewpoint. After financial liberalisation, and with an increased emphasis on reducing inflation, the debt position became unsustainable, as the gap between interest rates and nominal GDP growth narrowed substantially and the primary deficit increased. These two adverse developments resulted in a sharp increase of the consolidated debt of central and state governments, which reached 81 percent of GDP in March 2003 after rising by almost five percentage points of GDP per year in the previous four years.

The central government decided to move away from discretionary fiscal policy and limit its future fiscal freedom by passing the Fiscal Responsibility and Budget Management Act (FRBMA) in 2003. This Act set an upper deficit ceiling of 3 percent of GDP for the central government to be reached by fiscal year 2008. Under the influence of the Twelfth Finance Commission, nearly all state governments have introduced similar acts.

As a result, the overall fiscal deficit was targeted to be reduced to 6 percent of GDP by 2008. Such a deficit, while still high, will be sufficient to ensure that debt starts falling relative to GDP. The benefits of this consolidation policy are beginning to be seen; interest payments are now falling as a share of national income, and total government capital spending (including the repayment of some forms of debt) is starting to raise once again, a process that is being helped by buoyant tax revenues.

In India, government saving (net of depreciation) has been persistently negative since the early 1980s implying a significant use of private savings to finance current government spending. Net dissavings of general government peaked in 2001. The government was then absorbing almost half of the nation's saving in order to finance its own consumption outlays. In addition, the government was borrowing to finance its investment, capital transfers and loans to state-owned enterprises. As a result, the borrowing requirement (fiscal deficit) of state and local governments reached nearly 10 percent of GDP by 2001 and public debt rose significantly.

To end this unsustainable situation, the central government

enacted legislation to improve the fiscal discipline. After close to three years of discussion, the Fiscal Responsibility and Budget Management Act (FRBM), was adopted in August 2003. The Act set a medium-term target of achieving a balance between current revenue and current spending (i.e. a zero-revenue deficit) and limited the overall fiscal deficit for central government to 3 percent of GDP. By 2006, the revenue deficit was reduced to 2 percent of GDP and the fiscal deficit had been reduced to 3.7 percent of GDP.

The 2007 Budget confirmed the faster adjustment of the fiscal deficit, which is only slightly greater than the target for 2008 incorporated in the FRBM Act. However, the current deficit is expected to be 1.5 percent of GDP, indicating that a very sharp reduction would be necessary to meet the target of the FRBM for this balance.

In effect, the central government has not been able to stem the increase in current expenditure as much as had been planned and, consequently, the hoped-for increase in the extent of investment, which would have raised the fiscal deficit relative to the current deficit, has not materialised.

The FRBM Act also improved the transparency of the budgetary policy. The Act provides that the government has to lay three documents before Parliament every year: one with an assessment of economic prospects, another with its strategy with regard to taxation and expenditure, and the final one giving a three-year rolling target for the revenue balance and the overall fiscal balance.

Quarterly progress reviews also have to be placed before the Parliament. The second quarter review is the most important because a statement of the remedial steps that will be taken to offset any shortfall from targets has to be provided to the Parliament.

The government now also publishes its asset register annually, permitting the calculation of a net asset position for the government. Its revenue account, though, does not account for capital consumption.

Estimates of the revenue foregone through exemptions and concessions from standard tax rates are now also published annually, and the central government has made a first step towards accrual accounting by publishing the outstanding amounts of tax and non-tax revenue. During 2005, 23 state governments introduced similar legislation and, by the middle of 2006, only three states–West Bengal, Sikkim and Jharkhand had not introduced such laws, mandating a fiscal deficit of 3 percent of state GDP. To some extent, this move reflected the incentivisation process of the Finance Commission, a body established by the Constitution to advise on the sharing of tax revenues between the centre and the states. Standardised and rapid accounting procedures are still lacking at the state level and are almost non-existent at the municipal level with most local authorities not even using a double-entry accounting system.

States have reduced their fiscal deficits at a quicker pace than the central government in reaction to the more severe financial pressures that they faced at the beginning of this decade. These pressures were the result of a failure to adjust other expenditures after large centrally determined pay and pension increases at the end of the 1990s. With increased outlays funded from borrowing that amounted to nearly 40 percent of income, outlays on wages, pensions and interest increased to almost 70 percent of current revenues on average in the period 2000-03. The process of consolidation started in 2004 and has continued since then with the states planning to almost eliminate (on average) their revenue deficit in 2006 and reduce their fiscal deficit of 2.5 percent of GDP. The increase in the states' own tax revenues has been helped by a significant increase in transfers from central government which came in the form of higher shared taxes, increased grants and write-offs of interest due to the central government.

The process of consolidation is, however, far from uniform across the states. In 2005, the remaining revenue deficit of the states was concentrated in just four states (Jharkhand, Kerala,

Uttarakhand and West Bengal) where the fiscal deficit still amounted to between 35 percent and 60 percent of state government revenues, with similarly large revenue deficits for three of them. Indeed, these four states accounted for the whole of the revenue deficits of states–small deficits elsewhere were offset by surpluses in a number of states. As a result, debt levels of these four states continued to increase, rising from 37 to 47 percent of state GDP between 2000 and 2005, a particularly high burden given that their total revenue from taxation and transfers from central government amounted to just 14 percent of their GDP.

The current FRBM targets run until fiscal year 2008 and have provided a marked check to the growth of public debt. The combined fiscal deficit of state and local governments has fallen to 6.3 percent of national GDP and should reach 5.7 percent of national GDP in fiscal year 2008, if deficit targets are met, slightly less than might be thought given that the both levels of government are aiming for a 3 percent deficit. The combined liabilities of the states and central government fell from a peak of 82 percent of GDP in 2004 to 76 percent in 2006 and are likely to fall a further 6 percentage points by 2008. Assuming medium-term annual growth of nominal GDP of around 13 percent and interest rates of no more than 8 percent, the current fiscal targets would result in a further gradual decline of the debt to GDP ratio. While a gradual decline in the debt to GDP ratio indicates a sustainable fiscal position, the general government's balance sheet reveals a further deterioration of the government's net asset position as government borrowing continues to exceed the level of net capital formation.

Currently, net capital formation by the general government sector (including departmental enterprises such as the post office and state road transport agencies) amounts to 2.5 percent of GDP, with a further small and declining amount of capital transfers. Part of these transfers represent infusions of capital to loss-making enterprises. They should be considered as a form of subsidy rather than capital formation. Consequently, if governments wished to restrict their borrowing to a level that covered net investment, a fiscal deficit of no more than 3 percent (at current levels of investment) for both levels of government, rather than the current 6 percent deficit, would be needed. This would ensure that government debt returns to the level of the mid-1990s by 2013.

## 8.5 Response of the Economy to Reforms

India has achieved a higher growth path consistently after economic reforms. Overall, the performance of the economy has improved markedly since the1980s. Since 2000, the annual trend growth of GDP and GDP per capita has been 6.5 percent and 4.75 percent respectively, almost three times the growth rate in the first three decades after Independence. Moreover, there is evidence more recently that the sustainable growth rate of the economy has reached 8.5 percent. If this growth path continues, then average income levels will double in a decade, while with the growth path experienced prior to 1980, it would have taken 55 years to reach such income levels. This pace of growth has brought a steady catch-up in Indian per capita incomes from 5.5 percent of the US level in 1985 to 8 percent in 2005, when income is valued at estimated purchasing power parity (PPP).

Compared to all non-OECD countries, India's recent growth performance has also been good, outperforming all but 10 percent of this group of economies. Some of the larger Indian states (with population sizes above 50 million) have out performed many of the much smaller economies in this best performing non-OECD group. Given that India is a large and diverse country of sub-continental size with a population of 1.1 billion, it is more appropriate to compare its growth performance to four country groupings, with a similar population size (China), countries that had incomes per head below US$ 3000 measured at international prices, countries with incomes between US$ 3,000 and US$ 8,000, and all other countries. The level of income in India has moved above that of the low-income group and is growing faster than the middle-income countries, though it has fallen behind both the level and growth of incomes in China. Although India's average income level is still low–India ranked 107 out of 186 countries and territories for which data was available in 2005, the size of its population, and its rapid growth during the past 25 years, made it the fourth largest economy in the world in 2005 when measured at current prices and using purchasing power parities, and continued rapid growth suggests that it was the third largest economy in 2006. Note that on these estimates, in 1980 the Indian economy was smaller than that of Germany, France, Italy, Japan, the United Kingdom and even Brazil; and had by 2006 overtaken all of these economies, even if it had, itself, been overtaken by China.

## 8.6 Gains in Labour Productivity: Main Driver of Growth

Labour productivity growth has been the dominant factor behind the catch-up in incomes between 1990 and 2005. Over this period, average labour productivity growth in India outstripped that of all OECD countries with the exception of Korea, but was lower than in China. Demographic change has also boosted India's GDP per capita growth, especially since 2000, as India is currently in a beneficial phase, with the working age population growing faster than the total population.

Since reforms started in the mid-1980s, the growth in labour productivity has been driven by increases in total factor productivity (TFP) and capital deepening, suggesting that economic reforms have had a positive impact on both economic efficiency and capital formation. After 2000, the analysis is complicated by sharp cyclical swings in the economy. A slight easing of TFP growth was partially compensated for by an increase in capital deepening, resulting in somewhat lower labour productivity growth. Total GDP growth, however, was supported by a marked increase in labour inputs. All these estimates are still tentative as there is considerable uncertainty about recent factor inputs due to the time lag in the availability of investment and employment data.

## 8.7 Total Factor Productivity Growth and GDP

Total factor productivity growth can be further decomposed into the effect of human capital formation and a residual which reflects all other impacts. Overall, improvements in human capital formation added about 0.4 percent per year to productivity and output growth in the1980s and the 1990s. This contribution eased to around 0.2 percent after 2000 as the share of people in the workforce with at least primary education is now rising less sharply than previously as more workers have now completed primary education.

Estimating potential output growth by eliminating cyclical effects allows a more nuanced view of the impact of liberalisation on economic growth, as reforms should have boosted supply factors and thus trend growth. The estimate of potential output made by the OECD is based on a Cobb-Douglas production function estimated for the whole economy, using capital stock data from the 2007 National Accounts and employment data generated from both the annual and quinquennial National Sample Surveys.

Total factor productivity has been modelled with a time-varying trend. Given the importance of fluctuations in agricultural output stemming from fluctuations in rainfall during the monsoon season, rainfall has been treated as an input into the production process by estimating the impact of weather conditions on agricultural output and then deducting their impact from overall GDP. These fluctuations can be particularly important in certain years. The statistical results suggest a relatively large contribution of capital formation to economic growth compared to OECD countries, reflecting a low labour share in value added. The growth of total factor productivity is estimated to have improved in the mid-1980s, but there is no evidence of any further improvement since then. Potential output has been estimated from this production function by replacing actual employment input by a trend labour input calculated by smoothing the year to year movements in the ratio of employment to working age population. The labour input used in the production function was then taken as the product of the smoothed employment ratio and the working age population.

The strong performance of potential growth since 2000 has its origins mainly in an investment boom of a scale similar to that seen at the beginning of the 1990s. By 2005, the last year for which official data is available, the capital stock was growing by 7.5 percent. Since then, available data on production and imports of capital goods suggests that net fixed capital formation has continued to rise at over 20 percent, as in 2005, with the result that the growth of the capital stock has risen by a further percentage point and is now growing some three percentage points faster than its average growth rate over the previous two decades. In contrast to developments in the early 1990s, the increase appears to be firmly based on strong profitability and an acceleration of exports in key sectors. On the other hand, there is no statistical evidence of an improvement in the growth of total factor productivity in this decade. Nonetheless, these favourable supply side factors appear to have boosted the growth rate of the potential output to 8.5 percent by 2006.

While estimated potential growth has picked-up significantly, actual output growth has surged at an even faster pace. Growth has now averaged over 9 percent for two years running and, given the continuing rapid growth in credit, seems likely to maintain a high pace in 2007. So far this expansion has been possible because of the availability of spare capacity in the economy. A broad measure of inflation, such as the non-agricultural GDP deflator, has not accelerated and increased by less than 5 percent in the fourth quarter of the calendar year 2006. On the other hand, a number of other inflation indicators, such as the CPI, have moved well above the government's objective of keeping inflation in the 5-5.5 percent range. This increase has mainly been due to the high weight of food and commodities in these indices. The Reserve Bank has been progressively raising interest rates and this is likely to slow growth to 8 percent in 2008. Such an easing should be sufficient to ensure that the non-agricultural GDP deflator does not accelerate. The Reserve Bank has lowered its desired medium-term inflation rate to 4-4.5 percent, as measured by the wholesale price index, and this should help contain inflation expectations.

### 8.8 Sterling Performance of Services and the IT Sector

The performance of individual sectors of the economy also supports the view that changes in government policies have boosted growth. In the five years between 1999 and 2004, the growth of the service sector has risen markedly above that of the overall non-agricultural business sector. Within the service sector, a number of sectors have performed significantly better than others. In particular, in areas where government regulation has been eased, output has grown more rapidly. Three sectors stand out: communications, insurance and information technology (IT) services. All of these sectors have been significantly liberalised: telecommunications saw the transformation of the historic state monopoly operator into a corporation and the introduction of private competitors (notably for wireless telephony); insurance saw the end of the domination of the state-owned companies with the opening of the sector and the creation of a new regulator; and computer services also benefited from an improved business environment in the special zones, established for the software industry, which benefited from better infrastructure and tax advantages. On the other hand, the sectors that remained dominated by state-owned companies performed well below average.

The most noticeable increase in service sector output has come from the development of the information technology enabled services (ITES) sector. This sector started poorly in India with the exit of multinational firms and the creation of a government monopoly to manufacture and service computers in the 1970s. This move did, however, provide the initial market for two of what are now the largest ITES service companies. This policy ended in the mid-1980s when 100 percent investment by foreign companies was allowed in this area prompting a number of US companies to enter the market. This new computer-oriented investment policy reduced tariffs on hardware to 60 percent in 1984 and exempted all profits on export sales of software from corporate taxation (Dossani, 2005). The initial location chosen by these multinationals was Bangalore, perhaps as the result of the concentration of government research laboratories in that area (Balakrishnan, 2006).

The growth of ITES firms was at first driven by the provision of contract labour at the sites of foreign clients–a process that was aided by the ready availability of H1B non-immigrant visas in the United States, with almost 60 percent of the revenues of the major ITES companies coming from this form of activity in 1999 (Kumar, 2001). One spill-over of the supply of temporary staff to the US market was to create strong longer-term links between the US software industry and Indian companies, as temporary workers initially stayed in the country, with a significant minority creating their own businesses. More than half of these Indian-born American entrepreneurs went on to establish companies in India, mainly in the areas of software development and production (Saxenian, 2002). The extent of foreign investment in the software industry is substantial and has come either through established foreign firms or through venture capital, mainly from the US, though mostly established in Mauritius as a result of its double taxation treaty with India (Upadhyaya, 2004).

The initial advantage of Indian companies was the availability of trained staff who had mainly graduated from public universities and colleges. The supply was subsequently boosted by the growth of private sector colleges, helped by changes in the government licensing criteria. Having established credibility through repeated contracts, the Indian companies were able to diversify into domestic production of software and the lower value added area of business process outsourcing (Banerjee and Dufflo, 2000). Poor infrastructure was seen as a major constraint to software companies, and government policy became oriented to overcoming this problem through the establishment of software parks. These parks were developed by the Software Technology Parks of India and provide basic infrastructure, such as broadband satellite communication facilities and back-up generation facilities for electricity. Since 1998, private sector companies have been able to develop these parks. For firms within these zones, imports are duty free and can also be financed through foreign leases or rental agreements. In addition, the zone administration processes all necessary government forms, acting as a "one-stop shop" window for the entrepreneur. Decision-making is also devolved: zone directors can authorise smaller projects and take decisions in one day, with larger projects taking a week for approval (Bajpai, et al. 1998).

Two other government policies have also favoured the software industry: labour and tax laws. The restrictive labour laws that constrain large manufacturing companies do not apply to the service sector and, indeed, a number of state governments have eased regulations that restrict the employment of women and the use of round-the-clock shift working. Companies established within software parks are eligible for a complete tax holiday for five of their first eight years of operation. In addition, when this period is over, profits on export sales can be tax free within certain limits.

According to INFOSYS, about one-quarter of industry sales are tax free. Views on the role of tax concessions vary. Larger companies take the view that government support in the form of tax incentives and other benefits has been instrumental in the growth of software exports. Moreover, the industry is concerned that these concessions, which costs 0.2 percent of GDP, will expire in 2009. On the other hand, surveys of Indian entrepreneurs in the US, considering investing in India, put the availability of a skilled workforce well ahead of fiscal incentives as a reason for starting a business there, in contrast to the views of US-based Chinese entrepreneurs who considered low taxation and market access prime reasons for investing in China. International experience suggests that tax concessions have little impact on the destination of FDI if other general framework conditions for doing business are not also favourable.

Whatever the respective roles of human capital, infrastructure provision and tax concessions are, nearly all exports of IT-enabled services come from software parks. By 2005, about 85 percent of IT-enabled sales took place from the 60 software parks (25 government-owned). Although parks are now widely spread out across the country, the most successful are in Karnataka, the National Capital Region (Delhi, Haryana), Andhra Pradesh and Tamil Nadu. In the first mentioned state, IT-related sales now represent almost one-quarter of state GDP. Employment in the IT sector has risen sharply and now amounts to 1.2 million, or 0.3 percent of total employment. Exports of IT-related services have risen markedly, especially since the new private sector park development policy was established in1998. In the five years to1998, exports expanded from 0.3 percent to 1.3 percent of GDP, only to soar to 3.7 percent of GDP by 2005.

The manufacturing sector should have performed well. The GDP share of the manufacturing sector in India was high in 1980 relative to other countries at a similar stage of economic development. Although this was, in part, a legacy of autarkic economic polices, it also reflects the sheer size of India, which made it less likely to rely on imports. However, since the 1980s, industry had continually lost ground to services–with the result that its share in output has remained constant, despite the continual fall in the share of agriculture–

though there was some reversal of this trend in 2005 and 2006. In general, the poor performance of the manufacturing sector may be related to regulatory factors; tighter labour market legislation for goods-producers; higher indirect taxation on manufactured goods rather than services. Poor infrastructure, particularly for transport and electricity, may also have held back the production of goods more than services. In an attempt to stimulate export industries, the government has announced a policy of creating special economic zones that have many of the features of the successful software technology parks.

### 8.9 Special Economic Zones (SEZs)

The success of software parks in stimulating the development of the information technology service industry has led the government to progressively introduce legislation to enable the development of Special Economic Zones (SEZs), oriented to the manufacturing sector. The development of SEZs has, until recently, been slow. Even though India created the first such zone in Asia in 1965, only eight existed by 2004 and they provided only 5 percent of goods' exports, though the shares for jewellery was 55 percent.

The slow development of existing SEZs led the government to introduce a new policy at the beginning of 2006. The previous policy, while giving considerable tax advantages, had not overcome the administrative barriers to business that typify India nor did it overcome infrastructure barriers, notably for road and electricity. The new policy relies on private developers to create the zone and provide all infrastructure, with the objective of generating additional economic activity and creating employment. The new policy focuses on changes to the laws and regulations that govern SEZs and allows:

- Single window clearance for development in the zone; simplified administrative procedures and exemptions from many restrictive policies; exemption from selected central laws.

- Application of all municipal and many state laws by the SEZ Authority.
- Separate court system with internal security provided by the SEZ Authority.
- Labour laws have also been modified at the state level, with 14 states abolishing previous constraints, freely allowing contract labour, and a significant number deeming all enterprises in a SEZ to be public utilities and hence making wildcat strikes (i.e. those without due notice) illegal. Significant tax concessions have also been granted:
- Total corporate tax exemption for five years, 50 percent for a further five years and a further exemption for reinvested earnings derived form exports, with developers allowed a ten-year window of tax exemption. Zone developers are exempt from the minimum alternate corporate tax and the dividend distribution tax.
- Imports into the SEZ are tax and tariff free, but sales to the domestic market are regarded as imports into India. By February 2007, while 234 SEZ projects had been approved, 162 projects have been given "in-principle" approvals. Of the 234 approvals, 91 have full legal approval. The fully approved projects cover 67 square kilometres. The total area for proposed SEZs is 1750 square kilometres, at most 0.11 percent of total agricultural land. Two major projects of a much larger size (greater than 100 square kilometres) had been approved under previous legislation in Maharashtra and Haryana. These zones will be on par with the size of two (Zhuhai and Xiamen) of the three largest SEZs in China, though only one-third the size of the Shenzen development.

At end-January 2007, the government had announced a temporary freeze on granting permission for new SEZs, but this freeze has been lifted in April 2007 with the condition that there would be no compulsory land acquisition by the state governments. This policy change followed demonstrations against a proposed car plant in West Bengal and in Haryana. These demonstrations have certainly benefited farmers in terms of compensation, but more evolving policy is required to acquire land. Small states like Haryana should have been restricted to particular limit and barred to acquire fertile agriculture land. A new policy on compensation for land acquired from farmers should be announced after taking all considerations in mind to avoid farmer's resentment. As in September 2008, 260 SEZs have been approved.

### 8.10 Faster Growth in Relatively Developed States

The acceleration of economic growth has helped reduce poverty, both nationally and at the state level. The poverty rate has now dropped to 21.8 percent when a short recall period is used for measuring consumption, down markedly from 26.1 percent in 1991. Comparisons over a longer time period are only possible using a long recall period, which tends to lower estimated consumptions and so raise estimates of poverty. These estimates show that the poverty rate has fallen markedly from 45 percent in 1983 to 27.5 percent in 2004. Thus, in the two decades since reform began in1984 (and the period in which the growth of total factor productivity has increased), the poverty rate has fallen 15 percentage points, after having remained constant in the previous three decades. In addition, the speed of decline of poverty was markedly greater in the period from 1999 to 2004. Using the short recall period measure, the poverty rate fell by 17 percent in this period, sufficient to generate an 8 percent fall in the absolute number of people living below the poverty line, which is the first drop in the absolute number of people below the poverty line in a five-year period since Independence.

The reasons for the more rapid fall in the poverty rate since 1999 cannot yet be decomposed with certainty but appear to be linked to a better employment performance and a reduction in the relative price of food. Employment growth has outstripped population growth since 1999, in contrast to the previous six-year period. In addition, relative food prices fell by over 4 percent annually between 1999 and 2004 against a very slight fall in the period 1993 to 1999. Food prices are a major factor in determining the number of people living in poverty since the weight of food in the expenditure of households below the poverty line is particularly large.

General well-being is affected by more than just the measured poverty rate, and a number of other indicators also point to a more rapid improvement in well-being this decade, though the picture is mixed. There has been quite rapid growth in housing quality and the ownership of some consumer durables. Health indicators also suggest a more rapid improvement in recent years. Infant mortality and maternal mortality have improved significantly, and there has been a marked decline in the overall death rate, increasing life expectancy. Nonetheless, infant mortality remains high and maternal mortality is of particular concern. The latter is three times higher than in China and even within India there are marked variations in maternal mortality, with a much lower rate in Kerala. The government is increasing health spending; but it will be difficult to reach current targets for reducing maternal mortality without changes in health care delivery, especially in poorer states since 40 percent of staff at publicly funded medical centres are absent at any point in time with even higher absences for doctors.

There appears to have been a reasonably close relationship between economic prosperity and reductions in poverty. Growth in average per capita consumption is linked to the proportionate decline in the poverty rate across states. In urban areas there is a close linage between state GDP growth and consumption, but there is less of a relation in rural areas, weakening the overall relationship between state GDP growth and poverty reduction. Indeed, there were a number of states (Haryana, Tamil Nadu and Rajasthan) where poverty rates increased between 1999 and 2004 despite significant economic growth, suggesting that other factors also influence the evolution of poverty. There has been some increase in income inequality, both in urban and rural areas. This slight increase in inequality reduced the extent to which the poverty rate would have fallen, given economic growth, offsetting about one-third of the fall in poverty that might have occurred with unchanged overall growth and a constant distribution of income. However, such calculations are questionable in that the increase in inequality may be linked to the process that generated the increase in income growth. Overall, the evolution of poverty headcount at the national level suggests that faster economic growth is a powerful means of reducing poverty, and this effect becomes even bigger if steps are taken to make growth more inclusive.

The wide disparities in economic growth that have occurred over the past 15 years have increased the dispersion of incomes across the country. There has been considerable variation in the extent of income growth across the country, with lower growth concentrated in the north (from east to some parts of west), where the reduction in poverty has been markedly less than in southern, western and north-western states which have grown more rapidly. The spread in economic performance across states is of all the more concern as there is evidence that states that were initially poor have grown less than the states that were initially better-off. Despite the rapid improvement at the national level, there are six states (accounting for 40 percent of the population) where the growth of per capita GDP was less than 2.5 percent annually in the period 1993 to 2004 and where there has been little improvement in the proportion of the population living under the poverty line. If a more uniform distribution of economic activity could have been achieved, then the speed of reduction in poverty could have been doubled (Datt and Ravallion, 2002).

## 8.11 Prospects and Challenges

While India has significantly improved its economic performance, by raising its potential output growth from 3.5

percent in 1980 to 7.5 percent currently, the potential for further catch-up remains large. The average level of productivity is only 9 percent of that in the United States and 75 percent of that in China, so with appropriate framework conditions in place, India should be able to reap large productivity gains. Such gains could be achieved through enlarging and modernising its fixed capital stock including infrastructure, improving the skill level of the workforce, and through shifting resources towards higher productivity sectors, in particular from agriculture to manufacturing.

Unlike many OECD and a number of non-OECD countries, India's demographic profile continues to favour the catching up of average incomes. There are two channels for this positive outcome: first, following the decline in birth rates, population growth declines faster than growth of the working age population, resulting in a decline in the dependency ratio. The higher share of workers in total population tends to boost GDP per capita growth. On the other hand, the rate of increase of the labour force is declining over the medium term, thereby lowering potential output growth. Second, the demographic change could also have a positive effect on savings and thus contribute to capital formation. Indeed, cross-country studies of the impact of demography on savings suggest that a fall in the dependency ratio is generally associated with an increase in the private savings rate, and this result has also been found in a time series study for India.

However, increases in private savings are not necessarily channelled into productive investment, in particular, if governments absorb private savings to finance their current spending, as has been the case in India during the past decades. Channelling savings to the most productive use also requires efficient financial intermediation. At the same time, attracting FDI inflows can add directly to domestic capital formation and contribute to TFP growth. Sound public finances, efficient financial markets and openness to FDI inflows are therefore of great importance for building up a productive capital stock.

Longer term projections of economic growth are subject to a large degree of uncertainty, but it would seem that there is scope for a further acceleration in the growth of per capita incomes in India over the medium to long term. A wide range of scenarios can be imagined. Here just two are presented: one that maintains the status quo, the other which introduces a series of reforms designed to achieve the government's target of 10 percent growth.

In the first scenario, domestic investment rises in line with the increase in private household saving that may follow from the likely fall in the dependency ratio and the acceleration in per capita incomes that has already occurred. Government saving remains negative and the current account deficit remains at the relatively low level of 1.5 percent of GDP. In such a scenario, the domestic capital stock would accelerate, but only sufficiently to offset the likely slowdown in the growth of the labour force, with the result that output might continue to grow at 8.5 percent annually. However, given the demographic transition that is occurring, the growth of per capita income would accelerate somewhat to over 7 percent which is almost five times higher than experienced in three decades 1950 to 1980.

A more optimistic scenario can be imagined. In this scenario, the business environment is improved significantly by further fiscal consolidation, a marked reduction in the extent of control, and by policies that allow greater private sector involvement in both infrastructure and the financial sector. Such polices could result in a continued strong inflow of FDI and portfolio investment. These inflows have averaged 2.5 percent of GDP in the five years to 2006 and were even close to 3 percent of GDP in 2006. At the average level of the past five years, capital inflows were 12 times greater than total net flows of foreign aid in the same period. FDI inflows have the scope to expand considerably given a favourable environment. If inflows of foreign direct investment were to rise, it would be possible to sustainably finance a current account deficit of 3 percent of GDP. At the same time, if the government embarks on a major restructuring of public expenditure that substantially reduces government dissaving at both the central and state level, a further 3.5 percent of GDP could be invested. If these reforms were introduced over a five-year period, then the growth of the capital stock might rise to close to 11 percent annually, and the sustainable growth rate of the economy could rise to over 9.5 percent. Further, efficiency gains could flow from improvements in the tax system and a more neutral tax tariff structure and more rapid human capital formation.

## 8.12 Need for Further Deregulation

India's product market regulations are strict compared to most other countries. A central determinant of India's future growth rate will be the extent to which the regulations and laws governing economic activity are conducive to competition in the markets for goods and services. In order to benchmark India against other countries, a comprehensive set of indicators that measure the extent of product market regulation (PMR) has been constructed for India, both nationally and across states. These indicators draw on the framework developed for OECD countries to assess the extent to which the regulatory environment is conducive to competition in areas of the product market where technology and market conditions make competition viable. These indicators summarise data covering 139 formal rules and regulations that have a bearing on competition. The indicators cover most of the important aspects of general regulatory practice as well as some aspects of industry-specific regulatory policy.

At the economy-wide level, India has made good progress in improving some aspects of product market regulation and a few low-level PMR indicators are on a par with best practice in the OECD area. Overall, however, despite considerable deregulation during the past 20 years, product market regulation remains much more restrictive than in typical OECD countries. In particular, the degree of public sector involvement in product markets remains high. For example, despite gaining in importance, the private sector still only accounts for slightly more than half of economic activity in the formal non-farm business sector. Compared with OECD countries, India has a higher level of public sector presence in product markets. Barriers to entrepreneurship are also higher, reflecting high administrative burdens on business start-ups which could also be indicative of more widespread transaction costs in government administration.

Experience in other countries suggests that reducing regulation and increasing competition enhances productivity growth by improving the efficiency of resource use and encouraging a stronger effort on the part of managers to improve efficiency, but efficiency does not come at the expense of lower employment. Greater product market competition has also been found to improve employment and fixed investment. The link between increased competition and productive performance is related to the stimulus that a competitive market gives to innovation and technological diffusion. These are potentially key sources of productivity growth in India and are likely to be improved by more liberal product market regulation.

As seen above, raising economic growth in poorer states in India is the key to reducing poverty, and so benchmarking the extent to which individual states have created an environment conducive to competition may throw light on how poorer states can improve their performance. States in India have direct responsibility for a number of areas of economic policy as well as shared responsibility with central government in other areas.

Moreover, the implementation and administration of all laws is the responsibility of state governments. State government attitudes toward the role of the public sector in the economy and the efficiency with which they administer basic laws can therefore differ considerably. For example, delays in processing applications for establishing new businesses vary quite a lot across states and can impose large barriers to market entry. Cross-state differences in the regulatory environment may also be representative of the state governments' attitude towards economic efficiency that can also be seen in the way in which state-owned enterprises are operated, notably in the electricity sector, where economic performance also differs a lot between states. On the basis of a detailed study of the policies of 21 states, it appears that there are significant differences in product market regulation across states that impact on economic performance. To assess the extent of these differences, the PMR indicators have been estimated for 21 Indian states, which cover 98 percent of India's population and GDP.

While these state-level indicators are not entirely directly comparable with the national indicators, they are comparable across states in areas where the influence of state policy on the regulatory environment may be important. Furthermore, these differences in the regulatory environment are found to have an important bearing on various aspects of economic performance at the state level. For example, states in which the regulatory environment is more conducive to competition have a higher level of labour productivity in comparison to the relatively more restrictive states.

## 8.13 Employment Aspect of Accelerated Growth

The acceleration of output growth since the introduction of reforms eventually increased employment growth. After stagnating in the mid-1990s, employment growth picked up in the six years to 2004. The ratio of employment to the total population has increased, both for men and women, with particularly high ratios for men (around 97 percent between age 30 and 59) but much lower rates for women, especially in urban areas.

The Indian labour market is, however, characterised by a

high degree of informality. People with regular employment contracts account for only 15 percent of total employment and most of these are concentrated in urban areas. Total regular employment fell during most of the 1990s but started to grow after 1998. Since then there has been a marked increase in regular employment outside the "organised" sector of the economy. This sector broadly includes all companies except in the manufacturing sector, where only firms employing more than 10 people, or 20 people if no electrical machinery is used, are counted. Based on the National Sample Survey data, regular employment outside the organised sector almost doubled between 1998 and 2004, rising from 6 percent to over 9 percent of total employment. The increasing supply of people looking for regular employment has resulted in the real wages of such employees falling between 1999 and 2004, with the exception of graduates in urban areas. In larger enterprises, real wages have risen slightly in the same period, but by much less than the growth in productivity. As a result, there has been a considerable increase in the share of profits in total national income.

Self-employment is the predominant employment status in both urban and rural areas, with casual labour by far outweighing regular employment in rural areas. According to one measure, which only counts people as unemployed if they have not worked for a week, the rate of unemployment was low in the period July 2004 to June 2005, averaging 4.7 percent for the country as whole for people aged between 15 and 59. Information for the two years to 2007 is not available as there is no timely national labour force survey.

Moreover, much of this unemployment is a consequence of initial job search on entering the labour force: The unemployment rate is only 2.3 percent for those who have had at least one job. There are, however, other definitions of unemployment used in India that give a wide range of unemployment rates, especially when the extent of casual work is considered. The broadest definition of unemployment counts the shortfall in hours worked relative to the desired work week as unemployment, and shows an unemployment rate of nearly 8 percent. The bulk of the growth in employment has been created in very small enterprises. There is much evidence that the main reason for the lack of job creation in larger firms in the "organised" or formal part of the private sector is the restrictive legislation governing regular employment in larger firms. Larger firms in this sector have markedly increased the capital intensity of their production techniques. Rigid labour legislation makes it extremely difficult for firms to lay-off workers, and even changing job descriptions can be problematic.

The extent of the regulatory intervention can be judged by estimating the standard OECD indicator of employment protection legislation, which shows that employment protection legislation is more restrictive in India than in all but two OECD countries and is also markedly more restrictive than in Brazil, Chile and China. There are variations in employment protection legislation across Indian states. This affects job creation and destruction. The empirical evidence on whether employment legislation affects the total level of employment is mixed in the OECD area, but there is much evidence that restrictive labour market regulations lead to dual labour markets and prevent the upgrading of workers from irregular to regular jobs. The lack of formal sector employment reduces productivity growth as most new jobs are created in the informal sector, where productivity is much lower.

## 8.14 Need for Enhanced Efficiency of the Financial System

An efficient financial system is a key requirement for allocating capital to its most efficient use. In India, there are five major constituents of the money and capital markets: banks, insurance companies, pension funds, mutual funds and stock exchanges. These institutions have in the past been largely government-owned (with the exception of the stock markets). While private and foreign institutions have been allowed into the market, and minority stakes in some public sector banks have also been allowed, three of these four groups remain dominated by government-owned institutions, with only the mutual fund industry dominated by private sector companies. In contrast to the goods sector of the economy, the government continues to exert considerable control over banking sector operations as well as holding majority shareholdings in most banks. The banks are obliged to provide 40 percent of their loans to priority areas defined by the government and must lend 25 percent of their assets to the government to comply with the statutory liquidity ratio requirement.

New banks are required to have one-quarter of their branches in rural areas, and all banks are required to obtain central bank approval for the opening of new branches and off-site cash dispensers. Publicly owned banks have been allowed to sell minority shareholding to the public, subject to the overall shareholding of the government not falling below 51 percent, but the voting rights of private shareholders in banks are limited. The private shareholding in state-owned banks currently averages 36 percent, when weighted by operating profits, so that the government's role in the banking sector remains large in international comparison. Moreover, until 2007, a majority of the shares in the largest publicly owned bank were owned by the central bank, though this shareholding will be sold to the Ministry of Finance in 2007.

Overall, the expansion of the private sector has been quite limited: privately owned banks accounted for only 25 percent of banking assets by 2006, in part because regulations restrict the ability of foreign banks to invest in India. International evidence has been that high state-ownership of banks tends to depress financial development, the more so if the initial level of financial development is low. Moreover, there is evidence that economic growth is lowered by a higher share of publicly owned banks with evidence that the negative impact on economic growth is stronger for countries with relatively low financial depth such as India. On the basis of one cross-country study, a reduction in the share of public bank assets in total assets to the same share as in Brazil might raise economic growth by 0.7 percentage points annually.

## 8.15 Reorientation of Public Expenditure

Achieving the government's higher growth target requires greater investment. In part, that could be achieved by holding the growth of expenditure below that of revenue and thereby increasing saving and investment. However, some restructuring of public expenditure might also be possible. All levels of government have devoted a significant amount of resources to subsidising economic activities. Measuring the extent of subsidies is complicated. One approach to measuring subsidies is to use the definition of national accounts, which is similar to that used in the budget. With this definition, subsidies paid by all three levels of government amounted to 3.1 percent of GDP in 2003, markedly higher than most OECD countries and about seven times higher than in China and Brazil.

These direct measures of subsidies understate their full amount as they only measure cash flows and not the opportunity costs which arise from the government providing goods and services below cost. Estimating the opportunity cost of the provision of subsidized economic services (excluding education, healthcare and labour market services, which are generally provided by government), central government outlays on subsidies were more than double the explicit subsidies measured in the budget and the national accounts in 2003. At the state government level, in 1998 total subsidies were four times greater than the budgetary estimate due to the large implicit subsidies to agriculture, irrigation, power, water and sanitation, and road transport. No update is available for total state subsidies, but it seems likely that this broad measure of total subsidies for both state and central government exceeded 8 percent of GDP in 2003. In addition to subsidies, there are considerable cross-subsidies in India. These occur in many of the sectors where the state is a monopoly provider. Examples are electricity, railway transport, kerosene, road passenger transport and telephone calls. In total these cross-subsidies amounted to 2.3 percent of GDP in 1999.

### 8.16 Modernization of Tax Structure

India has made much progress in modernizing its tax system. First attempts to rationalize the tax system were made in the second half of the 1980s, but more fundamental tax reforms were implemented in the early 1990s as part of the market-oriented structural reforms. These reforms reduced tax distortions by cutting the very high marginal income and corporate tax rates. At the same time, and as part of trade liberalisation, import tariffs were significantly reduced and the system of excises was rationalized with the introduction of a central government value added tax for the production of goods. The latest major reform was the transformation of the state sales tax into a value added tax in April 2005. A further reform is planned for 2010 with the introduction of a nationwide Goods and Services Tax (GST). This has however been delayed further to 2011 as announced in the recent Union Budget 2010-2011 on February 26, 2010.

Tax reforms over the past 15 years have made a major contribution to the improvement in India's economic performance. Nonetheless, there is still scope for further improvements. India's tax system continues to be riddled with many loopholes and exemptions, which create distortions and increase complexity. Furthermore, trade of goods within India is hampered by physical controls at state borders to prevent fraud in states' VAT.

### 8.17 Centre-State Financial Relations

Within the federal structure of government, significant imbalances between the constitutional responsibilities for expenditure and the distribution of the powers of taxation are resolved by large transfers from central government to the states. These transfers result in the overall level of devolution to state, in terms of tax revenue, being at the high end of the experience of OECD federal countries. As well as dealing with the vertical imbalances, the transfers also attempt to deal with the extreme differences in income levels between states that make it difficult to provide a similar level of basic public services across the union. The transfers to states come from three sources: a constitutional body (the Finance Commission), the Planning Commission and through various central government programmes. The flows through the first two channels are largely formula driven, though it is noticeable that the first is markedly more redistributive than the second. Moreover, the second channel involves a high degree of micro-management of the uses to which the transfers are put, whereas the first essentially gives freedom to the states to use funds according to their own priorities. Increasingly, the third channel (transfers from ministries) is being used to influence state behaviour in areas that are not, constitutionally, within the sole competence of the central government.

Overall, two areas stand out from the current fiscal relations between the centre and the states: the difficulty of ensuring an adequate level of public services in the poorest states given their size and low relative income level and the difficulty of limiting the extent of state-level borrowing. To date, despite its constitutional powers, the centre has not exercised such control; rather it has encouraged borrowing through requirements to match grants with borrowing and through debt write-offs.

Central government policy has now changed and the move to market control of state borrowing is now underway. The extent of devolution to the third tier of government is as yet underdeveloped relative to that seen in OECD countries. Although local government has existed in many urban areas for several centuries, the Constitution only recognised devolution to local bodies in 1992. Local authorities are extremely under funded with the resultant under-provision of local services. Their total tax and grant income is only one-third that of local governments in OECD federal countries, despite the much larger average size of states in India. State governments continue to control local bodies by appointing key personnel and because of the very limited span for which elected heads of local governments remain in power.

Moreover, the State Finance Commissions (that determine the extent of revenue sharing between states and their local bodies) are often not as well-staffed or competent as the Central Finance Commission. In general, states have been unwilling to share their principal revenue stream (sales tax in the past and VAT presently) with local authorities, while the latter have been unwilling to develop local property taxes as a source of revenue.

### 8.18 High Demand for Infrastructure Services

As a result of rapid economic growth, there is a high and rapidly growing demand for infrastructure services across a range of sectors. On the supply side, although capital formation by the private sector has been growing relatively strongly, the public sector capital stock has been growing at half the pace of the capital stock in the private sector. Moreover, its growth has been less than half the growth rate of GDP growth. As a result, access to infrastructure is extremely low by world standards, and bottlenecks in public infrastructure could become a major obstacle for future growth. At the state level, an unequal distribution of infrastructure is an important reason why state performance has been diverging since the 1990s.

As well as being in short supply, India's infrastructure is often not very productive except when provided by the private sector. Private sector operators in the wireless phone market have transformed the availability of telephone communications in a few years. Relatively productive private sector operators are also making rapid inroads into the civil aviation market, and the productivity at some of India's ports has improved over recent years (albeit from a low base) as private contractors have been permitted to run port facilities. The government-run international airports at Delhi and Mumbai typically handle only 25 to 28 flights per runway per hour in comparison to 40 in a number of OECD countries, while India's rail network is also much less efficient than China's. Agreement has been reached for airport reconstruction in Delhi and Mumbai to start through a public-private partnership. Given fiscal constraints, the government is turning increasingly to private sector participation in infrastructure provision. It has instituted a Viability Gap Fund and the India Infrastructure Finance Company to provide partial grants and funding respectively for the private-sector in infrastructure projects. It is also trying to improve the regulatory framework and improve the governance of independent regulators in infrastructure sectors. However, unless the supply of savings is raised, a greater private sector involvement in infrastructure investment may crowd out other private sector capital formation, and so it is essential that involving the private sector is not used to bypass the fiscal constraints imposed by the FRBM legislation, but rather where there is clear evidence of greater efficiency of private sector operators.

Notwithstanding the launch of a major new investment programme, the rate of capital formation in India's electricity sector has been low in comparison to other emerging Asian countries and the coverage of the power network and quality of electricity supplied are poor. This imposes high costs on the economy, particularly electricity-intensive sectors such as manufacturing, through the need for high-cost backup generators and investment in self-generation facilities for larger users. The government has launched a "Power for All" programme that is due for completion by 2012. This programme is aimed at increasing capacity by just under 6 percent annually, for a total addition to capacity of 47 GW with total investment commitment of about US$ 44 billion (slightly less than 1 percent of GDP per year) against a capacity expansion of just over 3 percent annually in the previous five years. Moreover, plants representing a further 40 GW (a further 22 percent expansion) are in the pipeline for placement of orders. This represents the second largest planned capacity addition worldwide.

The weakness of public sector investment in electricity reflects the inability of the state electricity companies and boards to operate profitably given the governance structure of the industry. However, new regulatory agencies, with the necessary policy framework, are starting to ensure that tariffs are set on commercial principles, independent of political interference. The objective of the state companies has, in most cases, been to extend the coverage of the electricity network to rural villages, even though they have been in most cases unable to provide a regular power supply to the resulting network. Basic low-level investment in distribution systems has been neglected and electricity theft has been widespread. Aggregate technical and commercial losses of electricity from the system have been extremely high and have only fallen from 39 percent to 35 percent in the past five years. In its "Power for All" programme, the government has set a target of reducing these losses to 20 percent by 2012. For consumers, prices have typically been held below cost or electricity is provided without a meter.

Three states, namely, Punjab, Andhra Pradesh and Tamil Nadu, are giving free power to the farmers. In other states, farmers are being charged subsidised tariffs. Overall, gross subsidies to agricultural and domestic consumers have been falling slightly this decade, from 1.5 percent of GDP to just under 1.25 percent by 2005. Direct subsidies from the state government budgets amount to 0.4 percent of GDP, with the remainder coming from excess payments by industrial and commercial customers and enterprise losses. In addition, even if the electricity industry did not make losses, there would still be an opportunity cost stemming from its poor rate of return on assets, which is almost 6 percentage points below the cost of capital in the private sector. All this uncompensated subsidisation results in lower revenues for the state government electricity companies and reduces their ability to invest and increase supply. State electricity companies generally produce well below optimal levels of production, given their existing resources, with one study of Uttar Pradesh finding that better organisation alone could raise production by one-third (IIB, 2005). The combined losses of the state electricity boards are around 0.6 percent of GDP.

Three key policy initiatives are beginning to have a positive impact on the electricity sector. First, states were obliged to settle all debts for electricity purchased from the central government generator by issuing power bonds. The government then sold a stake in this company to the private sector. Second, the Electricity Act (2003) sets out a policy framework for addressing issues in distribution and creating a competitive electricity market that is conducive to private sector involvement. In addition, it is beginning to create a favourable environment for private sector generation and will also reduce the scope for overcharging industry for electricity supply. Finally, the Accelerated Power Development and Reform Programme uses financial incentives to encourage reform of the distribution sector at the state level. States that have been more successful in implementing the Electricity Act have had some success in reducing the extent of the aggregate technical and commercial loss of the system, which is an important and necessary step for making the sector more attractive for private sector investment. However, only the states of Orissa and Delhi have privatised distribution.

Until recently, investment in roads in India has been extremely low. In1998, however, the government launched the National Highway Development Project (NHDP) in order to substantially upgrade the interurban road network and the connectivity of ports. The first stage of this programme was substantially completed at the end of 2006, linking four cities

(Delhi, Mumbai, Kolkata and Chennai) in a dual-carriageway system nearly 6,000 km long, representing a density of 1.8 kilometres per 1,000 square kilometres. This density is still only 60 percent of that in Turkey and Mexico and, moreover, the Indian roads are not built to motorway standard. The overall road density in India is higher than in most developing countries due to the emphasis on constructing unpaved village roads. Even including other expressways that have been opened, the overall investment level in better quality roads has been modest (1060 km per year), against an expansion rate of 4,800 km per year in China between 2001 and 2005. Outlays for road building amount to only 0.4 percent of GDP annually.

The next phases of the NHDP involve a significant increase in investment in highway completion. Public funds are unable to finance such an ambitious expansion programme, and the government plans to fund all subsequent investment in highways on a PPP basis. A number of state governments are also funding roads in this way. The early indications are that PPPs are working reasonably well in the roads sector and are a significant improvement on the previous policy of 100 percent government funding via construction contracts and self-provision. The early experience with toll collection has generally been positive and some recent bids from private partners for viability gap funding have been negative, implying that they are prepared to pay for the right to collect tolls on some sections of highway, reflecting expectations of high traffic flow. The right to collect toll is applicable for all "build-operate-transfer" projects.

### 8.19 Urban Renewal and Development

The development of urban areas has lagged well behind developments in comparable countries. As a result, the level of urbanization in India is well below that in other countries with similar income levels. Such a development is significant in that productivity levels are much higher in urban areas (one-quarter of the population produces 60 percent of output). In addition,

90 percent of tax revenues are also generated in urban areas. The development of urban areas has been neglected in part because of the political structure of the country. As discussed above, the Constitution did not formally recognize the existence of levels of local government below that of the state prior to the constitutional amendment of 1992. That amendment required states to establish locally elected bodies and specified the area of competencies for local authorities. However, it established no point in time by which such authorities were to be established nor did it specify the funding mechanism for the local authorities.

Key local activities have been retained in state-run boards and authorities with little or no local input. Local finances suffer from being dependent on transfers from state government rather than having independent sources of finance. Local entry tariffs at one time generated most municipal revenue but with their abolition in all but two states, cities have become even more dependent on transfers from states. Property taxes are not used as a significant source of revenue, in part because of the poor state of property registers. Strict land development and rental controls that exist in many cities restrict the most efficient use of land. Land assembly is also held back by the difficulty in establishing title. Recognizing the key role of local governments, the central government established a new initiative in 2005 to induce states to strengthen their urban local governments (although less has been done in rural areas). This should help with their capacity to provide education and other public services. The program, the Jawaharlal Nehru National Urban Renewal Mission (JNURM), offers conditional transfers of resources based on a memorandum of understanding by states that requires them to implement wide-ranging reforms to strengthen local self-governance, with a particular focus on strengthening land markets, whose reform has the potential to not only stimulate urban development but also to give localities a more solid revenue base.

The focus on land development recognises a longstanding problem, as strong restrictions on land use exist in many cities, and poor quality of land title records limits property markets. The JNURM incentives focus on several areas, including reducing the land transfer tax to below 5 percent, repealing land ceiling laws, easing building requirements and reducing rent control acts, which is much needed as rent control acts have been exceedingly difficult to revise, with a major effort by New Delhi in 1995 never notified. A number of major reforms have already taken place, such as a reduction of stamp duty in West Bengal from 10 percent to 6 percent and a repeal of the land ceiling act in Maharashtra (including Mumbai). The Ministry of Urban Development is also providing technical assistance in targeted areas such as property records through the computerization of land title and use of geographic information systems, with a goal of doubling property tax compliance from less than 40 percent in the next five years. State run boards have proved to be inadequate suppliers of local services with water and sanitation boards generally being very inefficient. Labour productivity is about five times lower than in the best-managed Asian cities such as Singapore and Bangkok. Water supply is intermittent and poor in quality.

One government report found that staff in charge of disinfecting water had little knowledge of the underlying processes involved, with the result that bacteriological infection of domestic water supplies was widespread. This same report indicated that 10 percent of urban water samples in Maharashtra were contaminated by bacteria rising to 14 percent in Mumbai. Even worse findings have been reported from Jaipur and Kolkata. The water boards also have poor records in financing their activities, which necessarily holds back investment. Metering is not widespread and, in many cases, meters are not adequately maintained. Even when meters exist, billing is problematic and there is little enforcement of payment. In Mumbai, outstanding water bills amounted to almost two years of revenue. Even if bills were collected, water tariffs are set in an inefficient manner. Most boards use an increasing block tariff, with the idea that a basic water supply is provided at a low price and then larger users (presumed to be well-off) are charged a higher price. The limits for the "basic block" are generally much higher than basic needs with the result that around 70 percent of consumers in Hyderabad and Bangalore consume in the basic block. With low metering, low productivity and poor collection of bills, few major cities even cover operating costs. Across the country, subsidies to urban water supply are estimated to cost 0.5 percent of GDP.

The growth of urban areas is also held back by both inefficient land and rental markets. In the land market, most state governments charge high transfer taxes when land and buildings change ownership, so making the market illiquid. All states have rent control acts in force that strictly limit rent levels, allowing little increase in the initial nominal rental rate. As result, the private rental market has declined. A number of states have controls over the extent of ownership of land, in some cases limiting the holding of vacant land in urban areas to 500squaremetres. Land title can also be difficult to establish as the land registry is poorly organised and not computerised in most states. Low rental levels also help lower property taxes as the building is generally assessed on a value basis that takes into account whether there is a rent-controlled tenant. Land development plans were developed many decades ago with little regard for the evolution of the urban economy in intervening periods. Finally, one of the few licensing restrictions that remain on new investment is location control. There is a ban on new industrial development within 25 kilometres of the outer limit of cities with over one million habitants in order to preserve the environment.

The central government is trying to give an incentive to state governments to change a large number of these policies by offering grants for urban improvement if state governments are willing to change laws. States have signed memorandums of agreement with the centre, but it remains to be seen whether the money offered by the centre will be sufficient to change state-level policies.

Urban development since the 1990s has not been associated with increased air pollution; rather various policies have lowered its extent, but it remains critically high. Most air pollution in large Indian cities comes from particles; other sources (sulphurdioxide and nitrogenoxides) are of lesser concern. In southern cities, concentrations of these particles have been falling and were close to the national air quality standards. In northern cities, concentrations have also fallen but are well above national standards, and these cities account for 80 percent of the monitored towns where concentrations are worse than air quality standard for residential areas. Small particles cause the most damage to health and, in India, come from a number of sources, including vehicles, road dust and biofuels. A wide range of policies is thus needed to combat pollution. These policies need to vary according to the climate, with northern cities being more vulnerable to winter-time pollution from residential and commercial space-heating.

Policies to discourage the use of solid fuels, especially biofuels, for heating may be needed. State governments are moving to enforce legislation following Supreme Court judgements requiring them to respect their constitutional duty to protect the environment. This led Delhi to convert its public transport fleet to run on compressed natural gas. Improving education The low average level of educational achievement of the population has been a concern of the government for the past decade. Average spending per student is similar to that in other countries, once allowance is made for private spending. Nonetheless, relative to other countries, the performance of the Indian educational system has been poor and out of line with expenditure levels. Despite expenditure on primary school education that is not out of line with that of other countries, the level of literacy amongst young people was markedly lower than in other rapidly growing emerging economies in 2000. In fact, the cumulative performance of the education system over the period 1950 to 2000 left the country with a youth literacy rate some 30 percentage points below that in central and south America, 25 points below other emerging Asian countries and even 5 points below the average for Africa. Against this poor level of overall literacy, the percentage of the population with a tertiary education is relatively high.

Although primary and secondary education is a state government responsibility, the central government has embarked on a number of projects in the past decade that are beginning to turn the situation around. The first success was the programme to give a meal to all children attending school, which drew pupils from poorer backgrounds into the education system. As a result, there was a marked gain in literacy amongst children that completed their education during the 1990s. It was particularly marked amongst girls, but there still remained an imbalance between boys and girls in their literacy rates. While school, attendance and completion rates did improve in the decade to 2001, still only half of all children completed primary education at that date. A second scheme is designed to transfer funds to state governments in order to achieve the goal of all children completing an eight-year education programme by 2010. This decade, there is evidence of a further improvement, with the illiteracy rate dropping 10 percent for the age group 10-14 for the country as a whole. Moreover, this rate has been determined on the basis of probing questions by an interviewer rather than the self-assessment basis used in the census. Such an improvement has almost halved the gap in youth literacy that was apparent at the beginning of the decade, moving India markedly ahead of Africa but still lagging behind the 90-100 percent youth literacy rates that are typical of many emerging economies.

The key problem in improving literacy would appear to be ensuring that school attendance remains as high as school enrolment and that children indeed learn in school. Amongst those in the 5-14 age group actually attending school, illiteracy rates are now below 10 percent with little difference between rural and urban areas. The major difference between rural and urban areas lies in the degree of illiteracy amongst those who do not attend school which are extremely high, especially in rural areas. Some of those shown to be absent from school in the period of the sample survey will return to school at some point, and some of the younger children in the sample will learn to read, which will no doubt result in a further fall in the illiteracy rate.

There is evidence that concerted efforts between schools, administrators and parents can improve the quality of education in primary schools. The association *Pratham* has undertaken widespread field trials of methods that can be used to improve results and address deficiencies in the sometimes poor quality of education. The association found in its nationwide survey that a significant proportion of the 11-year-olds actually in school were unable to undertake basic linguistic and arithmetic tasks that should be within the capabilities of such an age group. The absence of teachers from schools is also a major problem, especially in smaller schools, as is the poor infrastructure of many schools. This latter factor is a reflection of the high proportion of the education budget that is spent on salaries, which also corresponds to an internationally high level of salaries relative to GDP per capita. About half of parents decide to send their children to private schools. In this sector, teacher attendance and school facilities are better, but the evidence for better performance in standardised tests in a few core areas is weak, though the private schools generally teach a much wider range of subjects, notably including English.

### 8.20 Summing Up

India has made much progress in making its economy more open and more market-based. As a result, and helped by political stability and favourable international conditions, the economy has achieved a higher growth path, poverty is declining and a number of indicators of health are improving. However, average living standards remain low and there are large income gaps across states, regions and socio-economic groups. India's main challenge is to sustain, and possibly accelerate, its catch-up process and to ensure that improvements in living standards are spread as widely as possible.

# Appendix

# Appendix

## Fiscal Policy Strategy Statement, as Part of the Budget Papers, Presented to Parliament by Shri Pranab Mukherjee, Minister of Finance, on February 26, 2010

---

**A. Fiscal Policy Overview**

1. In order to minimise the impact of the global slowdown on the Indian economy, the Government took a conscious decision to continue with the fiscal expansionary measures in the Budget 2009-10. The aim of the policy was to enhance public expenditure so as to boost demand and spur the process of development and economic revival. The above decision of the Government to increase public expenditure, even with lower revenue receipts, and stimulate the economy by creating demand was guided by the principle of insulating the vulnerable sections of society and sectors of economy from the impact of economic downturn and at the same time ensure revival of the economy with higher growth. These measures were expected to spur growth and restore revenue buoyancy in medium term and provide the required fiscal space to revert to the path of fiscal consolidation. The fiscal deficit of 6.8 percent of GDP in BE 2009-10 may therefore be seen against this background.

2. The positive impact of these measures could be seen with Indian economy recording 7 percent growth in real GDP in the first half of 2009-10 when most of the developed economies of the world were trying their best to stay afloat. Indian economy is estimated to grow at 7.2 percent in 2009-10 as per the latest data, although there are possibilities that it may actually be slightly higher.

3. The measures taken by Government to counter the effects of the global meltdown on the Indian economy have

resulted in shortfall in revenues and substantial increase in Government expenditures, leading to deviation from the fiscal consolidation path mandated under the FRBM Act. The gross tax to GDP ratio which increased to an all time high of 12 percent in 2007-08, thanks to the economy riding on high growth trajectory, has steadily declined to 10.9 percent in 2008-09 and 10.3 percent in RE 2009-10 due to moderation in growth in economy and reduction in tax/duty rates. At the same time total expenditure as percentage of GDP has increased from 14.4 percent in 2007-08 to 15.9 percent in 2008-09 and 16.6 percent in RE 2009-10. The fiscal expansion in the last 2 years has resulted in higher fiscal deficit of 6 percent of GDP in 2008-09 and 6.7 percent in RE 2009-10. Moreover, the revenue deficit as percentage of GDP has worsened to 4.5 percent and 5.3 percent in 2008-09 and RE 2009-10 respectively. The revenue deficit and fiscal deficit in RE 2009-2010 are higher than the targets set under the FRBM Act and Rules. The deviation from the mandate under FRBM Act and Rules was resorted to with the objective of keeping the economy on the higher growth trajectory amidst global slowdown by creating demand through increased public expenditure in identified sectors.

4. It is however important to note that the fiscal deficit in RE 2009-10 is broadly in line with BE 2009-10. Furthermore, against fiscal deficit of 7.8 percent of GDP in 2008-09 (inclusive of oil and fertiliser bonds), the comparable fiscal deficit including the impact of Rs. 10,306 crore of oil bonds towards under recoveries of the previous financial year, is 6.9 percent of GDP as per RE 2009-10. Both these deficit figures are based on the revised GDP numbers published by the Central Statistical Organisation. It clearly marks an improvement of about 1 percent of GDP in fiscal deficit in 2009-10 compared to 2008-09. The Government has made a conscious effort to avoid issuing Government securities in lieu of cash subsidies to oil and fertiliser companies. The Government would like to maintain this trend of extending

Government subsidy in cash rather than by way of bonds. This is a major step towards bringing all subsidy related liabilities into Government's fiscal accounting.

5. The medium term objective as enumerated in the Fiscal Policy Strategy Statement presented in July 2009 is to revert to the path of fiscal consolidation at the earliest with emphasis on structural fiscal reforms and prudent fiscal management with improvement in the economic situation. Without putting at risk the revival process, the Government is looking at exit strategies with improvement in economic conditions.

6. The Budget 2010-2011 is being presented in this backdrop with signs of recovery in the Indian economy along with a few other economies in the world. However, it is still early to predict complete revival in the world economy and the Government has to be cautious in its exit strategy. The growth rate of 7.9 percent in GDP in the second quarter of 2009-10 compared to the average growth of 5.8 percent during the second half of 2008-09 shows that the impact of fiscal stimuli has started showing results. Better than estimated direct tax receipts coupled with impressive growth data from manufacturing sector in recent months provide opportunities for the Government to revert back to the path of fiscal consolidation in a gradual manner staring from 2010-11. The 13th Finance Commission in its recommendations has also provided a roadmap for fiscal consolidation.

**B. Fiscal Policy for 2010-11**

7. The fiscal policy of 2010-11 is being guided by the principles of gradual adjustment from the fiscal expansion undertaken during 2008-09 and 2009-10. The adjustment path is being so calibrated that it would not affect the revival process and at the same time stabilize the debt to GDP ratio of the Government in the medium term. In the Medium Term Fiscal Policy Statement of 2009-10, the Government had enumerated the roadmap for fiscal consolidation during 2010-11 and 2011-12. The Government is adhering to these

commitments made in July 2009 and has also benefited from the recommendations of the 13th Finance Commission on fiscal consolidation. Accordingly fiscal deficit in BE 2010-11 has been reduced to 5.5 percent of GDP. This correction of fiscal deficit is attributed to reduction in total expenditure by 0.6 percent of GDP (from 16.6 percent in BE 2009-10 to 16.0 percent in BE 2010-11), increase in gross tax revenue by 0.4 percent of GDP (from 10.4 percent in BE 2009-10 to 10.8 percent in BE 2010-11) and increase in non debt capital receipt by 0.6 percent of GDP (from 0.1 percent in BE 2009-10 to 0.7 percent in BE 2010-11). All the above numbers are with reference to the revised GDP numbers.

8. Total expenditure of the Government has shown compounded average annual growth rate of 19.6 percent during the fiscal expansion period of 2008-2010. This level of growth in expenditure is not sustainable. In the fiscal policy strategy for ensuing financial year and the next two years, the Government has made efforts to moderate the growth rate of expenditure in order to bring down the deficit. Accordingly, non-plan expenditure as percentage of GDP has been reduced from 11.3 percent in BE 2009-10 to 10.6 percent in BE 2010-11. At the same time, adequate resources for plan expenditure have been provided at 5.4 percent of GDP in BE 2010-11 as against 5.3 percent in BE 2009-10. Total expenditure as percentage of GDP for the year 2011-12 and 2012-13 would be further brought down to 15.2 percent and 14.6 percent respectively. This would result in correction to the extent of 2 percent of GDP from the level of 16.6 percent in BE 2009-10. This adjustment in expenditure would be primarily on non-plan account and after factoring in adequate allocations for flagship schemes, Bharat Nirman programme and infrastructure sector. The correction in composition of expenditure would translate into deployment of borrowed resources largely for plan expenditure (97.8 percent in BE 2010-11). This is further estimated to go up to 122.9 percent in 2012-13 against only 81.1 percent in BE 2009-10.

9. Intent of the Government to bring the fiscal deficit under control with institutional reform measures encompassing all aspects of fiscal management such as subsidies, taxes, disinvestment and other expenditures were indicated in the Budget 2009-10. The decision of the Government to move towards nutrient based subsidy (NBS) regime in fertiliser subsidy along with increase in the MRP of urea is one of the steps in order to translate the above intentions into concrete action. Under the NBS regime, the subsidy on subsidized nutrients will remain fixed and the retail prices of subsidized fertilisers at farm gate level will be decided by the manufacturers/importers. The government in consultation with the fertilizer industry will make interventions in such a manner that the farm gate prices of non-urea fertilizers are as far as possible near the current prices so that farmers are not adversely affected. It is also expected to promote balanced use of fertilizer with increase in agricultural productivity. Unshackling of fertilizer industry is also expected to attract fresh investments into this sector.

10. With respect to rationalization of petroleum subsidy, the report of the Parikh Committee on the above subject is under consideration of the Government. In a departure from past practice, the Government has agreed to provide petroleum subsidy in cash instead of securities in the year 2009-10. Government would like to continue to pay compensation for under recoveries, if any, to oil marketing companies in cash only.

11. It is estimated that subsidy expenditure as percentage of GDP would decline from 2.1 percent in RE 2009-10 to 1.7 percent in BE 2010-11 and further to 1.6 percent and 1.4 percent respectively in 2011-12 and 2012-13.

## Tax Policy

### Direct Taxes

12. The last decade has witnessed a substantial growth in direct taxes. The direct tax to GDP ratio has gone up from 2.97

percent in 1999-2000 to 6.36 percent in 2008-09. The contribution of direct taxes to the total taxes collected by the Centre has increased from 33.8 percent to 55.5 percent during the same period.

13. The following policy measures have driven this increase in direct tax contributions: (i) Distortions within the tax structure have been minimised by expanding the tax base and by maintaining moderate tax rates; (ii) Tax administration has been geared up to provide better taxpayer services and also to enhance deterrence levels. Both these objectives reinforce each other and have promoted voluntary compliance. (iii) Business Processes in the Income-tax Department have been re-engineered through extensive use of information technology, viz., electronic reporting of tax collections, e-filing of returns, issue of refunds through ECS and refund bankers, computer assisted selection of returns for scrutiny, electronic reporting of foreign remittances liable to tax, online reporting and e-mailing of tax deduction at source details to taxpayers, etc. These measures have modernized the Department and enhanced its functional efficiency.

14. The Union Budget for 2009-10 announced that a draft Direct Taxes Code would be released within 45 days. The draft Code along with a Discussion Paper was released in August, 2009 inviting comments from the public. The proposed Direct Taxes Code is a new legislation which will replace the current Income Tax and Wealth Tax Acts. It is written in direct and simple language and is based on the philosophy of a wide tax base, moderate tax rates and an effective enforcement strategy. The Code proposes to minimise exemptions and deductions to widen the tax base. It also proposes to do away with profit-linked deductions and introduce investment-linked deductions for priority areas. At the same time, it advocates moderate tax rates with broad slabs. These measures will help to reduce litigation and free up the tax administration to provide better taxpayer services and focus on tackling tax evasion. The draft Code and Discussion Paper have generated healthy debate and

a number of suggestions. After analysing the inputs received, the draft legislation will be finalized and introduced in Parliament.

15. The major policy proposals in the Union Budget 2010-11 intended to consolidate and carry forward the past achievements are:

- Rationalisation of the Personal Income Tax (PIT) rate structure for individuals by broadening the income slabs. This will reduce the tax liability of a majority of individual taxpayers.
- Reducing the surcharge on Corporate Income Tax (CIT) from 10 percent to 7.5 percent. This is part of the initiative to phase out surcharges. Surcharge on PIT has already been removed last year.
- Increasing the rate of Minimum Alternate Tax (MAT) on companies to 18 percent from the existing level of 15 percent. This will enhance the *inter* se equity in taxation of companies and will also raise the effective tax rate which is currently around 22 percent as against the nominal rate of 33.99 percent.
- Raising the threshold limits on a number of transactions which are subject to Tax Deduction at Source (TDS). This will reduce the compliance burden for deductors as well as deductees and enable the tax administration to efficiently process claims for TDS credit.
- Reducing the compliance burden on small taxpayers by increasing the threshold level of turnover beyond which accounts of the business are to be compulsorily audited from Rs. 40 lakh to Rs. 60 lakh. The compliance burden of small taxpayers is being further reduced by providing a presumptive rate of taxation of 8 percent of turnover and allowing the tax liability to be paid as self assessment tax instead of several advance tax instalments.
- Enabling small companies to reduce their regulatory and compliance burden by converting to Limited Liability Partnerships (LLPs) by proposing that such conversion

shall not attract capital gains tax liability under the Income-tax Act.

- Expediting the resolution of major tax disputes by widening the scope of cases which can be admitted by the Income Tax Settlement Commission to also include assessment proceedings relating to search proceedings.

16. The use of information technology for providing better taxpayer services has been a cornerstone of direct tax policy. The mass processing of income tax returns is a key recommendation of the business process reengineering study conducted by the Income-tax Department. A Centralised Processing Centre (CPC) has been set up at Bengaluru for processing all e-filed income-tax returns as well as paper returns filed in the State of Karnataka. The CPC has commenced operations during this year and is currently processing 20,000 returns daily. Two more CPCs are proposed to be rolled out in the coming year. This initiative will help provide better tax payer service through faster processing of returns and issue of refunds.

**Indirect Taxes**

17. The medium term objective of the policy for indirect taxes in recent years has been to achieve fiscal consolidation through an improvement in the tax-GDP ratio. This is sought to be achieved through the widening of tax base and removal of exemptions coupled with moderation in the rates of tax. It is expected that these measures would foster voluntary compliance. There is an equally strong emphasis on procedural simplification and the adoption by tax departments of internal business processes leveraged on Information Technology so as to minimize day-to-day physical interface between the tax payer and tax administration.

18. In specific terms, the declared goal is to move to a comprehensive Goods and Services Tax (GST) both at the Centre and in the States. By addressing the problems of cascading and double taxation, this key reform in the realm of indirect taxation is expected to contribute significantly to

efficiency and growth in the economy which, in turn, would augment the buoyancy of tax collections. The current fiscal year 2009-10 has seen considerable movement in the discussions on finalization of the model for the proposed GST. The Empowered Committee of State Finance Ministers released its First Discussion Paper on the model and roadmap for GST in November, 2009. Further work on the refinement of this model based on the feedback received from trade, industry and other stakeholders is underway.

19. The global financial crisis in September, 2008 and the resultant collapse of export markets triggered off an economic slowdown in India. Faced with the threat of a deepening crisis, the Government had to inject three rounds of fiscal stimulus packages to boost aggregate demand. An important element of these packages was the sharp, across the board reduction in the rates of Central Excise duty for non-petroleum products and the reduction in the rate of Service Tax from 12 percent to 10 percent.

20. Prior to the onset of the financial crisis, the surge in international prices of crude petroleum and other commodities posed a serious macro-economic challenge. Consequently, in June 2008, the import duty on crude petroleum and refined petroleum products was reduced by 5 percentage points each and the excise duty rates on motor spirit and diesel were also dropped significantly.

21. All these measures, taken together, strongly impacted revenue collections from indirect taxes in 2008-09. Their continuation in the current fiscal year has meant that revenue collections from customs, central excise and service tax continued to be under stress during 2009-10. The objective of fiscal consolidation, therefore, had to be temporarily suspended in the interest of economic recovery and maintenance of growth momentum. These measures have had a very positive impact in turning around the economy, particularly the manufacturing sector. As such, the Government seeks to return to the path of fiscal correction or

consolidation in a gradual manner so as not to affect recovery and growth adversely. Some of the proposals contained in the Budget for 2010-11 aim to subserve this purpose. The important ones in this direction are as under:

**Central Excise Duty**

- After two successive reductions in December, 2008 and February, 2009, the standard rate of excise duty (Cenvat) of 8 percent has been increased to 10 percent.
- Duty on petrol and diesel has been increased by Re. 1 per litre.
- Duty has been increased on cigarettes and other tobacco products.
- Ad-valorem component of excise duty on large cars, Multi Utility Vehicles and Sports Utility Vehicles has been increased from 20 percent to 22 percent. The specific component of duty remains unchanged.
- Cement, at present attracting 8 percent duty, would now suffer a higher incidence of 10 percent. In cases where cement attracts specific rates of duty, the same have also been hiked proportionately.
- Full or partial excise duty exemptions/concessions available to many items have been withdrawn and duty imposed on them @ 4 percent or 10 percent.

**Customs Duty**

- No change has been made in the peak rate of customs duty on non-agricultural items, which remains at 10 percent.
- Customs duty on serially numbered gold bars (other than tola bars) and gold coins has been increased from 'Rs. 200 per 10 gram' to 'Rs. 300 per 10 gram'. On other forms of gold the duty has gone up from 'Rs. 500 per 10 gram' to 'Rs. 750 per 10 gram'. In case of silver, the duty has been increased from 'Rs. 1,000 per kg to Rs. 1,500 per kg.' Platinum would now attract customs duty of 'Rs. 300 per 10 gram' as compared to earlier rate of 'Rs. 200 per 10 gram'.

- In the petroleum sector, customs duty has been increased on: crude petroleum from Nil to 5 percent; petrol and diesel from 2.5 percent to 7.5 percent; and other specified petroleum products from 5 percent to 10 percent.

**Service Tax**

- The rate of service tax of 10 percent applicable since 24.02.2009 has been continued.
- Eight new services are being brought under the service tax net.
- Scope of many existing services has been modified to plug the loopholes and check evasion of tax.

**Contingent and other Liabilities**

22. The FRBM Act mandates the Central Government to specify the annual target for assuming contingent liabilities in the form of guarantees. Accordingly the FRBM Rules prescribe a cap of 0.5 percent of GDP in any financial year on the quantum of guarantees that the Central Government can assume in the particular financial year. The Central Government extends guarantees primarily on loans from multilateral/bilateral agencies, bond issues and other loans raised by various Public Sector Undertakings/Public Sector Financial Institutions. The stock of contingent liabilities in the form of guarantees given by the Government has increased from Rs. 1,07,957 crore at the beginning of the FRBM Act regime in 2004-05 to Rs. 1,13,335 crore at the end of 2008-09. As a percentage of GDP, it has reduced from 3.3 percent in 2004-05 to 2.0 percent in 2008-09.

23. Assumption of contingent liability in the form of guarantee by the sovereign helps to leverage private sector participation in areas of national priorities. In the current situation, wherein several infrastructure projects are being cleared for implementation under the Public Private Partnership (PPP) mode, difficulties are being faced in reaching financial closure due to the current uncertainties in the global financial market. Within the given fiscal constraints

and with a view to supporting financing of above mentioned PPP projects, the India Infrastructure Financing Company Limited (IIFCL) has raised Rs. 10,000 crore through Government guaranteed tax free bonds in the previous financial year 2008-09. The IIFCL would raise additional amounts on the same basis as per requirement in the coming years. The capital so raised will be used by IIFCL to refinance bank lending of longer maturity to eligible infrastructure projects.

24. The assumption of contingent liability in the form of guarantee for 2009-10 up to January 2010 is Rs. 38,778 crore which is 0.6 percent of GDP during 2009-10, higher than the target of 0.5 percent of GDP set under the FRBM Rules. This deviation has been necessitated in the larger interest of re-invigorating the economy in the background of the economic slowdown, to stimulate demand and increase investment in infrastructure sector projects with assistance from multilateral agencies. In the medium term while this may not have a potential budgetary impact, the additional investment will help restore the economy to its higher growth path and contribute to higher revenue buoyancy.

**Government Borrowings, Lending and Investments**

25. The Government policy towards borrowings to finance its deficit continues to remain anchored on the following principles, namely (i) greater reliance on domestic borrowings over external debt, (ii) preference for market borrowings over instruments carrying administered interest rates, (iii) consolidation of the debt portfolio and (iv) development of a deep and wide market for Government securities to improve liquidity in secondary market. For better cash management, a new instrument namely "cash management bill" has been introduced during the year. The tenure of this instrument will be less than 91 days.

26. In order to finance high level of fiscal deficit during 2009-10, market borrowings for the Government increased

significantly. However, raising of indicated resources as per the published calendar for the current financial year has been completed without disrupting the market. The gross and net market borrowings (including dated securities and 364- day Treasury Bills) of the Central Government during 2009-10 up to 19th February amounted to Rs. 4,78,383 crore and Rs. 3,89,627 crore respectively as against Rs. 3,18,550 crore and Rs. 2,42,317 crore during 2008-09. The weighted average maturity of dated securities issued during 2009-10 is 11.2 years as compared to 13.8 years during 2008-09. The weighted average yield of dated securities issued during 2009-10 is 7.23 percent and is lower than 7.69 percent during 2008-09.

27. The gross and net market borrowings (dated securities) of the Central Government during 2010-11 is estimated at Rs. 4,57,143 crore and Rs. 3,45,010 crore (4.98 percent of GDP) respectively as against Rs. 4,51,000 crore and Rs. 3,98,411 crore (6.46 percent of GDP) during 2009-10.

28. During the year 2010-11, the financing of fiscal deficit is estimated to be done without taking recourse to short-term borrowings through Treasury Bills or cash draw down. The share of market borrowings, external debt and NSSF in the financing of deficit for 2010-11 is estimated at 90.5 percent, 5.9 percent and 3.5 percent respectively. However, to take care of temporary mismatch between receipts and expenditure, the Government may have to take recourse to ways and means advances from RBI.

29. The outstanding balance under Market Stabilization Scheme (MSS) on 1st April, 2009 was Rs. 88,773 crore. The outstanding balance under the MSS is estimated to decline to Rs. 2,737 crore at the end of 2009-10. As part of the Government decision to de-sequester Rs. 45,000 crore from MSS for using it in financing increased fiscal deficit during 2008-09 and 2009-10, Rs. 12,000 crore was de-sequestered during 2008-09. Of the balance Rs. 33,000 crore, the option of de-sequestering MSS to the tune of Rs. 28,000 crore was exercised (up to February, 2010) during 2009-10. New

accretion in MSS to the tune of Rs. 50,000 crore is estimated for BE 2010-11 and with redemption of existing securities of Rs. 2,737 crore during 2010-11, the closing balance is also estimated at Rs. 50,000 crore.

30. In order to have prudent management of debt and greater focus on carrying cost as well as meeting secondary market liquidity, the government has set up a Middle Office which in due course will transit into the proposed Debt Management Office. The Middle Office is now being strengthened appropriately.

31. There is a shift in policy on the uses of disinvestment proceeds from Central PSUs received under the National Investment Fund (NIF). The disinvestment proceeds received during 2009-2012 period will be reckoned as resources for the purpose of financing the social sector programmes which are creating capital assets. However, the income from investments made from proceeds received up to 2008-09 under NIF would continue to be used to finance social infrastructure and provide capital to viable public sector enterprises without depleting the corpus of NIF.

**Initiatives in Public Expenditure Management**

32. The focus has shifted from financial outlays to outcomes for ensuring that the budgetary provisions are not merely spent within the financial year but do result in intended outcomes. The Government had outlined in the President's address to the joint session of Parliament in June 2009 that an area of major focus would be reform of governance for effective delivery of public services. The following initiatives are being taken by the Government to achieve the above mentioned objective:

1. Establishing mechanisms for performance monitoring and performance evaluation in Government on a regular basis;

- At the beginning of the financial year with the approval of the Minister concerned, each Department will prepare a Result-Framework (RF) document;

- To achieve results commensurate with the priorities listed in the RF document, the Minister incharge will approve the proposed schemes and activities of the Department;
- The Minister incharge will also approve the corresponding success indicators (Key Performance Indicators-KPIs or Key Result Areas-KRAs) and time bound targets to measure progress in achieving these objectives;
- RF will be drawn up in such manner that quarterly monitoring becomes possible;
- During the year, the RF as well as the achievements against the KPIs will be reviewed by a Committee on Government Performance and the report of such review may be submitted to the Prime Minister through the concerned Minister for further action as deemed necessary;
- At the end of the year, all Ministries/Departments will review and prepare a report listing the achievements against the agreed goals (KPIs); and
- These results will be placed before the Cabinet for information by 1st June of each year.

2. Strengthening public accountability of flagship programmes by the creation of Evaluation Office which will concurrently evaluate the impact of these programmes and place it in public domain;
3. Putting up a public data policy to place all information covering non-strategic areas in the public domain which will help citizens to access the data and engage directly in governance reform.
4. All Ministries/Departments have been directed to make their Citizen's Charter more effective and mandatory adoption of the 'Seven Step Model for Citizen Centricity'.

33. The Revised Estimates for 2009-10 have been fixed after factoring in the unspent balances available with the Ministries/Departments and duly considering their absorptive capacity for the remaining months of the financial year. This has resulted in better estimation of overall expenditures and reprioritizing of resources to needy Ministries/Departments.

Initiatives have also been taken to evenly pace the plan expenditure during the year and also to avoid rush of expenditure at the year end which results in poor quality of outcomes. The practice of restricting the expenditure in the month of March to 15 percent of budget allocation within the fourth quarter ceiling of 33 percent is being enforced. The quarterly exchequer control based cash and expenditure management system which inter alia involves preparing a Monthly Expenditure Plan (MEP) continues to be followed in select Demands for Grants. The emphasis is on right pacing plan expenditure by ensuring adequate resources for execution of budgeted schemes. At the same time, steps have also been taken in the form of austerity instructions to reduce expenditure in non-priority areas without compromising operational efficiency. All these have resulted in availability of adequate resources from realised receipts for priority schemes.

34. Necessary monitoring mechanisms have been put in place with the help of the office of the Controller General of Accounts (CGA) to avoid parking of funds and to track expenditure.

35. A central monitoring, evaluation and accounting system for centrally sponsored schemes and central sector schemes of the Government has been instituted under the Central Plan Schemes Monitoring System. All sanctions issued by the Central Ministries under these schemes are now identified with a unique sanction ID that enables the tracking of release as per their accounting and budget heads across the different implementing agencies. This central system is hosted on the e-lekha portal of the CGA.

36. Expenditure data of all Ministries/Departments are being uploaded on a daily basis by the Pay and Accounts Offices on e-lekha. This is a significant step towards faster and accurate compilation of the accounts for the Government of India and will lead to the development of a core accounting solution. The monthly and annual Finance and Appropriation

Accounts are regularly updated on the CGA website: www.cgaindia.gov.in.

## C. Policy Evaluation

37. The process of fiscal consolidation is being restarted in 2010-11 after the deviations experienced during 2008-09 and 2009-10. Though the revenue base has not yet increased to the level of 2007-08, still, by doing expenditure reforms and with the help of disinvestment proceeds, the Government is able to bring down the fiscal deficit to earlier estimated level of 5.5 percent of GDP in 2010-11. With the introduction of the Direct Tax Code in 2011-12 and also the likely introduction of GST in 2011-12, it is expected that the fiscal deficit would be brought down in 2011-12 and 2012-13 in line with the recommendations of the Thirteenth Finance Commission. This level of deficit would reduce the debt to GDP ratio from 51.1 percent in RE 2009-10 to 48.2 percent in 2012-13. However, the mandated correction under the FRBM Act and Rules can be achieved once the revenue buoyancy is restored to the earlier level of 2007-08.

38. There are however difficulties in achieving revenue surplus. This has to be seen in the context of present composition of expenditure. Revenue expenditure of the Central Government also includes releases made to States and other implementing agencies for implementation of Government schemes and programmes. The outcomes of many of these schemes are not in the nature of the outcomes related to revenue expenditure. In most of the cases these schemes are primarily in the nature of creating durable assets but these assets are not owned by the Central Government. Therefore, in technical classification of revenue and capital account, the Central Government is not able to show expenditure on these schemes as capital expenditure. Examples of such schemes are Rajiv Gandhi Grameen Vidyutikaran Yojana, Jawaharlal Nehru National Urban Renewal Mission, Pradhan Mantri Gram Sadak Yojana, Accelerated Irrigation Benefit

Programme etc. Over the years, the number of such schemes funded by the Central Government and implemented by States/autonomous bodies has increased significantly. This has resulted in significant increase in funds transfer from Centre to States/autonomous bodies resulting in higher revenue expenditure. However, these revenue expenditures cannot be treated as unproductive in nature. On the contrary, they contribute to growth in economy.

39. At the same time in the current classification of expenditure, any release to a sick PSU in the form of loan is treated as capital expenditure. Similarly, defence capital expenditure constitutes bulk of the total capital expenditure of the Government. Presently, most of the infrastructure related expenditure is not directly funded from the capital account of the Central Government. The releases made to these agencies may not necessarily be reflected as capital expenditure of the Central Government. There are autonomous bodies or Central PSUs who are executing various infrastructure projects. There is a case for looking at Government of India expenditure classification in a more pragmatic way wherein more emphasis should be on the end outcomes of expenditure.

40. With the projected deficit targets the Government would be able to meet the targets set in by the 13$^{th}$ Finance Commission for debt to GDP ratio. However, the challenge remains for translating the outlays into outcomes.

# Bibliography

# Bibliography

Acharya, Shankar, 2002a, India's Medium Term Growth Prospects (unpublished: New Delhi: ICRIER).

Acharya, Shankar, 2002b, Macroeconomic Management in the Nineties (unpublished, New Delhi: ICRIER).

Agell, J., T. Lindh and H. Ohlsson. 1997. Growth and the Public Sector: A Critical Review Essay. – European Journal of Political Economy, 13, 33-52.

Agell, J., T. Lindh and H. Ohlsson. 1999. Growth and the Public Sector: A Reply. – European Journal of Political Economy, 15, 359-366.

Aghion, P., C.Harris, P.Howitt and J.Vickers (2001), "Competition, Imitation and Growth with Step-by- Step Innovation", Review of Economic Studies, Vol.68, No.3, pp.467-92.

Ahluwalia Montek, S. (2002) "Economic Reforms in India Since1991: Has Gradualism Worked.", Journal of Economic Perspectives, Vol.16, No.3, Summer, ss.67-88.

Ahluwalia, Montek, 2002, Economic Reforms in India since 1991: Has Gradualism Worked., • Journal of Economic Perspectives, 16,3 (Summer), pp.67-88.

Albala, J.M., and Mamatzakis, E.C. (2001), 'Is Productive Infrastructure Productive?

Alesina, A. and R. Perotti. 1996. Fiscal Adjustments in OECD Countries: Composition and Macroeconomic Effects. Washington, DC: IMF.

Alesina, A., S. Ardagna, F. Schiantarelli and G. Nicoletti (2003), "Regulation and Investment", NBER Working Papers, No.9560.

Alexander, W.R. 1990. Growth: Some Combined Cross-Sectional and Time Series Evidence from OECD Countries. – Applied Economics, 22, 1197-1204.

Allaudin, K. and P.V. Rajaraman.1996. Urban Infrastructure Financing in India: Tamil Nadu's New Financial Intermediary, Times Research Foundation, Calcutta.

Alonso, W.1971.'The economics of urban size", The Proceedings of the Regional Science Association'.

Anderson, D. 1989. "Infrastructure pricing policies and the public revenue in African countries", World Development, Vol. 17,

No. 4.

Aschauer, David. 1989. Is Public Expenditure Productive. Journal of Monetary Economics.

Bagchi, A. (2003), *Fifty years of Fiscal Federalism in India, an Appraisal*, Kale Memorial lecture at Gokhale Institute of Politics & Economics, Pune, December 8, 2001.

Bahl, R.W (Ed.) .1981."Urban Finances in Developing Countries", Urban Affairs Annual Reviews, Vol. 20, Sage Publishing, Beverly Hills, CA.

Bahl, R.W 1997. Fiscal Federalism in Uganda, Prepared for the Public Expenditure Reviews for Ethiopia and Uganda, 1994–1998, World Bank, Washington, DC.

Bahl, R.W and J. Linn 1992.Urban Public Finance in Developing Countries, Oxford University Press, New York.

Bahl, R.W, D. Holland And J. Linn.1983.Urban Growth and Local Taxes in Less-Developed Countries, Paper No. 89, East-West Population Institute, Honolulu, Hawaii.

Bahl, R.W. 2000a. "How To Design a Fiscal Decentralization Program", in Yusuf et al.

Bahl, Roy W. 1999. Implementation Rules for Fiscal Decentralization. *Public Budgeting and Finance 19 (2): 59-75.*

Bahl, Roy W. and Johannes F. Linn. 1992. Urban Public Finance in Developing Countries. Oxford: Oxford University Press.

Bahl, Roy W. and Shyam Nath. 1986. Public Expenditure Decentralization in Developing Economies. Government and Policy 4: 405-18.

Bahl, Roy W., Jorge Martinez-Vazquez, and Sally Wallace. 1996. State and Local Government Choices in Fiscal Redistribution. Research Paper No. 58, Georgia State University Policy Research Centre.

Bajpai, Nirupam and Vanita Shastri (1998) "Software Industry in India: A Case Study", Development Discussion Paper No.667, Harvard Institute for International Development, Harvard University, December.

Baker, J. (Ed.) 1990.Small Town Africa: Studies in Rural-Urban Interaction, The Scandinavian Institute of African Studies, Uppsala.

Balakrishnan, P.B. (2006) "Benign Neglect or Strategic Intent", Economic and Political Weekly. 9 September, Mumbai.

Ballassa, B. 1982."Structural Adjustment Policies in Developing

Economies", World Development, Vol. 10.

Banerjee, Abhijit V. and Esther Duflo (2000), "Reputation Effects and the Limits of Contracting: A Study of the Indian Software Industry,"Quarterly Journal of Economics, Vol.115, No.3, pp.989-1017.

Bardhan, Pranab. 1997. The Role of Governance in Economic Development. A Political Economy Approach. Paris: OECD Development Centre.

Bardnan, Pranab and Dilip Mookherjee 1999. Relative Capture of Local and Central Governments. An Essay in the Political Economy of Decentralization. Working Paper, University of California, Berkeley and Boston University.

Bardnan, Pranab and Dilip Mookherjee. 1998.Expenditure Decentralization and the Delivery of Public Services in Developing Countries. CIDER Paper C 98-104, University of California, Berkeley.

Barro, R. 1989. A Cross-Country Study of Growth, Saving, and Government. Cambridge, MA: National Bureau of Economic Research.

Barro, R. 1991. Economic Growth in a Cross-Section of Countries. – Quarterly Journal of Economics, 106, 407-444.

Barro, R. and X. Sala-i-Martin. 1995. Economic Growth. New York: McGraw-Hill.

Barro, R. J. 1997. Determinants of Economic Growth: A Cross-Country Empirical Study. USA: Massachusetts Institute of Technology.

Barro, Robert and Xavier Sala-i-Martin. 1995. Economic Growth. New York: McGraw-Hill.

Barro, Robert. 1999. Inequality, Growth, and Investment. NBER Working Paper 7038. Cambridge: National Bureau of Economic Research.

Barro, Robert. 1990. Government Spending in a Simple Model of Endogenous Growth." *Journal of Political Economy 98: 103-125.*

Bartik, Timothy J. 1985. Business Location Decisions in the United States: Estimates of the effects of Unionization, Taxes, and other Characteristics of States. Journal of Business and Economics Statistics *3 (1), January, 14-22*

Beede, D. and D. Bloom.1995."The Economics of Municipal Solid Waste", World Bank Research Observer, Vol. 10, No. 2.

Bennett, R.1990. Decentralization, Local Governments And Markets: Towards A Post-Welfare Agenda, Clarendon Press, Oxford.

Bhalla, Surjit. 2005. "Tax Rates, Tax Compliance and Tax Revenues: India,1988–2004" (www.oxusresearch.com/downloads/ce070704.pdf).

Bindra, A. (2006), "Civil aviation in India: Flying higher", downloaded from www.civilaviationweek.com/Civil Aviation in India Flying Higher.pdf.

Bird, R. and F. Vaillancourt (Eds.) 1998.Fiscal Decentralization in Developing Countries, Cambridge University Press, Cambridge.

Bird, R.M. and P.P. Gendron (1998), *Dual VATs and Cross-Border Trade: Two Problems, One Solution*? International tax and Public Finance 5, 429-42.

Bird, Richard M. 1986 . In Measuring Fiscal Centralization and Fiscal Balance in Federal States. Government and Policy 4: 384-404.

Bird, Richard M. and Edgard R. Rodriguez. 1999. Decentralization and poverty alleviation. International experience and the case of the Philippines. Public Administration and *Development 19: 299-319.*

Bird, Richard M. and Francois Vaillancourt. 1997. Fiscal Decentralization in Developing Countries: An Overview and Perspective. Paper prepared for the International Seminar *in Public Economics, Tokyo, August 1998.*

Birdsall, Nancy, David Ross, and Richard Sabot. 1995. Inequality and Growth Reconsidered: Lessons from East Asia. • World Bank Economic Review 9 (3), September, 477-508.

Biswas, R. and S. Marjit (2000), *Political Lobbying and discretionary Finance in India: An Aspect of Regional Political Influence in a Representative Democracy*, Working Paper, Centre for Studies in Social Sciences, Calcutta.

Blair, H.2000."Participation and Power at the Periphery: Democratic Local Governance in Six Countries", World Development, Vol. 28, No. 1.

Blair, Harry. 1988. spreading Power to the Periphery: An Assessment of Democratic Local Governance. USAID Program and Operations Assessment Report No. 21.

Bleaney, M., N. Gemmell and R. Kneller. 2001. Testing the

Endogenous Growth Model: Public Expenditure, Taxation and Growth over the Long-Run. – Canadian Journal of Economics, 34, 36-57.

Blinder, A. S. and R. M. Solow. 2005. Does Fiscal Policy Matter. In: A. Bagchi, ed. Readings in Public Finance. New Delhi: Oxford University Press, 283-300.

Boadway, Robin W. and David Wildasin. 1984. Public Sector Economics 2nd Edition. Boston: Little Brown.

Break, George. 1967. Intergovernmental Fiscal Relations in the United States. Washington DC, The Brookings Institution.

Brennan, Geoffrey and James Buchanan. 1980. The Power to Tax: Analytical Foundations of a *Fiscal Constitution. Cambridge: Cambridge University Press.*

Brenner, Y.S. 1966.Theories of Economic Development and Growth, Praeger Press, New York.

Bresser e Nakano", Brazilian Journal of Political Economy, 22 (4), Out./Dez.

Brillantes, A. 1994. "Redemocratization and Decentralization in the Philippines: The Increasing Leadership role of NGOs", International Review of Administrative Sciences, Vol. 60, No. 4.

Brown-Collier, Elba and Bruce Collier, "What Keynes Really Said About Deficit.

Bucovetsky, S.1991. "Asymmetric Tax Competition", Journal of Urban Economics, Vol. 30.

Campbell, T. Et Al.1991.Decentralization to Local Government in Latin American Countries: National Strategies and Local Response in Planning, Spending and Management, Latin America Regional Studies Program, World Bank, Washington, Dc.

Carbonara, Emanuela. 2000. Corruption and Decentralization. • WP 342/83 - Dipartimento di *Scienze Economiche, Bologna.*

Carey and Tchilinguirian (2000), *Average Effective tax rates on capital, labour and consumption*, OECD Economics Department Working Paper 207, October, Paris.

Carrol, R. and M. Wasylenko.1994."Do State Business Climates Still Matter. Evidence Of A Structural Change", National Tax Journal.

Cashin, P. 1994. Government Spending, Taxes, and Economic Growth. Washington, DC: IMF.

Castles, F. and S. Dowrick. 1990. The Impact of Government Spending Levels on Medium-Term Economic Growth in the OECD, 1960-85. – Journal of Theoretical Politics, 2, 173-204.

Cernea, M. 1985.Putting People First: Sociological Variables in Rural Development, Oxford University Press, Oxford.

Chambers, R.1986.Managing Rural Development: Ideas and Experience from East Africa, Kumarian Press, West Hartford, Ct.

Chaudhury, N., Hammer, J., Kremer M., Muralidharan, K. and F. Rogers (2006), "Missing in Action: Teacher and Health Worker Absence in Developing Countries", Journal of Economic Perspectives,Vol.20, No 1.

Cheema, G.S. And D.A. Rondinelli.1983.Decentralization and Development: Policy Implementation in Developing Countries, Sage Publishing, Beverly Hills, CA.

Chidambaram, (2007), Statement to the Chief Ministers' Conference on Pension Reforms, Government Press Information Bureau, New Delhi, January 22.

Chu, and Sanjeev Gupta (eds.) Economic Policy and Equity. Washington, D.C.:Clarendon Press, 1988.

Clarke, Peter, The Keynesian Revolution in the Making, 1924-1936, Oxford.

Cochrane, G.1983. Policies for Strengthening Local Government in Developing Countries, World Bank Staff Working Paper No. 582, World Bank, Washington, DC.

Cohen, J. 1995.Ethnic Federalism in Ethiopia, Development Discussion Paper, Harvard Institute For International Development, Cambridge, Ma.

Comparison of Fiscal Decentralization Experiences. • In Richard Lopez Murphy (ed.), *Fiscal Decentralization in Latin America. Washington, D.C.: Inter-American*

Conway P., D. deRosa, G. Nicoletti and F. Steiner (2006), "Regulation, competition and productivity convergence", OECD Economics Department Working Papers No.502,July.

Conway, P., V. Janod and G. Nicoletti (2005), "Product Market Regulation in OECD Countries: 1998 to 2003", OECD Economics Department Working Papers, No.419, OECD Publishing.

Conyers, Diana. 1990. Decentralization and Development Planning: A Comparative Perspective. In P. de Valk and K. Wekwete (eds.), Decentralizing for Participatory *Planning. Aldershot: Avebury, England.*

Crane, R.1994. "Water Markets, Market Reform and The Urban Poor: Results From Jakarta, Indonesia", World Development, Vol. 22.

Crook, R. and J. Manor. 1994. Enhancing Participation and Institutional Performance: Democratic Decentralization in South Asia and West Africa, Overseas Development Administration, London.

Datt, G. and Martin R. (2002), "Is India's Economic Growth Leaving the Poor Behind." Journal of Economic Perspectives, Vol. 16, No. 3 (Summer), pp. 89 108.

Davey, K.J 1988.Municipal Development Funds and Intermediaries, Policy, Planning And Research Paper No. 32, World Bank, Washington, DC.

Davey, K.J. 1989.Strengthening Municipal Government in Developing Countries, Policy, Planning And Research Paper No. INU 47, World Bank, Washington, DC.

Davoodi, H. and H. Zou. 1998. "Fiscal Decentralization and Economic Growth: A Cross-Country Study", Journal of Urban Economics, Vol. 43.

Davoodi, Hamid and Heng-fu Zou. 1998. Fiscal Decentralization and Economic Growth: A Cross-Country Study. • Journal of Urban Economics 43 (2): 244-57.

Davoodi, Hamid, Danyang Xie and Heng-fu Zou. 1995. Fiscal Decentralization and Economic Growth in the United States. • Mimeo. Policy Research Department. Washington, D.C. World Bank.

De la Fuente, A. 1997. Fiscal Policy and Growth in the OECD. London: Centre for Economic Policy Research.

De Los Reyes, R. and S. Jopillo.1995.Responding to Local Government Council Demands and Challenges, Institute of Philippine Culture, Ateneo de Manila University, Quezon City.

De Mello, Luiz R. Jr. 2000. Fiscal Decentralization and Intergovernmental Fiscal Relations: A Cross-County Analysis. • World Development 28 (2): 365-380.

Deaton, A. and J. Dreze (2002), "Poverty and Inequality in India: A re-examination", Economic and Political Weekly, 7 September.

Deaton,A. and Kozel (2005), "Data and Dogma: the Great Indian Poverty Debate", World Bank Research Observer, September.

Decentralizing the State. World Bank Latin America and Caribbean Studies. Washington, D.C: World Bank.

Deininger, Klaus and Lyn Squire. 1996. Measuring Income Inequality: a New Database" *World Bank Economic Review 10: 565-591.*

Dethier, Jean-Jacques, 2000. Governance, Decentralization, and Reform in China, India, and Russia. Kluwer Academic Press: Dordrecht, London, and Boston.

Dethier, Jean-Jacques. 1999. Governance and Economic Performance: A Survey. ZEF *Discussion Papers on Development Policy. Bonn: Center for Development Research,* Universitat Bonn.

Dev, S. and C. Ravi (2007), "Poverty and Inequality: All India and States, 1983 2005" Economic and Political Weekly, February, pp. 509 21

Devarajan, S. V., V. Swaroop and H. Zou. 1996. The Composition of Public Expenditure and Economic Growth. – Journal of Monetary Economics, 37, 313-344.

Devarajan, Shantayanan, Vinaya Swaroop and Heng-fu Zou. 1996. The Composition of Public Expenditures and Economic Growth. Journal of Monetary Economics 37: 313-344.

Diamond, P. 1997. Consolidating The Third Wave Democracies, Johns Hopkins University Press, Baltimore And London.

Dillinger, W. 1992.Urban Property Tax Reform: Guidelines and Recommendations, World Bank, Washington, DC.

Dillinger, W. 1995.Better Urban Services: Finding the Right Incentives, World Bank, Washington, DC.

Dillinger, William. 1994. Decentralization and its Implication for Urban Service Delivery." *Urban Management Programme Discussion paper No. 16. Washington, D.C.: World* Bank.

Dornbusch, R., S. Fischer and R. Startz. 1998. Macroeconomics. USA: The McGraw-Hill Companies, Inc.

Dossani, R. (2005), Origins and Growth of the Software Industry in India, Shorenstein APARC Working Paper, Stanford University.

Dowrick, S. 1993. Government Consumption: Its Effects on Productivity Growth and Investment. In: N. Gemmell, ed. The Growth of the Public Sector: Theories and International Evidence. Aldershot: Edward Elgar.

Easterly, W. and S. Rebelo. 1993a. Marginal Income Tax Rates and Economic Growth in Developing Countries. – European

Economic Review, 37.

Easterly, W. and S. Rebelo. 1993b. Fiscal Policy and Economic Growth. – Journal of Monetary Economics, 32, 417-458.

Easterly, W., C. A. Rodrigues and K. Schmidt-Hebbel. 1993. Fiscal Deficits and Macroeconomic Performance in Developing Countries. – World Bank Research Observer, 8, 211-238.

Easterly, W., C. A. Rodrigues and K. Schmidt-Hebbel. 1994. Public Sector Deficits and Macroeconomic Performance. New York: Oxford University Press.

Easterly, William and Sergio Rebelo. 1993. Fiscal Policy and Economic Growth: An Empirical Investigation. • Journal of Monetary Economics 32: 417-458.

Easterly, William. 2000. It's been a rough ride, Toto, but I think we're back in Kansas." Working Paper. Washington, D.C.: World Bank.

Economic Literature, 22 (4), Dec. 1984, pp. 1572-1575.

Economic Review, 34 (4), Dec. 1944, pp. 798-827.

Económica, LXII, No 246, 2003, pp. 15-45.

*Economics, 12 (1-2): 59-73.*

Edwards, S., "Why are Saving Rates so Different Across Countries.: An International Comparative Analysis" (April1995), NBER Working Paper No.W5097.

Ehdaie, Jaber. 1994. Fiscal Decentralization and the Size of Government, Policy Research *Working Paper 1387. Washington, D.C.: World Bank.*

Engen, E. M. and J. Skinner. 1992. Fiscal Policy and Economic Growth. Cambridge, MA: National Bureau of Economic Research.

Esman, M. and J. Montgomery.1982."The Administration Of Human Development", in P.T. Knight (Ed.), Implementing Programs of Human Development, World Bank Staff Working Paper No. 403, World Bank, Washington, DC.

Estache, A. and S. Sinha.1995.Does Decentralization Increase Public Infrastructure Expenditure", in A. Estache, Decentralizing Infrastructure: Advantages and Limitations, Discussion Paper No. 290, World Bank, Washington, DC.

Estache, Antonio. 1995. Decentralization Infrastructure: Advantages and Limitations, World *Bank Discussion Paper 290. Washington, D.C.: World Bank.*

Evans, H. 1992. "A Virtuous Cycle Model Of Rural-Urban

Development: Evidence From a Kenyan Small Town and its Hinterland", Journal of Development Studies, Vol. 28, No. 4.

Evans, H. and P. Smoke.1997.An Evaluation of the Local Development Fund in Palestine, UNCDF, New York.

Evidence from Chile', *Applied Economic Letters*, 8: 195-98.

Feder, Gershon. 1983. Exports and Economic Growth, Journal of Development.

Ferguson, B. 1993.The Design Of Municipal Development Funds", Review of Urban And Regional Development Studies, Vol. 5.

Fischer, Stanley. 1993. The Role of Macroeconomic Factors in Growth, Journal of Monetary *Economics 32: 485-512.*

Fisman, Raymond and Roberta Gatti. 2000. Decentralization and Corruption: Evidence Across Countries, Working Paper. Washington, D.C.: World Bank.

Fölster, S. and M. Henrekson. 1999. Growth and the Public Sector: A Critique of the Critics. –European Journal of Political Economy, 15, 337-358.

Forbes, Kristin. 2000. A Reassessment of the Relationship Between Inequality and Growth." *American Economic Review.*

Foster, V., S. Pattanayak and L. Prokopy (2003), "Do current water subsidies reach the poor.", Water Tariffs and Subsidies in South Asia Paper4, Water and Sanitation Programme –South Asia.

Gaile, G. 1992."Improving Rural-Urban Linkages Through Small Town Market-Based Development", Third World Planning Review, Vol. 14, No. 2.

Gale, William and Paul Orszag, "Economic Effects of Sustained Budget Deficits".

Gaurav, D. and M. Ravallion (2002), "Has India's Post-Reform Economic Growth Left the Poor Behind." Journal of Economic Perspectives, Vol.16, No.3, pp.89-108.

Gemmell, N. 2004. Fiscal Policy in a Growth Framework. In: T. Addison and A. Roe, eds. Fiscal Policy for Development: Poverty, Reconstruction and Growth. Great Britain: Palgrave Macmillan, 149-176.

Gertler, P. 1987. "Are User Fees Regressive: The Welfare Implications of Health Care Financing Proposals In Peru", Journal of Econometrics, Vol. 36.

Gertler, P. and J. Van Der Gaag.1990.The Willingness to pay for Medical Care: Evidence from two developing Countries, Johns Hopkins University Press, Baltimore, Md.

Government of India (2004), Central Government Subsidies in India, Ministry of Finance, Department of Economic Affairs, December.

Government of India, (2001), *Observations on the Customs Tariff*, Paper presented to the Inter Ministerial Group on the Customs Tariff Structures, Ministry of Finance, Department of Revenue, Delhi.

Gramlich, E.M.1987."Federalism and Federal Deficit Reductions", National Tax Journal, Vol. 40, No. 3.

Gramlich, Edward. 1987. Sub national Fiscal Policy. In John Quigley (ed.) Perspectives on *Local Public Finance and Public Policy. Greenwich: JAI Press. 3-27.*

Gramlich, Edward. 1993. A Policymaker's Guide to Fiscal Decentralization. National Tax Journal 46 (2): 229-35.

Grier, K. and G. Tullock. 1989. An Empirical Analysis of Cross-National Economic Growth,1951-80. – Journal of Monetary Economics, 24, 259-276.

Grote, Ulrike and Joachim von Braun. 2000. Does Decentralization Serve the Poor."

Gupta, S., B. Clements, E. Baldacci and C. Mulas-Granados. 2002. Expenditure Composition, Fiscal Adjustment, and Growth in Low-Income Countries. Washington, DC: IMF.

Gupta, Sanjeev, Keiko Honjo, and Marijn Verhoeven. 1997. The Efficiency of Government Expenditure: Experiences from Africa. • IMF Working Paper WP/97/153. Washington, D.C.: International Monetary Fund.

Gurgur, Tugrul and Anwar Shah. 2000. Localization and Corruption: Panacea or Pandora's Box, Working Paper. Washington, D.C.: World Bank.

Hansen, B. 1958, reprinted in 2003. The Economic Theory of Fiscal Policy. Great Britain: Routledge.

Hansson, P. and M. Henrekson. 1994. A New Framework for Testing the Effect of Government Spending on Growth and Productivity. – Public Choice, 81, 381-401.

Harral, C. (2006), "Highway and Railway Development in India and China, 1992-2002", Transport Note No.TRN-32, May, World Bank.

Herd, R. 1989. The Impact of Increased Government Saving on the Economy. Paris: OECD.

Herd, Richard and Sean Dougherty (2007), "Growth Prospects in China and India Compared", The European Journal of Comparative Economics, Vol. 4, No. 1, pp. 65-89.

Herd,Richard and W. Leibfritz (2008), ' Fiscal Policy in India :Past Reforms and Future Challenges', OECD Working Paper, 595.

Hermes, N. and R. Lensink. 2004. Fiscal Policy and Private Investment in Less Developed Countries. In: T. Addison and A. Roe, eds. Fiscal Policy for Development: Poverty, Reconstruction and Growth. Great Britain: Palgrave Macmillan, 177-198.

Hicks, U.K 1961. Development from Below: Local Government and Finance in the Developing Countries of The Commonwealth, Clarendon Press, Oxford.

Hicks, U.K et al. Federalism And Economic Growth In Underdeveloped Countries, George Allen and Unwin, Ltd., London.

Hicks, U.K.1978.Federalism: Failure and Success, Oxford University Press, London.

Himanshu (2007), "Recent Trends in Poverty and Inequality: Some Preliminary Results", Economic and Political Weekly, 10 February.

Hirschman, A.O.1958.The Strategy of Economic Development, W.W. Norton and Company, New York.

Huntington, S.1991.The Third Wave: Democratization in the Late Twentieth Century, University of Oklahoma Press, Norman, Ok.

Huther, J. And A. Shah 1996.Applying a Simple Measure of Good Governance to the Debate on Fiscal Decentralization, World Bank, Washington, DC.

Huther, Jeff and Anwar Shaw. 1998. Applying a Simple Measure of Good Governance to the Debate on Fiscal Decentralization. World Bank Policy Research Working Papers, no.1894.

IMF (2007), VAT Fraud and Evasion: What Do We Know, and What Can be Done? IMF Working Paper, 07/31, February.

J. Mccullough And R. Johnson 1989. "Analyzing Decentralization Policies in Developing Countries: A Political Economy Framework", Development and Change, Vol. 20.

J. Schiff, (eds.), International Monetary Fund. Rangarajan, C. (2005) —Strengthening Financial Management for Rural Employment Guarantee Scheme", paper presented to a workshop held at the

National Institute of Public Finance and Policy, New Delhi.

Jayanthakumaran, K. (2003), "Benefit-Cost Appraisals of Export Processing Zones: A Survey of the Literature", Development Policy Review, Vol.21, No.1.

Jimenez, E. 1990.Social Sector Pricing Policy Revisited: A Survey of Some Recent Controversies, Proceedings of The World Bank Annual Conference on Development Economics, World Bank, Washington, DC.

Kelly, R1993."Implementing Property Tax Reform in Developing Countries: Lessons from the Property Tax in Indonesia", Review of Urban and Regional Development Studies, No. 4.

Keynes, John M, The General Theory and After. Part II. Defence and Development.

Killick, T.1984. The Quest For Economic Stabilization: The IMF and the Third World, Heinemann Educational Books, London.

Kim, K.-H.1993.Urban Finances in Selected Eastern and Southern African Countries, Urban Management Program, United Nations Center for Human Settlement, Nairobi.

King, D. 1984. Fiscal Tiers: The Economics Of Multi-Level Government, George Allen and Unwin, London.

King, R. G and S. Rebelo. 1990. Public Policy and Economic Growth: Developing Neoclassical Implications. – Journal of Political Economy, 98, S126-51.

Kirman, Alan. 1992. Whom or What Does the Representative Individual Represent. Journal *of Economic Perspectives 6 (2): 117-36.*

Klitgaard, Robert. 1988. Controlling Corruption. Berkeley: University of California Press.

Kneller, R., M. Bleaney and N. Gemmell. 1999. Public Policy and the Government Budget Constraint: Evidence from the OECD. – Journal of Public Economics, 74, 171-190.

Kocherlakota, N. and K.-M. Yi. 1997. Is There Endogenous Long-Run Growth. Evidence from US and UK. – Journal of Money, Credit and Banking, 29, 2235-2262.

Koester, R. B. and R. Kormendi. 1989. Taxation, Aggregate Activity and Economic Growth: Cross-Country Evidence on Some Supply-Side Hypotheses. – Economic Inquiry, 27, 367-86.

Korpi, W. 1985. Economic Growth and the Welfare System: Leaky Bucket or Irrigation System. – European Sociological Review, 1, 97-118.

Kraay, A. (2006), "When is growth pro-poor. Evidence from a panel of countries", Journal of development Economics, Vol.80, No.1, June2006, pp.198-227.

Kumar, M. (2002), "Economic Reforms and their Macroeconomic Impact", in Kapila (ed.), A Decade of Economic Reforms, Academic Foundation.

Kumar, S. (2005), "Mortality Variations In India", Actuary Sahara India Life Insurance Company, Ltd, presentation to the 7th Global Conference of Actuaries, 15-16 February, 2005, New Delhi.

Landau, D. 1983. Government Expenditures and Economic Growth. – Southern Economic Journal, 10, 32-38.

Landau, D. 1985. Government Expenditures and Economic Growth in the Developed Countries: 1952-76. – Public Choice, 47, 459-477.

Landau, D. 1986. Government and Economic Growth in the Less Developed Countries: An Empirical Study for 1960-88. – Economic Development and Cultural Change, 35, 35-75.

Leibfritz, W., D. Roseveare and P. van den Noord. 1994. Fiscal Policy, Government Debt and Economic Performance. Paris: OECD.

Leibfritz, W., J. Thornton and A. Bibbee. 1997. Taxation and Economic Performance. Paris: OECD.

Lerner, Abba "Functional Finance and the Federal Debt," Social Research, 10,

Levine, Ross and David Renelt. 1992. A Sensitivity Analysis of Cross-Country Growth Regressions. American Economic Review 82 (4): 942-963.

Lewis, B.D.1998. "The Impact Of Public Infrastructure on Municipal Economic Development: Empirical Results From Kenya", Review of Urban and Regional Development Studies, Vol. 10, No. 2.

Lewis, W.A.1954. "Economic Development with Unlimited Supplies of Labour", The Manchester School, Vol. 22.

Lin, Justin Yifu and Zhiqiang Liu. 2000. Fiscal Decentralization and Economic Growth in China. Economic Development and Cultural Change 49 (1): 1-22.

Litvack, J., J. Ahmad and R. Bird. 1998. Rethinking Decentralization at the World Bank, Discussion Paper, World Bank, Washington, DC.

Litvack, Jennie, Junaid Ahmad, and Richard Bird. 1998. Rethinking Decentralization at the World Bank. World Bank Discussion Paper. Washington, D.C.: World Bank.

Litvack, Jennie. 1994. Regional Demands and Fiscal Federalism, In Wallich, Christine, ed.*Russia and the Challenge of Fiscal Federalism. Washington, D.C.: World Bank: 218-40.*

Majumder, R. (2005), "Infrastructure and Regional Development: Interlinkages In India", Indian Economic Review, Vol.40, No.2, pp.167-184.

Mankiw, N. Gregory, David Romer, and David N. Weil. 1992. A Contribution to the Empirics of Economic Growth. • The Quarterly Journal of Economics, May: 407-437.

Manor, J. 1998.The Political Economy of Democratic Decentralization, World Bank, Washington, DC.

Marsden, K. 1983. Links Between Taxes and Economic Growth: Some Empirical Evidence. Washington, DC: World Bank.

Martin, R. and M. Fardmanesh. 1990. Fiscal Variables and Growth: A Cross-Section Analysis. – Public Choice, 64, 239-259.

Martinez-Vazquez, Jorge and Robert M. McNab. 1998. Fiscal Decentralization, Economic Growth, and Democratic Governance, International Studies Program Working Paper. Atlanta: Andrew Young School of Policy Studies, Georgia State University.

Martinez-Vazquez, Jorge, Charles E. McLure, Jr. and Sally Wallace. 1995. Subnational Fiscal Decentralization in Ukraine, In Richard M. Bird, Robert D. Ebel and Christine I.

Masson, P.R., T. Bayoumi, H. Samiei (1998), "International Evidence on the Determinants of Private Saving", World Bank Economic Review, Oxford University Press, Vol.12, No.3, pp.483-501, September.

Mauro, Paolo. 1995. Corruption and Growth. • The Quarterly Journal of Economics, August, 691-712.

Mauro, Paolo. 1996. The Effects of Corruption on Growth, Investment, and Government Expenditure. • IMF Working Paper 96/98. Washington, D.C.: International Monetary Fund.

Mawhood, P.1987."Decentralization in the Third World in the 1980s", Planning and Administration, Vol. 14, No. 1.

McCallum, J. and A. Blais. 1987. Government, Special Interest Groups and Economic Growth. – Public Choice, 54, 3-18.

McDermott, C. J. and R. F. Wescott. 1996. An Empirical Analysis of

Fiscal Adjustments. Washington, DC: IMF.

McGillivray, M. and O. Morrissey. 2004. Fiscal Effects of Aid. In: T. Addison and A. Roe, eds. Fiscal Policy for Development: Poverty, Reconstruction and Growth. Great Britain:Palgrave Macmillan, 72-96.

McKenzie, D. and I. Ray (2004), "Household Water Delivery Options in Urban and Rural India," paper prepared for the 5th Stanford Conference on Indian Economic Development, 3-5 June.

McLure, Ch. Jr., (2000), Implementing Subnational Value Added Taxes on Internal Trade: The Compensating VAT (CVAT), International Tax and Public Finance 7 pp. 723-40.

McLure, Charles E. Jr. 1995. Comment of Prud'homme. World Bank Research Observer 10: 221-226.

McNab, Robert and Robert Moore. 1998. Trade Policy, Export Expansion, Human Capital, and Growth. • Journal of International Trade and Economic Development 7 (2): 237-256.

Mendoza, E., G. Milesi-Ferretti and P. Asea. 1997. On the Ineffectiveness of Tax Policy in altering Long-Run Growth: Harberger's Superneutrality Hypothesis. – Journal of Public Economics, 66, 99-126.

Michalopolous, C.1987.World Bank Programs for Adjustment and Growth, Development Policy Issue Series, Report No. Vpers 11, World Bank, Washington, DC.

Miller, S. and F. Russek. 1997. Fiscal Structures and Economic Growth: International Evidence. – Economic Inquiry, 35, 603-613.

Ministry of Finance (2001), An Assessment of the Government of India's pension liability, New Delhi, June.

Mishra, R.K. (1997), *The National Civil Service System In India: A Critical View*, Paper presented to a the conference on Civil Service Systems in Comparative Perspective, School of Public and Environmental Affairs, Indiana University, Bloomington, April 5-8.

Modigliani, F. (1990), "Recent Declines in the Saving Rates: A Life Cycle Perspective", Revista di PoliticaEcon., December, pp.5–42.

Mohan, R. and S. Dasgupta (2004), "Urban Development in India in the 21st Century: Policies forAccelerating Urban Growth", Stanford Centre for International Development, October.

Montgomery, J. 1972."Allocation Of Authority in Land Reform Programs: A Comparative Study of Administrative Processes and Outputs", Administrative Science Quarterly, Vol. 17.

Moser, C.1989.Approaches to Community Participation in Urban Development Programs in Third World Countries, Economic Development Institute, World Bank, Washington, DC.

Mosley, P. 2000. Globalisation, Economic Policy and Convergence. – World Economy, 23, 613-634. Musgrave, Richard, 1959, The theory of Public Finance (New York: McGraw Hill).

Mukerji, P. (2004), Essays in International Trade Liberalization and the Extensive Margin, Ph.D. Dissertation, University of Maryland.

Murgal and Ravallion (2005), *Employment Guarantee in Rural India: What Would It Cost and How Much Would It Reduce Poverty*? Economic and Political Weekly, July 30.

Musgrave, R.1959.The Theory of Public Finance, Mcgraw Hill, New York, 1959.

Musgrave, Richard. 1993. Fiscal Decentralization and Economic Development, National Tax Journal 46, (2):237-243.

Musgrave, Richard. 1959. The Theory of Public Finance. New York: McGraw-Hill.

Musgrave, Richard. 1990. Decentralization of the Public Sector: An Overview, In Robert Bennett (ed.) *Decentralization, Local Governments and Markets: Toward a Post Welfare Agenda* Oxford: Clarendon Press.

Mushkin, S.1972.Public Prices for Public Products, The Urban Institute, Washington, Dc, 1972.

Nam, Ch.W., R. Parsche and B. Schaden (2001), *Measurement of Value Added Tax Evasion in Selected EU Countries on the Basis of national Accounts Data*, Cesifo Working Paper No. 431, March.

Nazmi, N. and M. D. Ramirez. 1997. Public and Private Investment and Economic Growth in Mexico. – Contemporary Economic Policy, 15, 65-75.

Nicoletti, G. and S. Scarpetta (2003), "Regulation, Productivity and Growth: OECD Evidence", Economic Policy, No.36, pp.9-72, April.

Nicoletti, G. and S. Scarpetta (2005), "Product market reforms and employment in OECD countries", OECD Economics Department Working Papers, No.472, December.

Nicoletti, G., D. Hajkova, L. Vartia and Kwang-YeolYoo. (2006), "Taxation, business environment and FDI location in OECD countries", OECD Economics Department Working Papers, No.502, July.

Nicoletti, G., S. Scarpetta and O. Boylaud (1999), "Summary Indicators of Product Market Regulation with an Extension to Employment Protection Legislation", OECD Economics Department Working Papers, No.226.

Nirmal, A. (2004) *Study on transfer of resources from Centre to States*, 1st volume of the Official Statistics Seminar Series, November.

Nordstrum, H. 1992. Studies in Trade Policy and Economic Growth. Stockholm University Monograph no. 20, Stockholm.

Oates, W. 1972.Fiscal Federalism, Harcourt, Brace, Jovanovich, New York.

Oates, Wallace E. 1972. Fiscal Federalism. New York: Harcourt Brace Jovanovich.

OECD (2006a), Going for Growth, OECD, Paris.

OECD (2006b), OECD Economic Surveys: Brazil, OECD, Paris.

OECD (2007), Going for Growth, OECD, Paris.

OECD (2007*a*), Economic Survey: India 2007, OECD, Paris.

Olowu, D.1988.African Local Governments as Instruments of Economic and Social Development, International Union of Local Authorities, The Hague.

Oyugi, W.O.1978. Local Government and Development, Discussion Paper No. 131, Institute of Development Studies, University of Sussex, Brighton.

Palma and M. Sawyer, (eds.), Capital Controversy, Post-Keynesian Economics.

Panagariya, A. (2004), "India's Trade Reform", India Policy Forum, Vol.1, 2004, Brookings-NCAER Washington, D.C.

Panagariya, Arvind. 2005. "India's Trade Reforms." *India Policy Forum 2004*, pp. 1–57. Brookings and New Delhi: National Council of Applied Economic Research.

Panganiban, E.1994.Democratic Decentralization in Contemporary Times: The New Local Government Code of the Philippines, Conference Paper, Institute of Commonwealth Studies, University of London, London.

Panizza, Ugo. 1998. Politics and Macroeconomic Institutions: A Study of the Determinants of Fiscal Centralization and the Links between Income Distribution and Long-Run Growth. Johns Hopkins University, Ph.D. Dissertation.

Pant, Devandra Kirman, Suman Bery, and Deepak Lal, 2003 in the Growth Slowdown:

Patel, Urjit R., 1997, Aspects of Pension Fund Reform: Lessons for India, Economic and Political Weekly, September, pp. 2395–2402.

Pauly, M. 1973. "Income Redistribution as a Local Public Good", Journal of Public Economics, Vol. 2.

Peacock, A. and G.k. Shaw, 1976 The Economic Theory of Fiscal Policy, 80-95

Perotti, Roberto. 1996. Growth, Income Distribution, and Democracy: What the Data Say."*Journal of Economic Growth 1: 149-187.*

Persson, T. and G. Tabellini. 1994. Is Inequality Harmful for Growth. – American Economic Review, 84, 600-621.

Persson, Torsten and Guido Tabellini. 1994. Is Inequality Harmful to Growth, American *Economic Review 84 (3), June, 600-621.*

Petersen, J. and J. Crihfield. 2000. Linkages between Local Governments and Financial Markets: A Tool kit for Developing Sub-Sovereign Credit Markets in Emerging Economies, Urban and Local Government Background Series, No. 1, World Bank, Washington, DC.

Peterson, G. 2000.Building Local Credit Systems, Urban And Local Government Background Series, No. 3.

Peterson, George E. 1996. Decentralization in Latin America: Learning Through Experience." Washington, D.C.: World Bank.

Planning Commission (2002), 10th Five Year Plan (2002-2007)", *Chapter 6: Governance and Implementation*, December, New Delhi.

Planning Commission (2005), *Performance Evaluation of Targeted Public Distribution System*, Programme Evaluation Report 189, March, New Delhi.

Plosser, C. I. 1992. The Search for Growth. Federal Reserve Bank of Kansas City.

Poirson, H. (2006), —Making Tax Policy Pro-Growth", in: *India Goes Global*, C. Purfield and J. Schiff, (eds.), International Monetary Fund.

Pommerehne, Werner W. 1977. Quantitative Aspects of Federalism: A Study of Six Countries." in Wallace Oates, ed. The Political

Economy of Fiscal Federalism, Lexington, Mass.: D.C. Heath, 275-355.

PortaLa, R., F.Lopez-De-Silanes A. Shleifer (2002), "Government Ownership of Banks", The Journal of Finance, Vol.57, No.1, pp.265–301.

Porter, D. and M. Onyach-Olaa 1999."Inclusive Planning and Allocation for Rural Services", Development in Practice.

Prasad, Eswar; Ken Rogoff; Shang-Jin Wei; and Ayhan Kose, "Effects of Financial Globalization on Developing Countries: Some Empirical Evidence.

Prud'homme, R. 1995."The Dangers of Decentralization", World Bank Research Observer, Vol. 10, No. 2.

Prud'homme, Remy. 1991. Public Finance with Several Levels of Government: Proceedings of*the 46th Congress of the International Institute of Public Finance. The Hague:* Foundation Journal Public Finance.

Purfield, C. (2006), "Is Economic Growth Leaving Some States Behind.", India goes global: Its expanding role in the world economy, IMF, Washington, D.C.

Purfield, Catriona, 2003, State Government Finances, · in India—Selected Issues and Statistical Appendix (July), pp. 47-63.

Pursell, G. (2002), "Trade Policies in India", in D. Salvatore (ed.), National Trade Policies, Greenwood Press, New York.

Putnam, R.1993.Making Democracy Work: Civic Traditions in Modern Italy, Princeton University Press, Princeton, NJ.

Ram, R. 1986. Government Size and Economic Growth: A New Framework and Some Evidence from Cross-Section and Time Series Data. – American Economic Review, 76, 191-203.

Ram, Rati. 1986. Government Size and Economic Growth: A New Framework and Some Evidence from Cross-Section and Time-Series Data, American Economic Review (79):191-203.

Rangarajan, C. and D.K. Srivastava (2003), Dynamics of Debt Accumulation in India: Impact of Primary Deficit, Growth and Interest Rate", *Economic and Political Weekly* 38: 46, 4851-58.

Rao, C. Bhujanga, D.K. Srivastava, P. Chakraborty and T.S. Rangamannar (2003), Budgetary Subsidies in India: Subsidising Social and Economic Services, National Institute of Public Finance and Policy, March.

Rao, M.G. (2000), *Fiscal Decentralization in Indian Federalism*, Institute for Social and Economic Change, Bangalore.

Rao, M.G., R. Shand and K.P. Kalirajan (1999), —Convergence of Incomes across Indian States: A Divergent View", *Economic and Political Weekly*, March 27-April 2, 769-778.

Rao. M.G. and N. Singh (2004), *The Political Economy of India's Federal System and its Reform*, Working Paper No. 566, Department of Economics University of California, Santa Cruz.

Real Exchange Rate Misalignment, Fiscal Deficits and Capital Flows, (unpublished, NCAER).

Registrar General (2006), Maternal Mortality in India: 1997-2003, Trends, Causes and Risk Factors, New Delhi.

Richardson, H.W. 1977.City Size and National Spatial Strategies in Developing Countries, World Bank Staff Working Paper No. 252, World Bank, Washington, DC.

Richardson, P., C. Giorno and S. Thurman. 1994. Macroeconomic Performance and Fiscal Policy Adjustments in the Medium Term: Alternative Medium-Term Scenarios. Paris: OECD.

Romer, P. 1989. Endogenous Technological Change. – Journal of Political Economy, 98, S71-102.

Rondinelli, Dennis A. and John R. Nellis. 1986. Assessing Decentralization Policies in Developing Countries: A Case for Cautious Optimism, Development Policy Review 4(1): 3-23.

Rose-Ackerman, Susan. 1997. Corruption and Development. Proceedings of the Annual *Bank Conference on Development Economics. Washington, D.C.: World Bank.*

Rubinfeld, Daniel. 1987. The Economics of the Local Public Sector, In Alan Auerbach and Martin Feldstein (eds.) Handbook of Public Economics, Volume 2. Amsterdam: North Holland.

S. Peterson.1999.Administrative Decentralization: Strategies for Developing Countries, Kumarian Press, West Hartford, Ct.

Salmon, Pierre. 1987. Decentralizations as an Incentive Scheme. Oxford Review of *Economic Policy 3 (2): 24-43.*

Sau, R. (2007), "Second Industrialisation in India: Land and the State", Economic and Political Weekly, 17February, Mumbai.

Saxena, N.C. and Ravi, J.S. (2006) Rural Poverty Reduction through Centrally Sponsored Schemes", Paper prepared for the National Advisory Council, New Delhi.

Saxenian, A. (2002), Local and Global Networks of Immigrant Professionals in Silicon Valley, Public Policy Institute of California, San Francisco.

Schroeder, L.1988. Intergovernmental Grants in Developing

Countries, Planning, Policy and Research Paper No. 38, World Bank, Washington, DC.

Sengupta, N. (2005), *A civil servant remembers*, Samskriti, New Delhi. Murray, Christopher J. L., and Alan D. Lopez, 1996, The Global Burden of Disease, (WHO: Geneva).

Serres,deA., S. Kobayakawa, T. Sløk and L. Vartia (2006), "Regulation of financial systems and economic growth", OECD Economics Department Working Papers, No.506, August.

Sewell, David. 1996. The Dangers of Decentralization According to Prud'homme: Some Further Aspects. • World Bank Research Observer 11: 143-50.

Shah, A.1997a.Fiscal Federalism and Economic Governance: for Better or for Worse., World Bank, Washington, DC.

Shah, Ajay, 2000, Issues in Pension System Reform in India, Indira Gandhi Institute for Development Research (mimeographed; Bombay, India).

Shah, Anwar ,1999. Fiscal Federalism and Macroeconomic Governance: for Better or for Worse." *Fiscal Decentralization in Emerging Countries: Governance Issues, K. Fukasaku and* L.R. De Mello, Jr. (eds.), 37-54. Paris: Organization for Economic Cooperation and Development.

Shah, Anwar. 1994. The Reform of Intergovernmental Fiscal Relations in Developing and Emerging Market Economies. Policy Research Series 23. Washington D.C.: World Bank.

Shankar, R. 2000.Fiscal Decentralization and Economic Growth: Are We asking the right Questions., Department of Urban Studies and Planning, Massachusetts Institute of Technology, Cambridge, MA.

Shanmugam, K.R and P. Kulshreshtha (2005), "Efficiency analysis of coal-based thermal power generation in India during post-reform era", International Journal. Global Energy Issues, Vol.23, No.1.

Shannon, John. 1997. Middle-of-the-Road Federalism. • National Tax Association Forum, 28,August.

Shleifer, Andrei and Robert Vishny. 1993. Corruption. Quarterly Journal of Economics(109): 599-617.

Shleifer, Andrei. 1997. Government in transition. European Economic Review 41: 385-410.

Slemrod, J. 1995. What Do Cross-Country Studies Teach About Government Involvement, Prosperity, and Economic Growth. –

Brookings Papers on Economic Activity, 2

Smith, B.1985.Decentralization: The Territorial Dimension of the State, George Allen and Unwin, London.

Smoke, P 1999a ."Improving Infrastructure Finance in Developing Countries Through Grant-Loan Linkages", International Journal of Public Administration, Vol. 22, No. 12.

Smoke, P 1999c. "Understanding Decentralization in Asia: An Overview of key issues and Challenges", Regional Development Dialogue, Vol. 20, No. 2.

Smoke, P 2000b."Strategic Fiscal Decentralization In Developing Countries: Learning From Recent Innovations", In Yusuf et al.

Smoke, P and B. Lewis. 1996. "Fiscal Decentralization In Indonesia: A New Approach To An Old Idea", World Development, Vol. 24, No. 8.

Smoke, P.2000a.Beyond Normative Models and Donor Trends: Strategic Design and Implementation of Decentralization in Developing Countries, Mimeo, Management Development and Governance Division, Undp, New York.

Solow, Robert M. 1956. A Contribution to the Theory of Economic Growth. • Quarterly *Journal of Economics (70): 65-94.*

Spahn, Peter. 1997. Decentralized Government and Macroeconomic Control. • Infrastructure *Notes FM-12. Washington, D.C.: World Bank.*

Srinivasan, T. N., 2001, India's Fiscal Situation: Is A Crisis Ahead, Center for Research on Economic Development and Policy Reform Working Paper No. 92 (Palo Alto).

Srinivasan, T.N. 2000. Growth, Poverty Reduction, and Inequality. Working Paper, Department of Economics, Yale University.

Stren, R.E.1991. "Old Wine In New Bottles. An Overview of Africa's Urban Problems and the 'Urban Management' approach to dealing with them", Environment and Urbanization, Vol. 3, No. 1.

Strumpf, Koleman. 1999. Does Government Decentralization Increase Policy Innovation." Working Paper. Department of Economics, University of North Carolina at Chapel Hill.

Subhedar, S.P., A. Thanawala and R. Sane (2004), "Regulation and supervision of occupational pension funds and gratuity fund", Working Paper03/04, Indian Pension Research Foundation.

Sukthankar (2001), Committee Report on Operation, Maintenance and Management of Rural and Urban Water Supply Schemes, 28February, Government of India.

Taillant, J. Daniel. 1994. Decentralization: Local and Regional Government Development. A Literature Review mimeo, LATPS, World Bank, Washington, D.C.

Taylor, Lance, Reconstructing Macroeconomics, Cambridge, Harvard University The Collected Writings of John Maynard Keynes, vol. XIV, London and the Fiscal Affairs Department and the Policy Development and Review.

Ter-Minasian, Teresa (ed.). 1997. Fiscal Federalism in Theory and Practice. Washington, D.C.: The World Bank.

Ter-Minassian, T. (Ed.) 1997. Fiscal Federalism: Theory and Practice, IMF, Washington, DC.

Tiebout, C.1956. "A Pure Theory of Local Expenditure", Journal of Political Economy, Vol. 64, No. 5.

Tiebout, Charles. 1956. A Pure Theory of Local Expenditures. Journal of Political Economy, 64, October, 416-24.

Toye, John, "Fiscal Crisis and Fiscal Reform in Latin America," Cambridge *Transition Economies, Washington D.C.: The World Bank, 321-378.*Union. The Collected Writings of John Maynard Keynes, vol. XXV, London and University Press.

Treisman, Daniel. 1999. Decentralization and Corruption: Why are Federal States perceived to be more corrupt.Department of Political Science, University of California, Los Angeles, Working Paper.

Treisman, Daniel. 2000. Decentralization and the Quality of Government. Department of Political Science, University of California, Los Angeles, Working Paper.

Upadhya, C. (2004), "A New Transnational Capitalist Class. Capital Flows, Business Networks and Entrepreneurs", The Indian Software Industry Economic and Political Weekly Special Article, 27 November.

USAID (1995), India: Demographic and Health Surveys, 1992/93 – Final Report, Washington, D.C.

USAID (2000), India: Demographic and Health Surveys, 1998/99 – Final Report, Washington, D.C.

Wallis, John J. and Wallace E. Oates. 1988. Does Economic Sclerosis Set in with Age. An Empirical Study of the Olson Hypothesis. • Kyklos, 41 (3), 397-417.

Wallis, M.1991. "Local Governmental and Development: A Guide to the Literature", Environment and Urbanization, Vol. 3, No. 1.

Walsh, C.1992.Fiscal Federalism: An Overview of issues and a Discussion of their relevance to the European Community, Federalism Research Center Discussion Paper No. 12, Australian National University, Canberra.

Wasylenko, Michael and Therese McGuire. 1985. Jobs and Taxes: The Effect of Business Climate on States' Employment Growth Rates. National Tax Journal, 38 (4),December, 497-511.

Wasylenko, Michael. 1987. Fiscal Decentralization and Economic Development. Public *Budgeting and Finance 7: 57-71.*

Weede, E. 1986. Sectoral Reallocation, Distributional Collations and the Welfare State as Determinants of Economic Growth Rates in Industrialised Democracies. – European Journal of Political Research, 14, 501-519.

Whittington, D. Et Al. 1991. "A Study of Water vending and Willingness to Pay for Water in Nigeria", World Development, Vol. 19.

Williamson, John, "What Washington Means by Policy Reform," in J. Williamson, *Working Paper WPS1082,* The World Bank. Working Paper. Centre for Development Research (ZEF-Bonn), University of Bonn.

Woller, Gary M. and Kerk Phillips. 1998. Fiscal Decentralization and LDC Economic Growth: An Empirical Investigation. Journal of Development Studies 34 (4): 139-148.

World Bank 1999. World Development Report. Washington, D.C.: World Bank.

World Bank 2000. World Development Report 1999/2000: Entering The 21st Century, World Bank, Washington, DC.

World Bank. 1997. World Development Report. Washington, D.C.: World Bank.

Yeyati, E.L. A. Micco and U. Panizza (2004), "Should the Government be in the Banking Business. The Role of State-Owned and Development Banks" in Unlocking Credit: The Quest for Deep and Stable Lending, The Johns Hopkins University Press.

York, Harcourt Brace, 1964. [Originally published in 1936.] and Commodities. The Collected Writings of John Maynard Keynes, vol. XXVII, and the History of Economics: Essays in Honour of

Geoff Harcourt, Volume I,

Yusuf, W., W. Wu and S. Evenett.2000. Local Dynamics In An Era Of Globalization, Oxford University Press, Oxford.

Zanzi, Vito 2000. In Fiscal Federalism: Issues to Worry About. • Working Paper. Washington, D.C.: International Monetary Fund.

Zanzi, Vito 1996. Fiscal Federalism and Decentralization : A Review of Some Efficiency and Macroeconomic Aspects. • Annual World Bank Conference on Development Economics, M. Bruno and B. Pleskovic (eds.), 295-316. Washington D.C.: World Bank.

Zanzi, Vito 1998. Corruption Around the World: Causes, Consequences, Scope, and Cures. • IMF *Staff Papers, 45 (4), 559-594.*

Zanzi, Vito. 1994. Corruption, Governmental Activities and Markets, IMF Working Paper *94/99. Washington, D.C.: International Monetary Fund.*

Zhang, T. And H. Zou 1998. "Fiscal Decentralization, Public Spending and Economic Growth in China", Journal of Public Economics, Vol. 67, 1998.

Zhang, Tao and Heng-fu Zou. 1997. Fiscal Decentralization, the Composition of Public Spending, and Regional Growth in India. • Development Research Group Working *Paper. Washington, D.C.: World Bank.*

Zhang, Tao and Heng-fu Zou. 1998. Fiscal Decentralization, Public Spending and Economic Growth in China. Journal of Public Economics 67 (2): 221-40.

# Index

# Index


**A**

Adequate Enabling Environment, 106
Adequate Local Access to Investment Capital, 118
Allocative Efficiency and Growth, 13
Appropriate Inter-governmental Transfer System, 115
Assessment of Effectiveness of Local Bodies, 169
Assignment of Appropriate Functions to Local Governments, 108
Assignment of Appropriate Revenues to Local Governments, 111

**B**

Budget Policy, 22

**C**

Cash Reserve Ratio (CRR), 38
Central Public Enterprises (CPEs), 44
Centrally-biased Constitution, 154
Centre-State Financial Relations, 212
Chelliah Committee on tax reform (1993), 43
Constitutional and Legal Framework for Local Bodies, 165
Controlling Debt of States by Central Government 161
Corruption and Fiscal Decentralization, 143

**D**

Decentralization and Economic Development, 93
Decentralized Government Expenditure and Growth, 130
Direct and Indirect Linkages between Decentralization and Growth, 135
Disinvestment, Privatization and Restructuring of Public Sector, 43
Distribution of Powers between the Centre and the States, 152
District Planning Committees (DPCs),

167, 170

**E**

Economic Policies in the 1980s, 178
Effectiveness and Transparency of Subsidies, 75
Electricity Act (2003), 217
Elements of a Good Fiscal Decentralization Programme, 105
Eleventh Plan on Government Finances, 57
Emerging Fiscal Decentralization Trends, 83
Employment Aspect of Accelerated Growth, 207
Empowered Committee of State Finance Ministers, 74
Estimation of Relationship between Decentralization and Growth, 132
Expenditure Reforms Commission, 45
Extent of Fiscal Devolution to State Governments, 157

**F**

Faster Growth in Relatively Developed States, 199
Fiscal Consolidation in the Indian Economy, 184
Fiscal Decentralization and Accountability of Local Participation, 103
Fiscal Decentralization and Distribution, 100
Fiscal Decentralization and Revenue Generation, 101
Fiscal Responsibility and Budget Management Act (FRBM Act), 39, 48, 60, 185
Fiscal Sector Development at the Central Level, 42
Fiscal Sector Development at the Level of States, 46
FRBM Act and Transparency of Budgetary Policy, 60

**G**

Gains in Labour Productivity, 190
Global Financial Crisis and Set Back to Fiscal Consolidation, 49
Goods and Services Tax (GST), 212
Gross Budgetary Support

(GBS), 50
Gross Domestic Product (GDP), 3
Growth-retarding Effects of Fiscal Decentralization, 99

**H**
High Demand for Infrastructure Services, 214
Historical Basis of Fiscal Centralization, 81

**I**
Income Distribution and Growth, 27
India's Development Experience: Pre-reforms Period, 176
Indian Administrative Service (IAS), 155
Indian National Congress (INC), 154
Initiation of Economic Reforms in Early 1990s, 179
International Monetary Fund (IMF), 81
Introduction of CENVAT, 65
Introduction of VAT at the Level of States, 74

**J**
Jawaharlal Nehru National Urban Renewal Mission (JNURM), 219

**K**
Keynes on Fiscal Policy in General Theory, 4

**L**
Law on Popular Participation (1994), 108
Linkage between Efficiency and Measured Growth, 138
Local Bodies Remain Underdeveloped, 167

**M**
Macmillan Committee, 4
Macroeconomic Effects of Decentralization, 94
Market Stabilisation Scheme (MSS), 54
Mechanism of Transfer of Resources from the Centre to the States, 158
Memorandum of Understanding (MOU), 46
Metropolitan Planning Committees (MPCs) 167
Minimum Alternate Tax (MAT), 54

Modernisation of Public Pension System, 73
Modernization of Tax Structure, 211

N
National Capital Territory (NCT), 151
National Development Council, 46
National Highway Development Project (NHDP), 217
National Institute of Rural Development (NIRD), 173
National Small Savings Fund (NSSF) 163
Need for Enhanced Efficiency of the Financial System, 209
Need for Further Deregulation, 205
North-East Industrial and Investment Promotion Policy (NEIIPP), 52

O
Organisation for Economic Co-operation and Development (OECD), 81

P
Post-Keynesian Views, 6
Primary Responsibility of Stabilization, 84
Product Market Regulation (PMR), 205
Proposed National Goods and Services Tax (GST), 71
Prospects and Challenges, 202
Public Expenditure Policy, 17

R
Reorientation of Public Expenditure, 210
Response of the Economy to Reforms, 189
Richard Musgrave, 1
Robust Economic Growth and Buoyant Tax Revenue, 50

S
Sate Finance Commission (SFC), 172
Significant Role Played by Postal Savings System, 163
Small Towns Development Project (STDP), 110
South African Constitution (1996), 108
Special Economic Zones (SEZs), 197
Stability and Growth, 23
Statutory Liquidity Ratio

(SLR), 38
Sterling Performance of Services and the IT Sector, 193

**T**
Tax and Expenditure Policies, 23
Tax Policy, 13
Tax Structure Reforms at the Central Level, 63
Total Factor Productivity (TFP), 190
Total Factor Productivity Growth and GDP, 191
Trends in Fiscal Imbalances, 48
Twelfth Finance Commission's (TFC), 49

**U**
Urban Renewal and Development, 218

**W**
Ways and Means Advances (WMA), 39, 44
World Development Report 1988/1989, 84
World Financial Authority, 7